PHP

fast&easy™
web development

Send Us Your Comments

To comment on this book or any other PRIMA TECH title, visit our reader response page on the Web at **www.prima-tech.com/comments**.

How to Order

For information on quantity discounts, contact the publisher: Prima Publishing, P.O. Box 1260BK, Rocklin, CA 95677-1260; (916) 787-7000. On your letterhead, include information concerning the intended use of the books and the number of books you want to purchase. For individual orders, turn to the back of this book for more information.

PHP

fast&easy™
web development

Julie C. Meloni

A DIVISION OF PRIMA PUBLISHING

A Division of Prima Publishing

Prima Publishing and colophon are registered trademarks of Prima Communications, Inc. PRIMA TECH and fast&easy are trademarks of Prima Communications, Inc., Roseville, California 95661.

Publisher: Stacy L. Hiquet
Marketing Manager: Judi Taylor
Associate Marketing Manager: Heather Buzzingham
Managing Editor: Sandy Doell
Acquisitions Editor: Lynette Quinn
Project Editor: Estelle Manticas
Technical Reviewer: Jonathan Younger
Copy Editor: Gayle Johnson
Interior Layout: Marian Hartsough
Cover Design: Barbara Kordesh
Indexer: Jonna VanHoose Dinse

PHP was written by the PHP Development Team, and released under the GNU General Public License.

Important: Prima Publishing cannot provide software support. Please contact the appropriate software manufacturer's technical support line or Web site for assistance.

Prima Publishing and the author have attempted throughout this book to distinguish proprietary trademarks from descriptive terms by following the capitalization style used by the manufacturer.

Information contained in this book has been obtained by Prima Publishing from sources believed to be reliable. However, because of the possibility of human or mechanical error by our sources, Prima Publishing, or others, the Publisher does not guarantee the accuracy, adequacy, or completeness of any information and is not responsible for any errors or omissions or the results obtained from use of such information. Readers should be particularly aware of the fact that the Internet is an ever-changing entity. Some facts may have changed since this book went to press.

ISBN: 0-7615-3055-X
Library of Congress Catalog Card Number: 00-10540
Printed in the United States of America

00 01 02 03 04 DD 10 9 8 7 6 5 4 3 2 1

*To everyone who bought my first book
and told me it wasn't half bad.*

Acknowledgments

Congratulations to the PHP Association and Zend Technologies for making such a great product.

Great thanks to Lynette Quinn (for bringing up the idea of this book) and Estelle Manticas (for dealing with me and making this book actually work!).

A thank-you to every single PHP user and developer, because without you, I wouldn't have anything to write about.

Muchas gracias to SMD, for exercising all that patience.

About the Author

JULIE MELONI is the Technical Director for i2i interactive, a multimedia company located in usually-sunny Campbell, CA. She's been developing Web-based applications since the Web first saw the light of day, and remembers the excitement surrounding the first GUI Web browser.

She wholeheartedly believes that Linux is the OS of the present, not just the future, and feels guilty for once working for Sun Microsystems. She would like to list all the activities she likes to do in her spare time, but she hasn't had any spare time in five years, so that would be a short list.

Contents at a Glance

Contents

Introduction

About a month after the release of my first book, *PHP Essentials*, my editors decided that a *Fast & Easy* version was warranted, due to the explosion in PHP usage and the deluge of new developers. This book is what I came up with: a step-by-step, learn-by-example path to developing successful Web sites—with pictures included!

The wonderful world of Open Source and shareware software has allowed us to include with this book a CD-ROM containing a Web server, a database server, and the release version of PHP 4.0.0. The first three chapters are dedicated to getting these tools up and running on your Windows or Linux machine. You'll be surprised at how simple it is to do, and how good it looks on your resume.

Before jumping into all of that, take a moment to familiarize yourself with PHP and its history.

What Is PHP?

Its official name is PHP: Hypertext Preprocessor, and it is a server-side scripting language. When your Web browser accesses a URL, it is making a request to a Web server. When you request a PHP page, something like http://www.yourcompany.com/home.php, the Web server wakes up the PHP parsing engine and says, "Hey! You've got to do something before I send a result back to this person's Web browser."

Then, the PHP parsing engine runs through the PHP code found in home.php and returns the resulting output. This output is passed back to the Web server as part of the HTML code in the document, which in turn is passed on to your browser, which displays it to you.

A Brief History of PHP

In 1994, an incredibly forward-thinking man named Rasmus Lerdorf developed a set of tools that used a parsing engine to interpret a few macros here and there. They were not extravagant: a guest book, a counter, and some other "home page" elements that were cool when the Web was in its infancy. He eventually combined these tools with a form interpretation (FI) package he had written, added some database support, and released what was known as PHP/FI.

Then, in the spirit of Open Source software development, developers all over the world began contributing to PHP/FI. By 1997, more than 50,000 Web sites were using PHP/FI to accomplish different tasks—connecting to a database, displaying dynamic content, and so on.

At that point, the development process really started becoming a team effort. With primary assistance from developers Zeev Suraski and Andi Gutmans, the version 3.0 parser was created. The final release of PHP 3.0 occurred in June of 1998, when it was upgraded to include support for multiple platforms (it's not just for Linux anymore!) and Web servers, numerous databases, and SNMP (Simple Network Management Protocol) and IMAP (Internet Message Access Protocol).

So where are we now?

- Millions of Web servers run a version of PHP.
- PHP 4.0.0 has been released, featuring the Zend engine.
- Plug-in modules for code optimization and debugging are just around the corner.
- PHP 4.0.0 can work with just about any combination of Web server, operating system, and database you can think up.

What Does PHP Do?

PHP does anything you want, except sit on its head and spin. Actually, with a little on-the-fly image manipulation and Dynamic HTML, it could probably do that, too.

According to the PHP Manual, "The goal of the language is to allow Web developers to write dynamically generated pages quickly."

Here are some common uses of PHP:

- Perform system functions: create, open, read from, write to, and close files on your system; execute system commands; create directories; and modify permissions.
- Gather data from forms: save the data to a file, send data via e-mail, return manipulated data to the user.
- Access databases and generate content on-the-fly, or create a Web interface for adding, deleting, and modifying elements within your database.
- Set cookies and access cookie variables.
- Start sessions and use session variables and objects.
- Use PHP user authentication to restrict access to sections of your Web site.
- Create images on-the-fly.
- Encrypt data.

These are just everyday uses. PHP 4.0.0 includes support for Java, Java Servlets, XML, and a myriad of other higher-level functions. The possibilities are endless.

Is PHP Right For You?

Only you can decide if PHP should be your language, whether you're developing sites for personal or commercial use on a small or large scale. I can only tell you that in the commercial realm, I've worked with all of the popular server-side scripting languages—Active Server Pages (ASP), ColdFusion, Java Server Pages (JSP), Perl, and PHP—on numerous platforms and various Web servers, with varying degrees of success. PHP is the right choice for me: It's flexible, fast, and simple in its requirements, yet powerful in its output.

Before deciding whether to use PHP in a large-scale or commercial environment, consider your answers to these questions:

- Can you say with absolute certainty that you will always use the same Web server hardware and software? If not, look for something cross-platform that is available for all types of Web servers: PHP.

- Will you always have the exact same development team, comprised entirely of ASP (or ColdFusion) developers? Or will you use whomever is available, thus necessitating a language that is easy to learn and syntactically similar to C and Perl? If you have reason to believe that your ASP or ColdFusion developers might disappear on you, don't use those tools; use PHP.

- Are memory and server load an issue? If so, don't use bloated third-party software that leaks precious memory; use PHP.

Here's the bottom line: PHP is simple, so just try it! If you like it, continue using it. It's Open Source, so help improve it. Join a mailing list; help others. If you don't like it, you're only out 20 or 25 bucks for this book, and the software can be uninstalled without rendering your machine completely inoperable.

For More Information

This book has its own Web site. That figures, doesn't it? The URL is www.thickbook.com. At this site you can download all the code samples in this book, as well as all the samples I didn't include, such as those geared toward alternative database types. You can also use this site to alert me to bugs and other problems you have with the examples. Although the code has been tested many times, one errant semicolon or quotation mark can cause the dreaded "Parse error."

Conventions Used in This Book

This book contains elements that offer insight and key information related to the topic being discussed.

- **Notes** provide additional helpful or interesting information.
- **Tips** often suggest techniques and shortcuts to make your life easier.

PART I

Getting Started

1

Installing and Configuring MySQL

You might think that the first step in getting up and running with PHP4 would be to install PHP, but trust me—installing the MySQL database first will make the PHP installation process run a bit more smoothly. In this chapter, you'll learn how to do the following:

- Install MySQL on Windows or Linux
- Create a sample database
- Create a sample table

If You're Using Windows

The installation of MySQL on the Windows platform is a breeze, because an installation wizard does most of the work for you! You'll be working with a file from this book's CD-ROM , so track it down before you get started.

Installing MySQL for Windows

Installing MySQL as a stand-alone process is the same for Windows 95/98/2000/NT. If you encounter any problems, go to the MySQL Web site at http://www.mysql.com/ and read their manual.

Before you begin, find the CD-ROM included in this book, and put it in your CD-ROM drive. Now you're ready to install some files.

1. Using Windows Explorer, navigate through the CD-ROM filesystem.

2. Open the software directory.

3. Open the Windows directory.

4. Double-click on the file called mysql-shareware-3_22_34-win.exe. A dialog box will open, prompting for confirmation to unzip to C:\WINDOWS\TEMP\.

5. Click on Unzip to extract the temporary files.

6. Under the Start menu, select Run.

7. Browse to C:\WINDOWS\TEMP\Setup.exe and click on OK. The MySQL Setup program will begin.

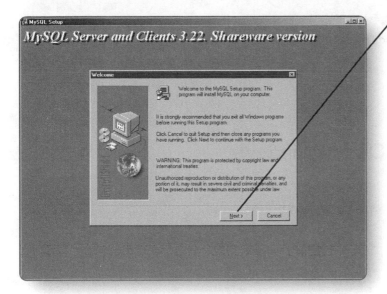

8. Read the setup information on the screen, and then click on Next.

9. Read the general MySQL information on the screen, and then click on Next.

10. Select your destination directory (C:\mysql\ or something else), and then click on Next.

11. Select Typical setup, and then click on Next. The installation program will extract and place files on your filesystem, and the installation program will end.

In the next section, you'll start MySQL and perform a few actions to familiarize yourself with the system.

Testing Your MySQL Installation

This section will have you start and work with the MySQL utilities via the command line in a DOS box. When using MySQL with PHP, you'll issue the same types of commands, except they'll be within the context of the PHP code. Use the information in this section to familiarize yourself with the types of commands and responses you'll be working with later in the book.

Starting MySQL

1. Open a DOS window.

2. At the prompt, type **cd c:\mysql\bin** and press Enter.

NOTE

If you installed MySQL in a different directory, substitute that directory name in the command in **step 2.**

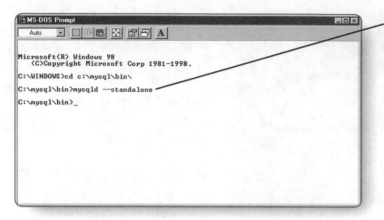

3. At the prompt, type **mysqld--standalone** and press Enter. The MySQL process will now be running in the background. You can now connect to MySQL and create databases and tables.

Keep the DOS window open, and move on to the next section to create a database.

Creating a Test Database

Before going any further, you should know the following:

- A database is a collection of tables.

- A table contains a set of records.

- All records have the same number of fields.

- Each field categorizes a piece of a data.

In this section, you'll create a database. The utility to use is the mysqladmin program, which allows you to administer MySQL from the command line.

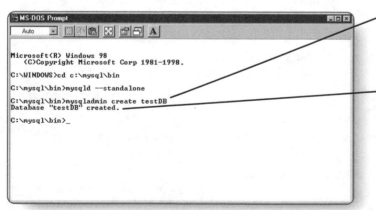

At the prompt, type **mysqladmin create testDB** and press Enter.

As you can see by the system response, a database called testDB has been created. Next, you'll add a table to that database.

Creating a Test Table

In this section, you'll create a table within the database you created in the preceding section. The utility to use is the mysql program, which allows you to work within the MySQL database system from the command line.

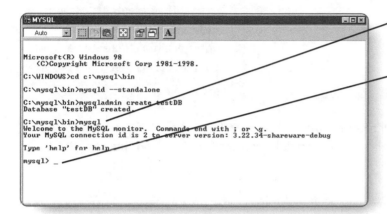

1. At the prompt, type **mysql** and press Enter.

When the MySQL Monitor starts, it provides its own prompt. At this prompt (mysql>) you will type commands used to create tables, explain tables, insert data, select data, and so on. Get used to ending your commands with a semicolon (;), because it's a common instruction terminator that is used in PHP as well.

Now that you've connected to the MySQL Monitor, you need to tell it which database to use.

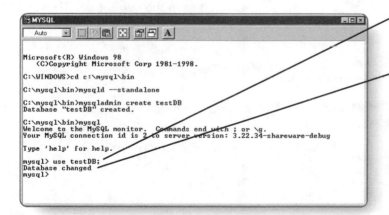

2. At the prompt, type **use testDB;** and press Enter.

The MySQL Monitor will respond with "Database changed" if the database exists and you have permission to access it.

It's time to create a test table. This table will have a column for an ID number and a column for some text.

NOTE

For more information about the specifics of creating tables, see Appendix C, "Basic MySQL Reference."

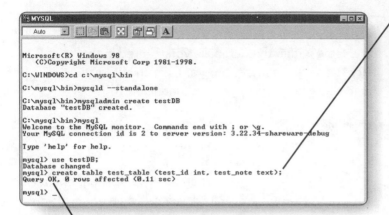

3. At the prompt, type **create table test_table (test_id int, test_note text);** and press Enter. This statement creates a table called test_table. Within the table, it creates a column called test_id of type int (integer). It also creates a column called test_note of type text.

The MySQL Monitor will respond with "Query OK." It will also tell you how many rows were affected and how long it took to complete the task (in this case, 0.11 seconds).

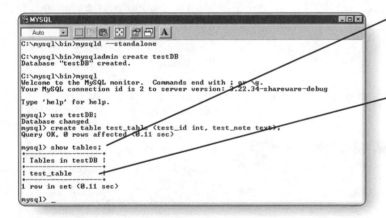

4. Verify the table creation by typing **show tables;** and pressing Enter.

The MySQL Monitor will respond with a list of all the tables in the current database.

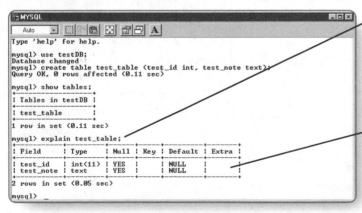

5. To verify the field names and types in a specific table, use the explain command. In this case, type **explain test_table;** and press Enter.

The MySQL Monitor will respond with a list of all the fields and their types in the selected table. This is a very handy command to use to keep track of your table design.

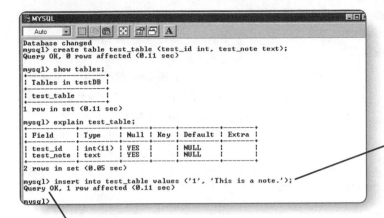

It's time to insert a few rows of data in your table, because this is getting pretty boring. The first row will have an ID of 1, and the note will be "This is a note."

6. To insert this row, type **insert into test_table values('1', 'This is a note.');** and press Enter.

The MySQL Monitor will respond with "Query OK." It will also tell you how many rows were affected and how long it took to complete the task.

7. Insert another row by typing **insert into test_table values('99', 'Look! Another note.');** and pressing Enter.

NOTE

For more information about the specifics of inserting data into tables, see Appendix C, "Basic MySQL Reference."

Now that you have some data in your table, even if it is only two rows, get familiar with selecting data. Keep the MySQL Monitor open, because you'll be using it in the next section as well.

Selecting Data from Your Test Table

The select command is very powerful and will likely be the command you use most often when working with PHP and MySQL. You can find more information about the select command in Appendix C, "Basic MySQL Reference," but for now, let's do some simple data selections.

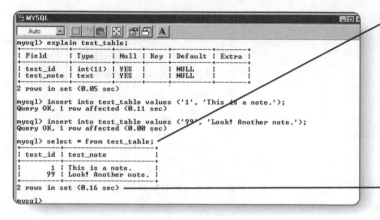

1. At the prompt, type **select * from test_table;** and press Enter. This command simply selects all fields from all rows (that's what the * does) in the table called test_table and returns the data to the screen in a nicely-formatted table.

The MySQL Monitor tells you how many rows were returned and how long it took the query to run.

Add a little order to the results. Try to get the results ordered by ID number—largest number first.

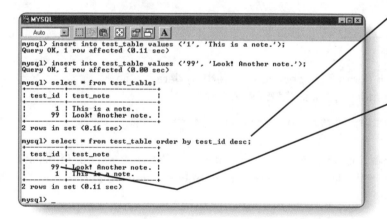

2. At the prompt, type **select * from test_table order by test_id desc;** and press Enter.

The result now shows the row with a test_id of 99 as the first row in the table. The "desc" in the command stands for "descending." There is another option, "asc," which stands for "ascending." Ascending order is the default order.

The next section is for the installation of MySQL on Linux, so assuming you don't have two machines, skip ahead to Chapter 2, "Installing Apache," to install the Apache Web server.

If You're Using Linux

This section will show you how to install MySQL on Linux using a file from this book's CD-ROM, so track it down before you get started. If you're using another flavor of UNIX, the instructions are the same but the file is different. Go to http://www.mysql.com/ to find the binary installation file specific to your system (Solaris, FreeBSD, and so on).

Installing MySQL for Linux

If you encounter any problems while installing MySQL for Linux, go to the MySQL Web site at http://www.mysql.com/ and read their manual.

Before you begin, find the CD-ROM included in this book, and put it in your CD-ROM drive. Mount the CD using your usual process, and you'll be ready to install some files.

1. Using the command line, type **cd [directory name]/software/linux/** and press Enter to reach the directory containing the file mysql-3.22.32-pc-linux-gnu-i686.tar.gz, from the CD-ROM.

> ### NOTE
> Replace [directory name] with the name of the mounted CD-ROM directory (/mnt, /cdrom, etc.)

2. Type **cp mysql-3.22.32-pc-linux-gnu-i686.tar.gz /usr/local/** and press Enter to copy the MySQL installation file to the /usr/local/ directory.

> ### NOTE
> You can put MySQL anywhere you want on your filesystem, such as /usr/local/bin/ or /opt/ or in another location. Just be sure to substitute your path for the path indicated in these directions.

3. Go to /usr/local/ by typing **cd/usr/local/** and pressing Enter.

```
mysql-3.22.32-pc-linux-gnu-i686/sql-bench/limits/pg.cfg
mysql-3.22.32-pc-linux-gnu-i686/sql-bench/limits/pg.comment
mysql-3.22.32-pc-linux-gnu-i686/sql-bench/limits/solid.cfg
mysql-3.22.32-pc-linux-gnu-i686/sql-bench/limits/sybase.cfg
mysql-3.22.32-pc-linux-gnu-i686/sql-bench/limits/Adabas.cfg
mysql-3.22.32-pc-linux-gnu-i686/sql-bench/limits/Adabas.comment
mysql-3.22.32-pc-linux-gnu-i686/sql-bench/limits/db2.cfg
mysql-3.22.32-pc-linux-gnu-i686/sql-bench/limits/solid-nt4.cfg
mysql-3.22.32-pc-linux-gnu-i686/sql-bench/limits/ms-sql65.cfg
mysql-3.22.32-pc-linux-gnu-i686/sql-bench/run-all-tests
mysql-3.22.32-pc-linux-gnu-i686/sql-bench/server-cfg
mysql-3.22.32-pc-linux-gnu-i686/sql-bench/test-ATIS
mysql-3.22.32-pc-linux-gnu-i686/sql-bench/test-alter-table
mysql-3.22.32-pc-linux-gnu-i686/sql-bench/test-big-tables
mysql-3.22.32-pc-linux-gnu-i686/sql-bench/test-connect
mysql-3.22.32-pc-linux-gnu-i686/sql-bench/test-create
mysql-3.22.32-pc-linux-gnu-i686/sql-bench/test-insert
mysql-3.22.32-pc-linux-gnu-i686/sql-bench/test-select
mysql-3.22.32-pc-linux-gnu-i686/sql-bench/test-wisconsin
mysql-3.22.32-pc-linux-gnu-i686/ChangeLog
mysql-3.22.32-pc-linux-gnu-i686/PUBLIC
mysql-3.22.32-pc-linux-gnu-i686/README
mysql-3.22.32-pc-linux-gnu-i686/INSTALL-BINARY
mysql-3.22.32-pc-linux-gnu-i686/manual.html
mysql-3.22.32-pc-linux-gnu-i686/manual.txt
mysql-3.22.32-pc-linux-gnu-i686/manual_toc.html
mysql-3.22.32-pc-linux-gnu-i686/MySQL-for-dummies
mysql-3.22.32-pc-linux-gnu-i686/configure
#
```

4. Unzip the MySQL installation file by typing **gunzip mysql-3.22.32-pc-linux-gnu-i686.tar.gz** and pressing Enter.

5. At the prompt, extract the files by typing **tar -xvf mysql-3.22.32-pc-linux-gnu-i686.tar** and pressing Enter.

A directory structure will be created, and you'll be back at the prompt. The parent directory will be /usr/local/mysql-3.22.32-pc-linux-gnu-i686/.

```
# ./scripts/mysql_install_db
Creating db table
Creating host table
Creating user table
Creating func table
Creating tables_priv table
Creating columns_priv table

To start mysqld at boot time you have to copy support-files/mysql.server
to the right place for your system

PLEASE REMEMBER TO SET A PASSWORD FOR THE MySQL root USER !
This is done with:
./bin/mysqladmin -u root password 'new-password'
See the manual for more instructions.

Please report any problems with the ./bin/mysqlbug script!

The latest information about MySQL is available on the web at http://www.mysql.com
Support MySQL by buying support/licenses at http://www.tcx.se/license.htmy.

# 
```

6. Enter the parent directory by typing **cd mysql-3.22.32-pc-linux-gnu-i686** and pressing Enter.

7. Type **./scripts/mysql_install_db** and press Enter.

The installation will be complete.

In the next section, you'll learn to start and work with the MySQL utilities via the command-line interface.

Testing Your MySQL Installation

This section will have you start and work with the MySQL utilities via the command line. When using MySQL with PHP, you'll issue the same types of commands; now, however these commands will be within the context of the PHP code. Use the information in this section to familiarize yourself with the types of commands and responses you'll be working with later in the book.

Starting MySQL

1. If you're not already there, enter the MySQL parent directory by typing **cd /usr/local/mysql-3.22.32-pc-linux-gnu-i686** and pressing Enter.

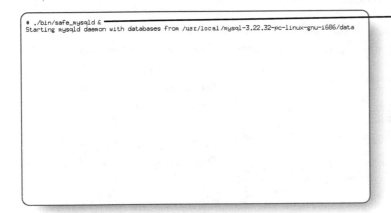

```
# ./bin/safe_mysqld &
Starting mysqld daemon with databases from /usr/local/mysql-3.22.32-pc-linux-gnu-i686/data
```

2. Start the MySQL process by typing **./bin/safe_mysqld &** and pressing Enter. The MySQL process will now be running in the background. You can now connect to MySQL and create databases and tables.

Creating a Test Database

Before going any further, you should know the following:

- A database is a collection of tables.
- A table contains a set of records.
- All records have the same number of fields.
- Each field categorizes a piece of a data.

In this section, you'll create a database. The utility to use is the mysqladmin program, which allows you to administer MySQL from the command line.

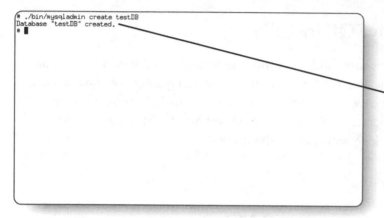

At the prompt, type **./bin/mysqladmin create testDB** and press Enter.

As you can see by the system response, a database called testDB has been created. Next, you'll add a table to that database.

Creating a Test Table

In this section, you'll create a table within the database you created in the preceding section. The utility to use is the mysql program, which allows you to work within the MySQL database system from the command line.

1. At the prompt, type **./bin/mysql** and press Enter.

When the MySQL Monitor starts, it provides its own prompt. At this prompt (mysql>) you will type commands used to create tables, explain tables, insert data, select data, and so on. Get used to ending your commands with a semicolon (;), because it's a common instruction terminator that is used in PHP as well.

Now that you've connected to the MySQL monitor, you need to tell it which database to use.

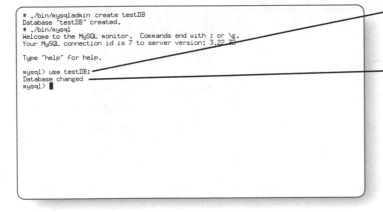

```
# ./bin/mysqladmin create testDB
Database "testDB" created.
# ./bin/mysql
Welcome to the MySQL monitor.  Commands end with ; or \g.
Your MySQL connection id is 7 to server version: 3.22.32

Type 'help' for help.

mysql> use testDB;
Database changed
mysql> █
```

2. At the prompt, type **use testDB;** and press Enter.

The MySQL Monitor will respond with "Database changed" if the database exists and you have permission to access it.

It's time to create a test table. This table will have a column for an ID number and a column for some text.

NOTE

For more information about the specifics of creating tables, see Appendix C, "Basic MySQL Reference."

```
# ./bin/mysqladmin create testDB
Database "testDB" created.
# ./bin/mysql
Welcome to the MySQL monitor.  Commands end with ; or \g.
Your MySQL connection id is 7 to server version: 3.22.32

Type 'help' for help.

mysql> use testDB;
Database changed
mysql> create table test_table (test_id int, test_note text);
Query OK, 0 rows affected (0.03 sec)

mysql> █
```

3. At the prompt, type **create table test_table (test_id int, test_note text);** and press Enter. This statement creates a table called test_table. Within the table, it creates a column called test_id of type int (integer). It also creates a column called test_note of type text.

The MySQL Monitor will respond with "Query OK." It will also tell you how many rows were affected and how long it took to complete the task (in this case, 0.03 seconds).

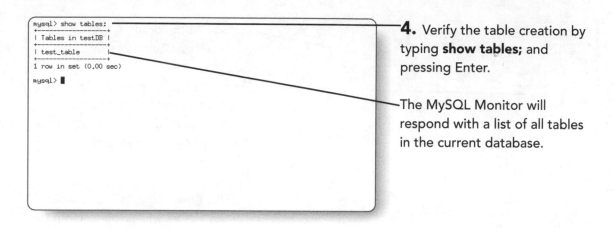

4. Verify the table creation by typing **show tables;** and pressing Enter.

The MySQL Monitor will respond with a list of all tables in the current database.

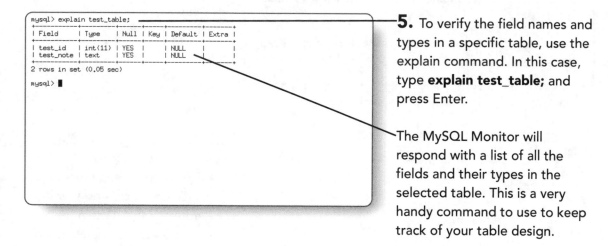

5. To verify the field names and types in a specific table, use the explain command. In this case, type **explain test_table;** and press Enter.

The MySQL Monitor will respond with a list of all the fields and their types in the selected table. This is a very handy command to use to keep track of your table design.

It's time to insert a few rows of data in your table, because this is getting pretty boring. The first row will have an ID of 1, and the note will be "This is a note."

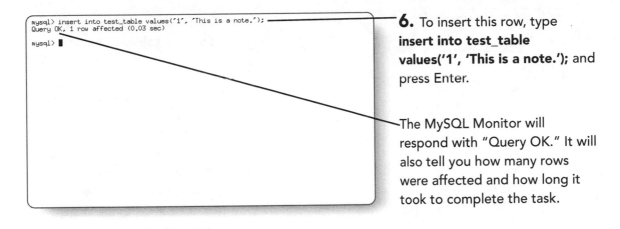

```
mysql> insert into test_table values('1', 'This is a note.');
Query OK, 1 row affected (0.03 sec)

mysql>
```

6. To insert this row, type **insert into test_table values('1', 'This is a note.');** and press Enter.

The MySQL Monitor will respond with "Query OK." It will also tell you how many rows were affected and how long it took to complete the task.

7. Insert another row by typing **insert into test_table values('99', 'Look! Another note.');** and pressing Enter.

> **NOTE**
>
> For more information about the specifics of inserting data into tables, see Appendix C, "Basic MySQL Reference."

Now that you have some data in your table, even if it is only two rows, get familiar with selecting data. Keep the MySQL Monitor open, because you'll be using it in the next section as well.

Selecting Data from Your Test Table

The select command is very powerful and will likely be the command you use most often when working with PHP and MySQL. You can find more information about select in Appendix C, "Basic MySQL Reference," but for now, we'll do some simple data selections.

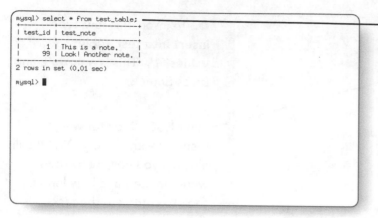

1. At the prompt, type **select * from test_table;** and press Enter.

This command simply selects all fields from all rows (that's what the * does) in the table called test_table and returns the data to the screen in a nicely-formatted table. The MySQL Monitor tells you how many rows were returned and how long it took the query to run.

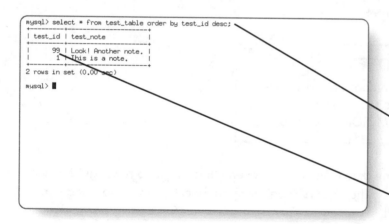

Add a little order to the results. Try to get the results ordered by ID number—largest number first.

2. At the prompt, type **select * from test_table order by test_id desc;** and press Enter.

The result now shows the row with a test_id of 99 as the first row in the table. The "desc" in the command stands for "descending." There is another option, "asc," which stands for "ascending." Ascending order is the default order.

In the next chapter, you'll install the Apache Web server and be one step closer to developing dynamic, database-driven Web sites!

2

Installing Apache

Since it's the most popular Web server in use these days, you might think that Apache is a complicated piece of software, but it's not difficult at all. In this chapter, you'll learn how to do the following:

- ● Install Apache on Windows or Linux
- ● Connect to your new Web server

If You're Using Windows

Installing Apache for Windows is even easier than installing MySQL. Apache also has an installation wizard, so track down the book's CD-ROM again, and hold on to your hat!

Installing Apache for Windows

Installing Apache is the same for Windows 95/98/2000/NT. If you encounter any problems, go to the Apache Web site at http://www.apache.org and read the server documentation.

Before you begin, find the CD-ROM included in this book and put it in your CD-ROM drive. Now you're ready to install some files.

1. Using Windows Explorer, navigate through the CD-ROM filesystem.

2. Open the software directory.

3. Open the Windows directory.

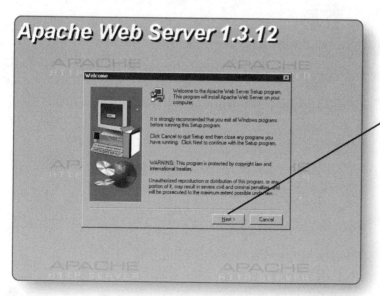

4. Double-click on the file called apache_1_3_12_win32.exe. The Apache Setup program will begin.

5. Read the setup information on the screen, and then click on Next.

6. Read the general Apache information on the screen, and then click on Next.

7. Read the note about Apache on Windows, and then click on Next.

8. Select your destination directory (for example, C:\Program Files\Apache Group\), and then click on Next.

9. Select Typical setup, and then click on Next.

10. Select a location for Apache links on the Windows Start menu, and then click on Next. The installation program will extract and place files on your filesystem, and the installation program will prompt you to read the README file.

11. Click on Finish to complete the installation.

In the next section, you'll make some minor changes to the Apache configuration file before you start Apache for the first time.

Configuring Apache

At this point, the only changes you'll make to the Apache configuration file are minor administrative changes. Configuration files are located in the conf directory, within the Apache installation directory. So, if your installation directory is C:\Program Files\Apache Group\Apache\, the configuration files will be in C:\Program Files\Apache Group\Apache\conf\.

```
#
# ServerAdmin: Your address, where problems with the server should be
# e-mailed.  This address appears on some server-generated pages, such
# as error documents.
#
ServerAdmin you@your.address


#
# ServerName allows you to set a host name which is sent back to clients for
# your server if it's different than the one the program would get (i.e., use
# "www" instead of the host's real name).
#
# Note: You cannot just invent host names and hope they work. The name you
# define here must be a valid DNS name for your host. If you don't understand
# this, ask your network administrator.
# If your host doesn't have a registered DNS name, enter its IP address here.
# You will have to access it by its address (e.g., http://123.45.67.89/)
# anyway, and this will make redirections work in a sensible way.
#
#ServerName new.host.name
```

1. Open a text editor.

2. Open the httpd.conf file, in the conf directory of the Apache installation directory.

3. Find this section of text.

4. Change the value of ServerAdmin to your e-mail address.

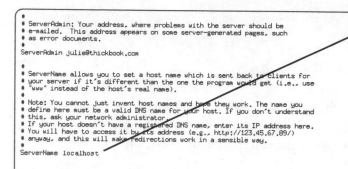

5. Change the value of ServerName to localhost.

6. Save the file.

Apache is now ready to run on your machine. In the next section, you'll start and connect to Apache.

Starting Apache

On the Windows platform, you can run Apache either on your own or as a service if you're using Windows NT.

Starting Apache as a Service

If you are using Windows NT and you want to run Apache as a service, follow these steps:

1. From the Windows Start menu, open the Apache Web Server menu and select the Install Apache as a service item.

2. Go to the Control Panel and open the Services window.

3. Select Apache from the list of services.

4. Click on Start.

Apache will now run in the background. In a few moments, you'll connect to your new Web server for the first time.

Manually Starting and Stopping Apache

If you cannot run Apache as a service, don't worry. You can still manually start and stop Apache.

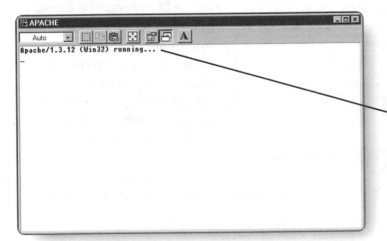

1. From the Windows Start menu, open the Apache Web Server menu and select the Start Apache item.

A DOS window will open.

Keep this DOS window open, or your Apache process will stop. You can minimize the window—just don't close it.

To stop Apache, select the Stop Apache item from the Apache Web Server menu on the Windows Start menu. For now, though, keep it running. In the next section, you'll connect to your new Web server for the first time.

Connecting to Apache

In the configuration section, you gave a value of localhost to ServerName in the httpd.conf file. You'll use this name to connect to your Web server.

NOTE

Only you can connect to your Web server using localhost. If you have a static IP and a machine name that resolves via DNS, you can substitute that name for localhost in the httpd.conf file, and other users can connect to that machine. This book assumes that you'll be using localhost for now, but it really makes no difference if you have a real machine name. Simply substitute your machine name for localhost in the examples.

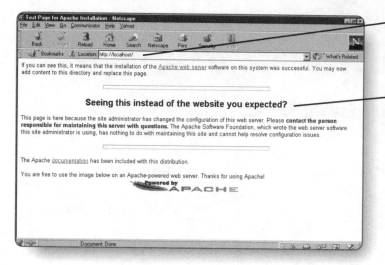

Open your Web browser, type **http://localhost/** in the location bar and press Enter.

This default start page comes from the htdocs directory within your Apache installation directory. You can go into that directory and delete all the default files if you want to, or you can leave them. They're not hurting anything, but you'll eventually be filling the htdocs directory with your own files and subdirectories, so you might want to delete the default files for the sake of good housekeeping.

Move ahead to the next chapter, where you'll install PHP and make a few more minor changes to your Apache configuration files before you're ready for some action.

If You're Using Linux

This section will show you how to install Apache on Linux using a file from this book's CD-ROM, so track down the CD before you get started. This same file should work for other flavors of UNIX as well, but if you have any concerns, go to http://www.apache.org/dist/ and find a better set of source files for your operating system.

Installing Apache for Linux

If you encounter any issues while installing Apache for Linux, go to the Apache Web site at http://www.apache.org and read the server documentation.

Before you begin, find the CD-ROM included in this book, and put it in your CD-ROM drive. Mount the CD using your normal process, and you'll be ready to install some files.

1. Using the command line, type **cd [directory name]/software/linux/** and press Enter to reach the directory containing the file apache_1.3.12.tar.gz from the CD-ROM.

NOTE

Replace [directory name] with the name of the mounted CD-ROM directory (/mnt, /cdrom, etc.).

2. Type **cp apache_1.3.12.tar.gz /usr/local/** and press Enter to copy the Apache installation file to the /usr/local/ directory.

3. Go to /usr/local/ by typing **cd /usr/local/** and pressing Enter.

4. Unzip the Apache installation file by typing **gunzip apache_1.3.12.tar.gz** and pressing Enter.

```
apache_1.3.12/icons/small/burst.gif
apache_1.3.12/icons/small/comp1.gif
apache_1.3.12/icons/small/comp2.gif
apache_1.3.12/icons/small/compressed.gif
apache_1.3.12/icons/small/continued.gif
apache_1.3.12/icons/small/dir.gif
apache_1.3.12/icons/small/dir2.gif
apache_1.3.12/icons/small/doc.gif
apache_1.3.12/icons/small/forward.gif
apache_1.3.12/icons/small/generic.gif
apache_1.3.12/icons/small/generic2.gif
apache_1.3.12/icons/small/generic3.gif
apache_1.3.12/icons/small/image.gif
apache_1.3.12/icons/small/image2.gif
apache_1.3.12/icons/small/index.gif
apache_1.3.12/icons/small/key.gif
apache_1.3.12/icons/small/movie.gif
apache_1.3.12/icons/small/patch.gif
apache_1.3.12/icons/small/ps.gif
apache_1.3.12/icons/small/rainbow.gif
apache_1.3.12/icons/small/sound.gif
apache_1.3.12/icons/small/sound2.gif
apache_1.3.12/icons/small/tar.gif
apache_1.3.12/icons/small/text.gif
apache_1.3.12/icons/small/transfer.gif
apache_1.3.12/icons/small/unknown.gif
apache_1.3.12/icons/small/uu.gif
apache_1.3.12/logs/
#
```

NOTE

You can put Apache anywhere you want on your filesystem, such as /usr/local/bin/ or /opt/. Just be sure to substitute your path for the path indicated in these directions.

5. At the prompt, extract the files by typing **tar -xvf apache_1.3.12.tar** and pressing Enter.

A directory structure will be created, and you'll be back at the prompt. The parent directory will be /usr/local/apache_1.3.12/.

6. Enter the parent directory by typing **cd apache_1.3.12** and pressing Enter.

7. Type the following and press Enter, to prepare to build Apache:

```
./configure --prefix=/usr/local/apache_1.3.12 --enable-module=so
```

> ### NOTE
>
> If the apache_1.3.12 directory resides elsewhere on your filesystem, such as /opt/ (as shown in the figures), use that path in the configuration directive in step 7.

```
# cd apache_1.3.12
# ./configure --prefix=/opt/apache_1.3.12 --enable-module=so
Configuring for Apache, Version 1.3.12
 + using installation path layout: Apache (config.layout)
Creating Makefile
Creating Configuration.apaci in src
Creating Makefile in src
 + configured for Linux platform
 + setting C compiler to gcc
 + setting C pre-processor to gcc -E
 + checking for system header files
 + adding selected modules
 + using -ldl for vendor DSO support
 + checking sizeof various data types
 + doing sanity check on compiler and options
Creating Makefile in src/support
Creating Makefile in src/regex
Creating Makefile in src/os/unix
Creating Makefile in src/ap
Creating Makefile in src/main
Creating Makefile in src/lib/expat-lite
Creating Makefile in src/modules/standard
#
```

The configuration script will run through its process of checking your configuration and creating makefiles, and then will put you back at the prompt.

```
passwd.o -lap -los  -lm -lcrypt -ldl
gcc -c  -I../os/unix -I../include   -DLINUX=2 -DUSE_HSREGEX -DUSE_EXPAT -I../lib/expat-lite `../apaci` htdige
st.c
gcc  -DLINUX=2 -DUSE_HSREGEX -DUSE_EXPAT -I../lib/expat-lite `../apaci` -o htdigest   -L../os/unix -L../ap ht
digest.o -lap -los  -lm -lcrypt -ldl
gcc -c  -I../os/unix -I../include   -DLINUX=2 -DUSE_HSREGEX -DUSE_EXPAT -I../lib/expat-lite `../apaci` rotate
logs.c
gcc  -DLINUX=2 -DUSE_HSREGEX -DUSE_EXPAT -I../lib/expat-lite `../apaci` -o rotatelogs   -L../os/unix -L../ap
rotatelogs.o -lap -los  -lm -lcrypt -ldl
gcc -c  -I../os/unix -I../include   -DLINUX=2 -DUSE_HSREGEX -DUSE_EXPAT -I../lib/expat-lite `../apaci` logres
olve.c
gcc  -DLINUX=2 -DUSE_HSREGEX -DUSE_EXPAT -I../lib/expat-lite `../apaci` -o logresolve   -L../os/unix -L../ap
logresolve.o -lap -los  -lm -lcrypt -ldl
gcc -c  -I../os/unix -I../include   -DLINUX=2 -DUSE_HSREGEX -DUSE_EXPAT -I../lib/expat-lite `../apaci` ab.c
gcc  -DLINUX=2 -DUSE_HSREGEX -DUSE_EXPAT -I../lib/expat-lite `../apaci` -o ab   -L../os/unix -L../ap ab.o -la
p -los -lm -lcrypt -ldl
sed <apxs.pl >apxs \
    -e 's%@TARGET@%httpd%g' \
    -e 's%@CC@%gcc%g' \
    -e 's%@CFLAGS@%  -DLINUX=2 -DUSE_HSREGEX -DUSE_EXPAT -I../lib/expat-lite `../apaci`%g' \
    -e 's%@CFLAGS_SHLIB@%-fpic -DSHARED_MODULE%g' \
    -e 's%@LD_SHLIB@%gcc%g' \
    -e 's%@LDFLAGS_MOD_SHLIB@%-shared%g' \
    -e 's%@LIBS_SHLIB@%%g' && chmod a+x apxs
make[2]: Leaving directory `/opt/apache_1.3.12/src/support'
<=== src/support
make[1]: Leaving directory `/opt/apache_1.3.12'
<=== src
# █
```

8. Type **make** and press Enter.

This second step of the installation process will produce many lines of output on your screen. When it is finished, you will be back at the prompt.

```
./src/helpers/install.sh -c -m 644 ./conf/httpd.conf-dist[*] /opt/apache_1.3.12/conf/httpd.
./src/helpers/install.sh -c -m 644 ./conf/httpd.conf-dist[*] /opt/apache_1.3.12/conf/httpd.
./src/helpers/install.sh -c -m 644 ./conf/access.conf-dist[*] /opt/apache_1.3.12/conf/acces
./src/helpers/install.sh -c -m 644 ./conf/access.conf-dist[*] /opt/apache_1.3.12/conf/acces
./src/helpers/install.sh -c -m 644 ./conf/srm.conf-dist[*] /opt/apache_1.3.12/conf/srm.conf
./src/helpers/install.sh -c -m 644 ./conf/srm.conf-dist[*] /opt/apache_1.3.12/conf/srm.conf
./src/helpers/install.sh -c -m 644 ./conf/mime.types /opt/apache_1.3.12/conf/mime.types.def
[PRESERVING EXISTING CONFIG FILE: /opt/apache_1.3.12/conf/mime.types]
./src/helpers/install.sh -c -m 644 ./conf/magic /opt/apache_1.3.12/conf/magic.default
[PRESERVING EXISTING CONFIG FILE: /opt/apache_1.3.12/conf/magic]
<=== [config]
make[1]: Leaving directory `/opt/apache_1.3.12'
+--------------------------------------------------------------------+
| You now have successfully built and installed the                  |
| Apache 1.3 HTTP server. To verify that Apache actually             |
| works correctly you now should first check the                     |
| (initially created or preserved) configuration files              |
|                                                                    |
|   /opt/apache_1.3.12/conf/httpd.conf                               |
|                                                                    |
| and then you should be able to immediately fire up                 |
| Apache the first time by running:                                  |
|                                                                    |
|   /opt/apache_1.3.12/bin/apachectl start                           |
|                                                                    |
| Thanks for using Apache.       The Apache Group                    |
|                                http://www.apache.org/              |
+--------------------------------------------------------------------+
# █
```

9. Type **make install** and press Enter.

This final step of the installation process will produce many lines of output on your screen. When it is finished, you will be back at the prompt.

In the next section, you'll make some minor changes to the Apache configuration file before you start Apache for the first time.

Configuring Apache

At this stage, the only changes you'll make to the Apache configuration file are minor administrative changes. Configuration files are located in the conf directory, within the Apache installation directory. So, if your installation directory is /usr/local/apache_1.3.12/, the configuration files will be in /usr/local/apache_1.3.12/conf/.

```
#
# ServerAdmin: Your address, where problems with the server should be
# e-mailed.  This address appears on some server-generated pages, such
# as error documents.
#
ServerAdmin you@your.address

#
# ServerName allows you to set a host name which is sent back to clients for
# your server if it's different than the one the program would get (i.e., use
# "www" instead of the host's real name).
#
# Note: You cannot just invent host names and hope they work. The name you
# define here must be a valid DNS name for your host. If you don't understand
# this, ask your network administrator.
# If your host doesn't have a registered DNS name, enter its IP address here.
# You will have to access it by its address (e.g., http://123.45.67.89/)
# anyway, and this will make redirections work in a sensible way.
#
#ServerName new.host.name
```

1. Open a text editor.

2. Open the httpd.conf file in the conf directory of the Apache installation directory.

3. Find this section of text.

```
#
# ServerAdmin: Your address, where problems with the server should be
# e-mailed.  This address appears on some server-generated pages, such
# as error documents.
#
ServerAdmin julie@thickbook.com

#
# ServerName allows you to set a host name which is sent back to clients for
# your server if it's different than the one the program would get (i.e., use
# "www" instead of the host's real name).
#
# Note: You cannot just invent host names and hope they work. The name you
# define here must be a valid DNS name for your host. If you don't understand
# this, ask your network administrator.
# If your host doesn't have a registered DNS name, enter its IP address here.
# You will have to access it by its address (e.g., http://123.45.67.89/)
# anyway, and this will make redirections work in a sensible way.
#
ServerName localhost
```

4. Change the value of ServerAdmin to your e-mail address.

5. Change the value of ServerName to localhost.

6. Save the file.

Apache is now ready to run on your machine. In the next section, you'll start and connect to Apache.

Starting and Stopping Apache

There's a handy utility in the bin directory within your Apache installation directory called apachectl. It allows you to issue start, stop, and restart commands. Use this utility to start Apache for the first time.

1. To get to the Apache installation directory, type **cd /usr/local/apache_1.3.12** and press Enter.

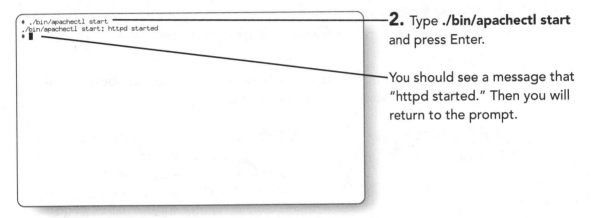

```
# ./bin/apachectl start
./bin/apachectl start: httpd started
#
```

2. Type **./bin/apachectl start** and press Enter.

You should see a message that "httpd started." Then you will return to the prompt.

To stop Apache, you can type **./bin/apachectl stop** and press Enter. For now, though, keep it running. In the next section, you'll connect to your new Web server for the first time.

Connecting to Apache

In the configuration section, you gave a value of localhost to ServerName in the httpd.conf file. You'll use this name to connect to your Web server.

> ## NOTE
>
> Only you can connect to your Web server using localhost. If you have a static IP and a machine name that resolves via DNS, you can substitute that name for localhost in the httpd.conf file, and other users can connect to that machine. This book assumes that you'll be using localhost for now, but it really makes no difference if you have a real machine name. Just substitute your machine name for localhost in the examples.

1. Open your Web browser, type **http://localhost/** in the location bar, and press Enter.

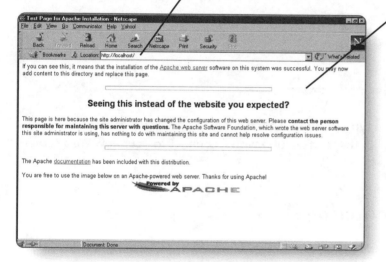

The default start page comes from the htdocs directory within your Apache installation directory. You can go into that directory and delete all the default files if you want to, or you can leave them. They're not hurting anything, but you'll eventually fill the htdocs directory with your own files and subdirectories, so you might want to delete them for the sake of good housekeeping.

Move ahead to the next chapter, where you'll install PHP and make a few more minor changes to your Apache configuration files before you're ready for some action.

3

Installing PHP4

This is it—the final piece of the puzzle that will get you started in the world of creating dynamic, database-driven Web sites. In this chapter, you'll learn how to do the following:

- Install PHP4 on Windows or Linux
- Make final modifications to Apache
- Use the `phpinfo()` function to retrieve system information

If You're Using Windows

Installing PHP4 for Windows doesn't occur through a wizard interface. Basically, you just unzip some files and move them around. It's no big deal, just follow along closely.

Installing PHP4 for Windows

Installing PHP4 with Apache on Windows is the same for Windows 95/98/2000/NT. If you encounter any problems, go to the PHP Web site at http://www.php.net/ and read the FAQ first and then the PHP Manual.

Before you begin, find the CD-ROM included in this book and put it in your CD-ROM drive. Now you're ready to install some files.

1. Using Windows Explorer, navigate through the CD-ROM filesystem.

2. Open the software directory.

3. Open the Windows directory.

4. Double-click on the file called php-4_0_0-Win32.exe. A dialog box will open, prompting for confirmation to unzip to C:\WINDOWS\TEMP\.

5. Change the unzip location to C:\php4\.

6. Click on Unzip to extract the files.

7. Confirm the action by clicking on OK.

8. Click on Close.

Organizing Your Installation Files

You now have all the basic PHP4 distribution files; you just need to move a few of them around.

1. Using Windows Explorer (or whatever method you prefer for moving through your filesystem), go to the C:\php4\ directory.

2. Rename the php.ini-dist file php.ini.

3. Move the php.ini file to C:\WINDOWS\, or wherever you usually put your *.ini files.

4. Move msvcrt.dll and php4ts.dll to C:\WINDOWS\SYSTEM\, or wherever you usually put your *.dll files.

NOTE

You might already have a copy of msvcrt.dll on your system. If you receive a warning when you try to move msvcrt.dll, you can ignore the warning and not copy the file. As long as this file is on your system, you don't necessarily need the one from the PHP4 distribution.

Configuring Apache to Use PHP4

To get a basic version of PHP4 working with Apache, you'll need to make a few minor modifications to the Apache configuration file.

The modifications you'll be making are to the same configuration file that you used in Chapter 2: the httpd.conf file located in the conf directory within the Apache installation directory.

```
#
# ScriptAlias: This controls which directories contain server scripts.
# ScriptAliases are essentially the same as Aliases, except that
# documents in the realname directory are treated as applications and
# run by the server when requested rather than as documents sent to the client.
# The same rules about trailing "/" apply to ScriptAlias directives as to
# Alias.
#

ScriptAlias /cgi-bin/ "C:/Program Files/Apache Group/Apache/cgi-bin/"
```

1. Open a text editor.

2. Open the httpd.conf file.

3. Find a section of text like this one.

```
#
# ScriptAlias: This controls which directories contain server scripts.
# ScriptAliases are essentially the same as Aliases, except that
# documents in the realname directory are treated as applications and
# run by the server when requested rather than as documents sent to the client.
# The same rules about trailing "/" apply to ScriptAlias directives as to
# Alias.
#

ScriptAlias /cgi-bin/ "C:/Program Files/Apache Group/Apache/cgi-bin/"
ScriptAlias /php4/ "C:/php4/"
```

4. Add a line like the following:

```
ScriptAlias /php4/ "C:/php4/"
```

NOTE

If you put your PHP files in a different directory, substitute that directory name in the ScriptAlias line.

```
#
# AddType allows you to tweak mime.types without actually editing it, or to
# make certain files to be certain types.
#
# For example, the PHP3 module (not part of the Apache distribution)
# will typically use:
#AddType application/x-httpd-php3 .phtml
#AddType application/x-httpd-php3-source .phps
```

Next, you have to add a directive to the httpd.conf file to define the file extensions used by PHP files. Common extensions are .php and .phtml, but you can use whatever you'd like.

5. Find a section of text like this one.

```
#
# AddType allows you to tweak mime.types without actually editing it, or to
# make certain files to be certain types.
#
# For example, the PHP3 module (not part of the Apache distribution)
# will typically use:
#AddType application/x-httpd-php3 .phtml
#AddType application/x-httpd-php3-source .phps

AddType application/x-httpd-php .phtml .php
AddType application/x-httpd-php-source .phps
```

6. Add the following two lines:

```
AddType application/x-httpd-php .phtml .php
```

```
AddType application/x-httpd-php-source .phps
```

Make one more modification to the httpd.conf file, and you'll be done.

```
#
# Action lets you define media types that will execute a script whenever
# a matching file is called. This eliminates the need for repeated URL
# pathnames for oft-used CGI file processors.
# Format: Action media/type /cgi-script/location
# Format: Action handler-name /cgi-script/location
#
```

7. Find a section of text like this one.

```
#
# Action lets you define media types that will execute a script whenever
# a matching file is called. This eliminates the need for repeated URL
# pathnames for oft-used CGI file processors.
# Format: Action media/type /cgi-script/location
# Format: Action handler-name /cgi-script/location
#

Action application/x-httpd-php  /php4/php.exe
```

8. Add the following line:

Action application/x-httpd-php /php4/php.exe

9. Save and close the httpd.conf file.

This final modification tells Apache that anytime a file with an extension of .php or .phtml is requested, Apache should first run that file through the PHP parser before sending any output to the Web browser.

Restarting Apache and Testing the PHP4 Installation

Now that all of your modifications have been made to the httpd.conf file, you can restart Apache.

If you're using Windows NT, do the following:

1. Go to Control Panel and open the Services window.

2. Select Apache from the list of services.

3. Click on Stop to stop the service.

4. Click on Start to start the service again.

Creating a Text Script

Now you'll create a simple PHP script to test your installation. PHP scripts and other files (HTML, images, and so on) should be located in the document root of your Web server. For Apache, the document root is the htdocs directory within your Apache installation directory.

> **TIP**
>
> If you need to manually start Apache, open the Apache Web Server menu from the Windows Start menu, and select the Start Apache item.

1. Open a new file in your text editor.

2. Type the following:

```
<? phpinfo(); ?>
```

3. Save the file with the name phpinfo.php.

4. Place this file in the document root of your Web server.

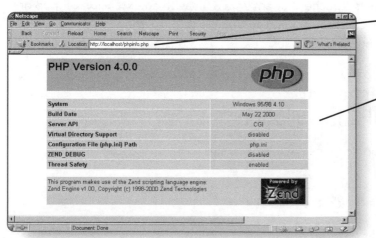

5. Open your Web browser and type **http://localhost/phpinfo.php**

The output of the phpinfo.php script should be a long page full of system and environment information. This information is very helpful when you're trying to figure out what's available to you.

If you browse through the results, you'll see that the following are pre-installed:

- Regular expression support
- Dynamic library support
- Internal sendmail support
- Perl-compatible regular expression support
- ODBC support
- Session support
- XML support
- MySQL support

Having these items preinstalled means that no additional .dll files are necessary for these functions to be available to you. For more information on obtaining .dll files for additional PHP functionality, see Appendix A, "Additional Configuration Options."

You're now ready to move on to Part II, "The Absolute Basics of Coding in PHP," and learn the fundamentals of the PHP language.

If You're Using Linux

This section will show you how to install PHP4 on Linux using a file from this book's CD-ROM, so track it down before you get started. This same file should work for other flavors of UNIX as well.

You will build PHP4 as a dynamic module for Apache. By building a dynamic rather than a static module, you can upgrade or recompile PHP4 without having to recompile Apache as well.

For example, all you'll be doing in this section is configuring PHP for MySQL support. If you decide you want additional options later in the game—such as image creation functions or additional encryption functions—you'll only have to change the configuration command for PHP4, recompile it, and restart Apache. No additional changes will be needed for the Apache installation.

Installing PHP4 for Linux

If you encounter any problems while installing PHP4 for Linux, go to the PHP Web site at http://www.php.net/ and read the FAQ first and then the PHP Manual.

Before you begin, find the CD-ROM included in this book, and put it in your CD-ROM drive. Mount the CD using your usual process, and you'll be ready to install some files.

1. Using the command line, type **cd [directory]/software/linux/** and press Enter to reach the directory containing the file php-4.0.0.tar.gz from the CD-ROM.

2. Type **cp php-4.0.0.tar.gz /usr/local/** and press Enter to copy the PHP4 installation file to the /usr/local/ directory.

NOTE

You can put PHP4 anywhere you want on your filesystem, such as /usr/local/bin/ or /opt/, or wherever you want to put the file. Just be sure to substitute your path for the path indicated in these directions.

```
php-4.0.0/Zend/zend-parser.output
php-4.0.0/Zend/zend-parser.h
php-4.0.0/Zend/zend-scanner.c
php-4.0.0/Zend/zend-scanner-cc.cc
php-4.0.0/TSRM/
php-4.0.0/TSRM/Makefile.in
php-4.0.0/TSRM/Makefile.am
php-4.0.0/TSRM/TSRM.c
php-4.0.0/TSRM/TSRM.dsp
php-4.0.0/TSRM/TSRM.h
php-4.0.0/TSRM/acconfig.h
php-4.0.0/TSRM/acinclude.m4
php-4.0.0/TSRM/build.mk
php-4.0.0/TSRM/buildconf
php-4.0.0/TSRM/configure.in
php-4.0.0/TSRM/threads.m4
php-4.0.0/TSRM/tsrm.m4
php-4.0.0/acconfig.h
php-4.0.0/php_config.h.in
php-4.0.0/buildmk.stamp
php-4.0.0/generated_lists
php-4.0.0/mkinstalldirs
php-4.0.0/install-sh
php-4.0.0/aclocal.m4
php-4.0.0/configuration-parser.output
php-4.0.0/configuration-parser.c
php-4.0.0/configuration-parser.h
php-4.0.0/configuration-scanner.c
#
```

3. Go to /usr/local/ by typing **cd /usr/local/** and pressing Enter.

4. Unzip the PHP4 installation file by typing **gunzip php-4.0.0.tar.gz** and pressing Enter.

5. At the prompt, extract the files by typing **tar -xvf php-4.0.0.tar** and pressing Enter.

A directory structure will be created, and you'll be back at the prompt. The parent directory will be /usr/local/php-4.0.0/

6. Enter the parent directory by typing **cd php-4.0.0** and pressing Enter.

7. Type the following and press Enter, to prepare to build PHP4:

```
./configure --with-mysql=/usr/local/mysql-3.22.32-pc-linux-gnu-i686/
--with-apxs=/usr/local/
apache_1.3.12/bin/apxs
```

> ### NOTE
> In configuration directives, use your own paths to the MySQL and Apache directories should they reside elsewhere on your filesystem (such as /opt/).

```
creating ext/pcre/pcrelib/Makefile
creating ext/posix/Makefile
creating ext/session/Makefile
creating ext/standard/Makefile
creating ext/xml/Makefile
creating ext/xml/expat/Makefile
creating ext/xml/expat/xmlparse/Makefile
creating ext/xml/expat/xmltok/Makefile
creating sapi/apache/Makefile
creating regex/Makefile
updating cache ./config.cache
creating ./config.status
creating php4.spec
creating Zend/Makefile
creating build-defs.h
creating php_config.h
creating internal_functions.c
+--------------------------------------------------------+
| License:                                               |
| This software is subject to the PHP License, available in this |
| distribution in the file LICENSE.  By continuing this installation |
| process, you are bound by the terms of this license agreement. |
| If you do not agree with the terms of this license, you must abort |
| the installation process at this point.                |
+--------------------------------------------------------+

Thank you for using PHP.

* ▮
```

The configuration script will run through its process of checking your configuration and creating makefiles. It then will put you back at the prompt.

8. Type **make** and press Enter.

```
/bin/sh /opt/php-4.0.0/libtool --silent --mode=compile gcc -DHAVE_CONFIG_H -I. -I/opt/php-4.0.0/ -I/opt/php-4
.0.0 -I/opt/apache_1.3.12/include -I/opt/php-4.0.0/Zend -I/opt/php-4.0.0 -I/usr/local/bin/mysql/include -I/op
t/php-4.0.0/ext/xml/expat/xmltok -I/opt/php-4.0.0/ext/xml/expat/xmlparse -DXML_BYTE_ORDER=12 -g -O2 -Wall -
c reentrancy.c
/bin/sh /opt/php-4.0.0/libtool --silent --mode=compile gcc -DHAVE_CONFIG_H -I. -I/opt/php-4.0.0/ -I/opt/php-4
.0.0 -I/opt/apache_1.3.12/include -I/opt/php-4.0.0/Zend -I/opt/php-4.0.0 -I/usr/local/bin/mysql/include -I/op
t/php-4.0.0/ext/xml/expat/xmltok -I/opt/php-4.0.0/ext/xml/expat/xmlparse -DXML_BYTE_ORDER=12 -g -O2 -Wall -
c php_variables.c
/bin/sh /opt/php-4.0.0/libtool --silent --mode=compile gcc -DHAVE_CONFIG_H -I. -I/opt/php-4.0.0/ -I/opt/php-4
.0.0 -I/opt/apache_1.3.12/include -I/opt/php-4.0.0/Zend -I/opt/php-4.0.0 -I/usr/local/bin/mysql/include -I/op
t/php-4.0.0/ext/xml/expat/xmltok -I/opt/php-4.0.0/ext/xml/expat/xmlparse -DXML_BYTE_ORDER=12 -g -O2 -Wall -
c php_ticks.c
/bin/sh /opt/php-4.0.0/libtool --silent --mode=compile gcc -DHAVE_CONFIG_H -I. -I/opt/php-4.0.0/ -I/opt/php-4
.0.0 -I/opt/apache_1.3.12/include -I/opt/php-4.0.0/Zend -I/opt/php-4.0.0 -I/usr/local/bin/mysql/include -I/op
t/php-4.0.0/ext/xml/expat/xmltok -I/opt/php-4.0.0/ext/xml/expat/xmlparse -DXML_BYTE_ORDER=12 -g -O2 -Wall -
c php_virtual_cwd.c
/bin/sh /opt/php-4.0.0/libtool --silent --mode=link gcc -g -O2 -Wall -o libphp4.la -rpath /opt/php-4.0.0/li
bs -avoid-version -L/usr/local/bin/mysql/lib/mysql -R /usr/local/bin/mysql/lib/mysql main.lo internal_functi
ons.lo snprintf.lo php_sprintf.lo configuration-parser.lo configuration-scanner.lo safe_mode.lo fopen-wrapper
s.lo php_realpath.lo alloca.lo php_ini.lo SAPI.lo rfc1867.lo php_content_types.lo strlcpy.lo strlcat.lo merge
sort.lo reentrancy.lo php_variables.lo php_ticks.lo php_virtual_cwd.lo Zend/libZend.la sapi/apache/libsapi.la
 regex/libregex.la ext/db/libdb.la ext/mysql/libmysql.la ext/pcre/libpcre.la ext/posix/libposix.la ext/sessio
n/libsession.la ext/standard/libstandard.la ext/xml/libxml.la -lgdbm -lpam -ldl -lmysqlclient -lresolv -lm -
ldl -lcrypt -lnsl -lresolv
make[1]: Leaving directory `/opt/php-4.0.0'
Making all in pear
make[1]: Entering directory `/opt/php-4.0.0/pear'
make[1]: Leaving directory `/opt/php-4.0.0/pear'
* ▮
```

This second step of the installation process will produce many lines of output on your screen. When it is finished, you will be back at the prompt.

```
make[2]: Leaving directory `/opt/php-4.0.0/sapi/apache'
make[2]: Entering directory `/opt/php-4.0.0/sapi'
make[2]: Nothing to be done for `install-p'.
make[2]: Leaving directory `/opt/php-4.0.0/sapi'
make[1]: Leaving directory `/opt/php-4.0.0/sapi'
Making install in regex
make[1]: Entering directory `/opt/php-4.0.0/regex'
make[2]: Entering directory `/opt/php-4.0.0/regex'
make[2]: Nothing to be done for `install-p'.
make[2]: Leaving directory `/opt/php-4.0.0/regex'
make[1]: Leaving directory `/opt/php-4.0.0/regex'
Making install in .
make[1]: Entering directory `/opt/php-4.0.0'
/opt/apache_1.3.12/bin/apxs -i -a -n php4 libs/libphp4.so
cp libs/libphp4.so /opt/apache_1.3.12/libexec/libphp4.so
chmod 755 /opt/apache_1.3.12/libexec/libphp4.so
[activating module `php4' in /opt/apache_1.3.12/conf/httpd.conf]
installing shared modules into /usr/local/lib/php/extensions/debug-non-zts-20000401
cp: modules/*: No such file or directory
make[1]: Leaving directory `/opt/php-4.0.0'
Making install in pear
make[1]: Entering directory `/opt/php-4.0.0/pear'
make[2]: Entering directory `/opt/php-4.0.0/pear'
creating header file hierarchy
creating phpize
creating php-config
make[2]: Leaving directory `/opt/php-4.0.0/pear'
make[1]: Leaving directory `/opt/php-4.0.0/pear'
# ▮
```

9. Type **make install** and press Enter.

This final step of the installation process will produce many lines of output on your screen. When it is finished, you will be back at the prompt.

To get a basic version of PHP4 working with Apache, you'll need to make a modification to the httpd.conf file.

Configuring Apache to Use PHP4

The installation process will have placed a module in the proper place within the Apache directory structure and will have automatically made some changes to the httpd.conf file. You'll need to make one more change to the httpd.conf file.

```
#
# AddType allows you to tweak mime.types without actually editing it, or to
# make certain files to be certain types.
#
# For example, the PHP 3.x module (not part of the Apache distribution - see
# http://www.php.net) will typically use:
#
#AddType application/x-httpd-php3 .php3
#AddType application/x-httpd-php3-source .phps
#
# And for PHP 4.x, use:
#
#AddType application/x-httpd-php .php
#AddType application/x-httpd-php-source .phps
```

1. Open your text editor.

2. Open the httpd.conf file.

3. Find a section of text like this one.

```
#
# AddType allows you to tweak mime.types without actually editing it, or to
# make certain files to be certain types.
#
# For example, the PHP 3.x module (not part of the Apache distribution - see
# http://www.php.net) will typically use:
#
#AddType application/x-httpd-php3 .php3
#AddType application/x-httpd-php3-source .phps
#
# And for PHP 4.x, use:
#
AddType application/x-httpd-php .phtml .php
AddType application/x-httpd-php-source .phps
```

4. Uncomment the last two lines by removing the #, and add .phtml as an option in the next-to-last line.

5. Save and close the httpd.conf file.

This final modification tells Apache that anytime a file with an extension of .php or .phtml is requested, Apache should first run that file through the PHP parser before sending any output to the Web browser.

Restarting Apache and Testing the PHP4 Installation

Now that all of your modifications have been made to the httpd.conf file, you can restart Apache.

1. To get to the Apache installation directory, type **cd /usr/local/apache_1.3.12** and press Enter.

2. Type **./bin/apachectl start** and press Enter.

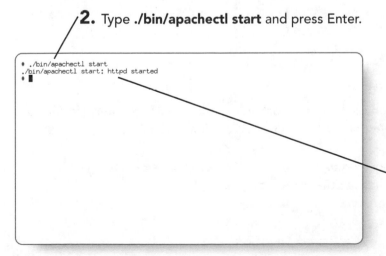

```
# ./bin/apachectl start
./bin/apachectl start: httpd started
#
```

NOTE
If the apache_1.3.12 directory resides elsewhere on your filesystem, such as /opt/, use that path in step 1.

You should see a message that "httpd started." Then you return to the prompt.

Now you'll create a simple PHP script to test your installation. PHP scripts and other files (HTML, images, and so on) should be located in the document root of your Web server. For Apache, the document root is the htdocs directory within your Apache installation directory.

1. Open a new file in your text editor.

2. Type the following:

```
<? phpinfo(); ?>
```

3. Save the file with the name phpinfo.php.

4. Place this file in the document root of your Web server.

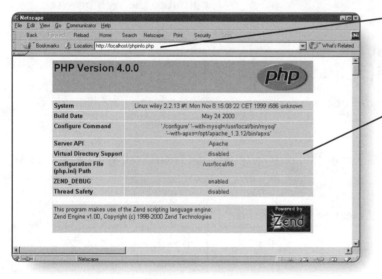

5. Open your Web browser, type **http://localhost/ phpinfo.php**, and then press Enter.

The output of the phpinfo.php script should be a long page full of system and environment information. This information is very helpful when you're trying to figure out what's available to you.

For more information on configuring and building additional functionality into your PHP4 installation, see Appendix A, "Additional Configuration Options."

You're now ready to move on to Part II, "The Absolute Basics of Coding in PHP," and learn the fundamentals of the PHP language.

PART II

The Absolute Basics of Coding in PHP

4

Mixing PHP and HTML

Now that you have a working development environment, with PHP, Apache, and MySQL happily running on your machine, it's time to delve into the PHP language. In this chapter, you'll learn how to do the following:

- Recognize and use the different kinds of PHP start and end tags
- Mingle PHP and HTML within your source code
- Escape special characters in your scripts to produce valid output

How PHP Is Parsed

So you have a file, and in that file you have some HTML and some PHP code. This is how it all works. Assume that PHP documents have an extension of .php.

1. The Web browser requests a document with a .php extension.

2. The Web server says, "Hey! Someone wants a PHP file. Something else needs to deal with it" and sends the request on to the PHP parser.

3. The PHP parser finds the requested file and scans it for PHP code.

4. When the PHP parser finds PHP code, it executes that code and places the resulting output (if any) into the place in the file formerly occupied by the code.

5. This new output file is sent back to the Web server.

6. The Web server sends it along to the Web browser.

7. The Web browser displays the output.

This method of code execution is called *server-side*. Code executed by the browser, such as JavaScript, is called *client-side*.

To combine PHP code with HTML, the PHP code must be set apart from the HTML. In the next section, you'll learn how this is done, using PHP start and end tags.

PHP Start and End Tags

The PHP parser recognizes a few different types of PHP start and end tags. It will attempt to execute anything between these tags, so it had better be valid code!

Study the following table to learn the three main sets of start and end tags recognized by the PHP parser.

Basic PHP Start and End Tags

Opening Tag	Closing Tag
<?php	?>
<?	?>
<script language="php">	</script>

Next, you'll use all three sets of tags in a script, which I promise will execute without errors.

1. Open a new file in your text editor.

2. Type the following code, which uses the first tag type:

```
<?php
echo "<P>This is a test using the first tag type.</P>";
?>
```

3. Type the following code, which uses the second tag type:

```
<?
echo "<P>This is a test using the second tag type.</P>";
?>
```

4. Type the following code, which uses the third tag type:

```
<script language="php">
echo "<P>This is a test using the third tag
type.</P>";
</script>
```

5. Save the file with the name phptags.php.

6. Place this file in the document root of your Web server.

7. Open your Web browser and type
http://localhost/phptags.php

> **NOTE**
> If you are using PHP on an external Web server while executing the example in this book, substitute that server's domain name for **localhost** in the URL.

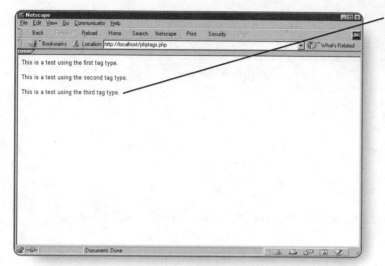

In your Web browser, you should see the results of your script.

In the next section, you'll learn that putting PHP blocks inside HTML is not scary at all.

Code Cohabitation

In the previous section, your file consisted of three chunks of PHP code, each of which printed some HTML text. In this section, you'll create a script that has PHP code stuck in the middle of your HTML, and you'll learn how these two types of code can peacefully coexist.

1. Open a new file in your text editor.

2. Type the following HTML:

```
<HTML>
<HEAD>
<TITLE>My First PHP Script</TITLE>
</HEAD>
<BODY>
```

3. Type the following PHP code:

```
<?
echo "<P><em>Hello World! I'm using PHP!</em></P>";
?>
```

4. Add some more HTML so that the document is valid:

```
</BODY>
</HTML>
```

5. Save the file with the name firstscript.php.

6. Place this file in the document root of your Web server.

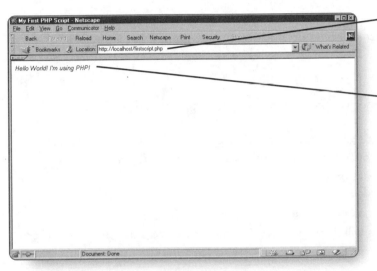

7. Open your Web browser and type **http://localhost/firstscript.php**

In your Web browser, you should see the results of your script.

8. In your Web browser, view the source of this document. Notice that the HTML source contains only HTML code. This block of PHP was executed:

```
<?
echo "<P><em>Hello World! I'm
using PHP!</em></P>";
?>
```

This block contains three elements: the command (echo), the string (<P>Hello World! I'm using PHP!</P>), and the instruction terminator (;).

Familiarize yourself now with echo, because it will likely be your most often-used command. The echo statement is used to output information—in this case, to print this HTML output:

```
<P><em>Hello World! I'm using PHP!</em></P>
```

The next section discusses a common error so that hopefully you'll be able to avoid it.

The Importance of the Instruction Terminator

The instruction terminator, also known as the semicolon (;), is absolutely required at the end of commands. The instruction terminator tells the PHP parser, "I'm done with this thing. Try the next one."

If you do not end commands with a semicolon, the PHP parser will become confused, and your code will display errors. These next steps show you how to get one of these errors and, more importantly, how to fix it.

1. Open a new file in your text editor.

2. Type the following HTML:

```
<HTML>
<HEAD>
<TITLE>Making an Error</TITLE>
</HEAD>
<BODY>
```

3. Type the following PHP code:

```
<?
echo "<P>I am trying to produce an error</P>"
echo "<P>Was I successful?</P>";
?>
```

4. Add some more HTML so that the document is valid:

```
</BODY>
</HTML>
```

5. Save the file with the name errorscript.php.

6. Place this file in the document root of your Web server.

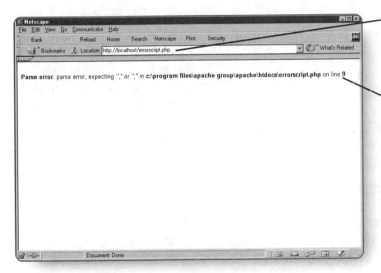

7. Open your Web browser and type **http://localhost/ errorscript.php**.

What a nasty error! The error message says that the error is on line 9. Take a look at lines 8 and 9 of the script:

```
echo "<P>I am trying to
produce an error</P>"
echo "<P>Was I
successful?</P>";
```

Fixing the Parse Error

Line 8 does not have an instruction terminator, and line 9 starts a new command. The PHP parser doesn't like this, and it tells you so by producing the parse error.

This error is easy enough to fix:

1. Open the errorscript.php file.

2. On line 8, add the instruction terminator (the ;) to the end of the line:

```
echo "<P>I am trying to produce an error</P>";
```

3. Save the file.

4. Place this file in the document root of your Web server.

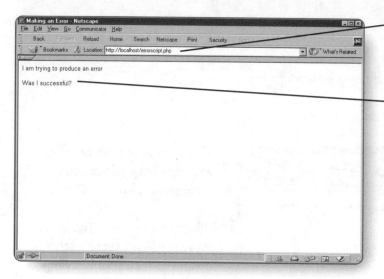

5. Open your Web browser and type **http://localhost//errorscript.php**.

After you fix line 8, the PHP parser can deal with the file, and the rest of the output is successful. Avoid this and other errors by paying close attention to things such as semicolons and, as you'll learn in the next section, quotation marks!

Escaping Your Code

Right up there with remembering to end your commands with semicolons is remembering to escape things such as quotation marks. When you use quotation marks inside other quotation marks, the inner pairs must be delineated from the outside pair using the escape (\) character (also known as a backslash).

The following steps show you what happens when your code isn't escaped, and how to fix it.

1. Open a new file in your text editor.

2. Type the following HTML:

```
<HTML>
<HEAD>
<TITLE>Trying For Another Error</TITLE>
</HEAD>
<BODY>
```

3. Type the following PHP code:

```
<?
echo "<P>I think this is really "cool"!</P>";
?>
```

4. Add some more HTML so that the document is valid:

```
</BODY>
</HTML>
```

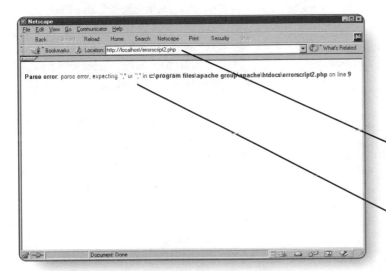

5. Save the file with the name errorscript2.php.

6. Place this file in the document root of your Web server.

7. Open your Web browser and type **http://localhost/ errorscript2.php**.

Another parse error! Take a look at the PHP code:

```
echo "<P>I think this is
really "cool"!</P>";
```

Fixing the Parse Error

Since you have a set of quotation marks within another set of quotation marks, that inner set has to be escaped.

This error also has a simple fix:

1. Open the errorscript2.php file.

2. On line 8, escape the inner quotation marks by placing a backslash before each one:

```
echo "<P>I think this is really \"cool\"!</P>";
```

3. Save the file.

4. Place this file in the document root of your Web server.

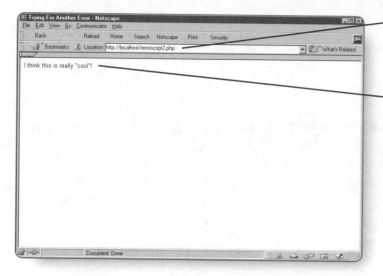

5. Open your Web browser and type **http://localhost errorscript2.php**.

Now that the inner quotation marks are escaped, the PHP parser will skip right over them, knowing that these characters should just be printed and have no other meaning.

In the next section, you'll learn a good programming practice: commenting your code so people know what the heck is going on in it.

Commenting Your Code

Commenting code is an excellent habit. Entering comments in HTML documents helps you (and others who might have to edit your document later) keep track of areas of large documents. Commenting also allows you to write notes to yourself during the development process.

HTML comments are ignored by the browser and are contained within <!-- and --> tags. For example, the following comment reminds you that the code following it contains your logo graphic:

```
<!-- logo graphic goes here -->
```

PHP uses comments, too, which are ignored by the PHP parser. PHP comments are usually preceded by double slashes, like this:

```
// this is a comment in PHP code
```

But you can use other types of comments, such as

```
# This is shell-style style comment
```

and

```
/* This begins a C-style comment that runs
onto two lines */
```

Create a script full of comments so that you can see how they're ignored (yes, I'm telling you to write a script that does absolutely nothing).

1. Open a new file in your text editor.

2. Type the following HTML:

```
<HTML>
<HEAD>
<TITLE>Code Comments</TITLE>
</HEAD>
<BODY>


<!-- This is an HTML comment. -->
```

3. Type the following PHP code:

```
<?


// This is a simple PHP comment.


/* This is a C-style, multiline comment. You can make this as
long as you'd like. */

# Used to shells? Use this kind of comment.

?>
```

4. Add some more HTML so that the document is valid:

```
</BODY>
</HTML>
```

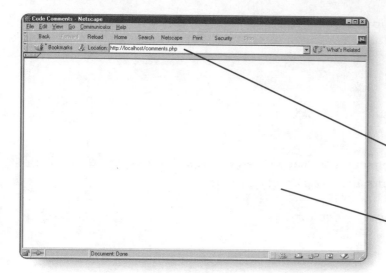

5. Save the file with the name comments.php.

6. Place this file in the document root of your Web server.

7. Open your Web browser and type **http://localhost/ comments.php**.

You should see absolutely nothing in your Web browser, because all you did was print an HTML comment (which is ignored). Since PHP comments are ignored by the PHP parser, the PHP block didn't contain any actual commands.

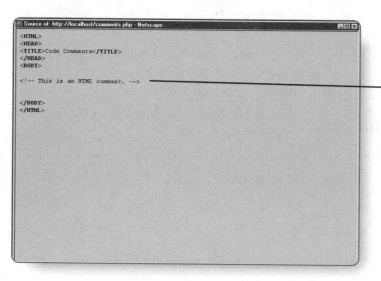

8. In your Web browser, view the source of this document. Notice that the HTML source contains the HTML comment.

HTML and PHP comments are used extensively throughout this book to explain blocks of code. Get used to reading comments, and try to develop the habit of using them. Writing clean, bug-free code, with comments and white space, will make you popular among your developer peers because they'll appreciate not having to work extra hard to figure out what your code is trying to do.

In the next chapter you'll learn all about variables, or, as I like to call them, "those things with the dollar signs."

5

Introducing Variables and Operators

In the last chapter, you were introduced to the process of parsing PHP code and how the code output is displayed in your Web browser. In the next few chapters, you'll learn a bit about the inner workings of the PHP language—all the bits and pieces that, when put together, actually produce a working program! In this chapter, you'll learn how to do the following:

- Recognize and use variables
- Recognize and use operators

What's a Variable?

A variable is a representation of a particular value, such as "blue" or "19349377". By assigning a value to a variable, you can reference the variable in other places in your script, and that value will always remain the same (unless you change it, which you'll learn about later).

To create a variable, do the following:

1. Think of a good name! For instance, if I want to create a variable to hold a username, I name my variable:

```
username
```

2. Put a dollar sign ($) in front of that name:

```
$username
```

3. Use the equal sign after the name (=) to assign a literal value to that variable. Put the value in quotation marks:

```
$username = "joe"
```

4. Assigning a value to a variable is an instruction, and as such should be terminated with a semicolon:

```
$username = "joe";
```

There you have it—a variable called "username" with a value of "joe". Later in this chapter, you'll do some exciting things (such as math) with your variables!

Naming Your Variables

As you've seen, variables begin with a dollar sign ($) and are followed by a meaningful name. The variable name cannot begin with a numeric character, but it can contain numbers and the underscore character (_). Additionally, variable names are case-sensitive, meaning that $YOURVAR and $yourvar are two different variables.

Creating meaningful variable names is another way to lessen headaches while coding. If your script deals with name and password values, don't create a variable called $n for the name and $p for the password—those are not meaningful names. If you pick up that script weeks later, you might think that $n is the variable for "number" rather than "name" and that $p stands for "page" rather than "password."

PHP Variable and Value Types

You will create two main types of variables in your PHP code: scalar and array. Scalar variables contain only one value at a time, and arrays contain a list of values, or even another array.

The example at the beginning of this chapter ($username = "joe";) created a scalar variable, and the code in this book deals primarily with scalar variables. You can find information on arrays in Appendix B, "Essential PHP Language Reference."

When you assign a value to a variable, you usually assign a value of one of the following types:

- **Integers**. Whole numbers (numbers without decimals). Examples are 1, 345, and 9922786. You can also use octal and hexadecimal notation: the octal 0123 is decimal 83 and the hexadecimal 0x12 is decimal 18.

- **Floating-point numbers ("floats" or "doubles")**. Numbers with decimals. Examples are 1.5, 87.3446, and 0.88889992.

- **Strings**. Text and/or numeric information, specified within double quotes (" ") or single quotes (' ').

As you begin your PHP script, plan your variables and variable names carefully, and use comments in your code to remind yourself of the assignments you have made.

Create a simple script that assigns values to different variables and then simply prints the values to the screen.

1. Open a new file in your text editor.

2. Type the following HTML:

```
<HTML>
<HEAD>
<TITLE>Printing Variables</TITLE>
</HEAD>
<BODY>
```

3. Add a PHP block and create a variable that holds an integer:

```
<?
$intVar = "9554215464";
```

4. Create a variable that holds a floating-point number:

```
$floatVar = "1542.2232235";
```

5. Create a variable that holds a string:

```
$stringVar = "This is a string.";
```

6. Add an echo statement for each variable:

```
echo "<P>integer: $intVar</P>";
echo "<P>float: $floatVar</P>";
echo "<P>string: $stringVar</P>";
```

7. Close your PHP block:

```
?>
```

8. Add some more HTML so that the document is valid:

```
</BODY>
</HTML>
```

9. Save the file with the name printvarscript.php.

10. Place this file in the document root of your Web server.

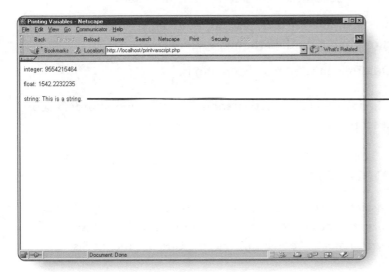

11. Open your Web browser and type **http://localhost/ printvarscript.php**.

You can see by this output that the values you assigned to the variables $intVar, $floatVar, and $stringVar were the values printed to the screen.

In the next section, you'll learn how to use operators to change the values of your variables.

What's an Operator?

In the previous section, you used an assignment operator (=) to assign values to your variables. There are other types of assignment operators, as well as other types of operators in general. The basic function of an operator is to do something with the value of a variable. That "something" can be to assign a value, change a value, or compare two or more values.

PHP Operators

Here are the main types of PHP operators and their functions:

- **Assignment operators**. Assign a value to a variable. Can also add to or subtract from a variable's current value.

- **Arithmetic operators**. You know all of these operators. Addition, subtraction, division, and multiplication occur when these operators are used.

- **Comparison operators**. Compare two values and return either true or false. You can then perform actions based on the returned value.

- **Logical operators**. Determine the status of conditions.

The rest of this chapter is devoted to discussing some of the main operators used in PHP. You'll be writing scripts for each, so hang on to your hat!

Assignment Operators

You've already seen an assignment operator at work; the equal sign is the basic assignment operator. Burn this into your brain: = does *not* mean "equal to"! Instead, == (two equal signs) means "equal to," and the single = means "is assigned to."

Take a look at the assignment operators in the following table and prepare to write a new script.

Assignment Operators

Operator	Example	Action
+=	$a += 3;	Changes the value of a variable to the current value plus the value on the right side.
-=	$a -= 3;	Changes the value of a variable to the current value minus the value on the right side.
.=	$a .= "string";	Concatenates (adds on to) the value on the right side with the current value.

Create a simple script to show how all of these assignment operators work. This script will assign an original value to one variable and then change that value as the script executes, all the while printing the result to the screen.

1. Open a new file in your text editor.

2. Type the following HTML:

```
<HTML>
<HEAD>
<TITLE>Using Assignment Operators</TITLE>
</HEAD>
<BODY>
```

3. Start a PHP block. Create a variable with a value of 100 and then print it:

```
<?
$origVar = 100;
echo "<P>Original value is $origVar</P>";
```

4. Add to that value and then print it:

```
$origVar += 25;
echo "<P>Added a value, now it's $origVar</P>";
```

5. Subtract from that value and then print it:

```
$origVar -= 12;
echo "<P>Subtracted a value, now it's $origVar</P>";
```

6. Concatenate a string and then print it:

```
$origVar .= " chickens";
echo "<P>Final answer: $origVar</P>";
```

7. Close your PHP block:

```
?>
```

8. Add some more HTML so that the document is valid:

```
</BODY>
</HTML>
```

9. Save the file with the name assignscript.php.

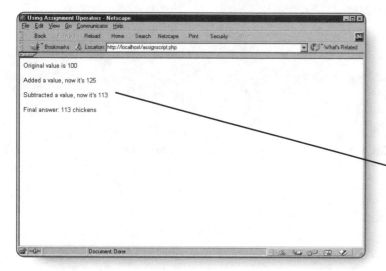

10. Place this file in the document root of your Web server.

11. Open your Web browser and type **http://localhost/ assignscript.php**.

The results of your calculations will be printed to the screen.

Next we move to arithmetic operators, none of which should be strange to you if you made it through your first few years of school.

Arithmetic Operators

Arithmetic operators are just basic math! Take a look at the table, be sure you remember your basic math, and start creating the test script for this section.

Arithmetic Operators

Operator	Example	Action
+	$b = $a + 3;	Adds values
-	$b = $a - 3;	Subtracts values
*	$b = $a * 3;	Multiplies values
/	$b = $a / 3;	Divides values
%	$b = $a % 3;	Returns the modulus, or remainder

Create a simple script to show how all of these arithmetic operators work. This script will assign original values to two variables, perform mathematical operations, and print the results to the screen.

1. Open a new file in your text editor.

2. Type the following HTML:

```
<HTML>
<HEAD>
<TITLE>Using Arithmetic Operators</TITLE>
</HEAD>
<BODY>
```

3. Add a PHP block, create two variables with values, and print the values:

```
<?
$a = 85;
$b = 24;
echo "<P>Original value of \$a is $a and \$b
is $b</P>";
```

> **NOTE**
>
> If you escape the dollar sign (\$), it will print literally instead of being interpreted as a variable.

4. Add the two values and print the result:

```
$c = $a + $b;
echo "<P>Added \$a and \$b and got $c</P>";
```

5. Subtract the two values and print the result:

```
$c = $a - $b;
echo "<P>Subtracted \$b from \$a and got $c</P>";
```

6. Multiply the two values and print the result:

```
$c = $a * $b;
echo "<P>Multiplied \$a and \$b and got $c</P>";
```

7. Divide the two values and print the result:

```
$c = $a / $b;
echo "<P>Divided \$a by \$b and got $c</P>";
```

8. Check the modulus of the two values and print the result:

```
$c = $a % $b;
echo "<P>The modulus of \$a and \$b is $c</P>";
```

9. Close your PHP block:

```
?>
```

10. Add some more HTML so that the document is valid:

```
</BODY>
</HTML>
```

11. Save the file with the name arithmeticscript.php.

12. Place this file in the document root of your Web server.

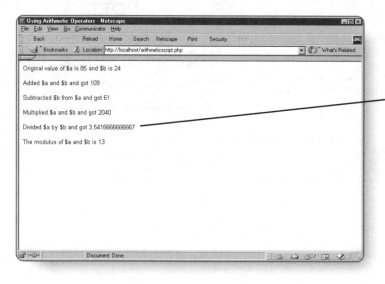

13. Open your Web browser and type **http://localhost/ arithmeticscript.php**.

Your original values, as well as the results of the various calculations, will be printed to the screen.

Next we move to comparison operators, which are quite necessary, but not nearly as much fun as arithmetic operators.

Comparison Operators

It should come as no surprise that comparison operators compare two values. As with the arithmetic operators, you already know most of the comparison operators but might not know what they are called. Take a look at the following table and then start creating the test script for this section.

Comparison Operators

Operator	Definition
==	Equal to
!=	Not equal to
>	Greater than
<	Less than
>=	Greater than or equal to
<=	Less than or equal to

The result of any of these comparisons is either true or false. This isn't much fun, but you can act on the result using control statements such as if[...]else and while to perform a specific task.

Create a simple script to show the result of some comparisons, using the if...else control statements to print a result to the screen.

1. Open a new file in your text editor.

2. Type the following HTML:

```
<HTML>
<HEAD>
<TITLE>Using Comparison Operators</TITLE>
</HEAD>
<BODY>
```

3. Start a PHP block, create two variables with values, and print the values:

```
<?
$a = 21;
$b = 15;
echo "<P>Original value of \$a is $a and \$b is $b</P>";
```

4. Within an `if[...]else` statement, test whether $a is equal to $b. Depending on the answer (true or false), one of the `echo` statements will print:

```
if ($a == $b) {
echo "<P>TEST 1: \$a equals \$b</P>";
} else {
echo "<P>TEST 1: \$a is not equal to
\$b</P>";
}
```

> **NOTE**
>
> Expressions are enclosed in parentheses.

5. Within an `if...else` statement, test whether $a is not equal to $b. Depending on the answer (true or false), one of the `echo` statements will print:

```
if ($a != $b) {
echo "<P>TEST 2: \$a is not equal to
\$b</P>";
} else {
echo "<P>TEST 2: \$a is equal to \$b</P>";
}
```

> **NOTE**
>
> The curly braces "{" and "}" separate the blocks of statements within a control structure.

6. Within an `if...else` statement, test whether $a is greater than $b. Depending on the answer (true or false), one of the `echo` statements will print:

```
if ($a > $b) {
echo "<P>TEST 3: \$a is greater than \$b</P>";
} else {
echo "<P>TEST 3: \$a is not greater than \$b</P>";
}
```

7. Within an `if...else` statement, test whether $a is less than $b. Depending on the answer (true or false), one of the `echo` statements will print:

```
if ($a < $b) {
echo "<P>TEST 4: \$a is less than \$b</P>";
} else {
echo "<P>TEST 4: \$a is not less than \$b</P>";
}
```

8. Within an `if...else` statement, test whether $a is greater than or equal to $b. Depending on the answer (true or false), one of the `echo` statements will print:

```
if ($a >= $b) {
echo "<P>TEST 5: \$a is greater than or equal to \$b</P>";
} else {
echo "<P>TEST 5: \$a is not greater than or equal to \$b</P>";
}
```

9. Within an `if...else` statement, test whether $a is less than or equal to $b. Depending on the answer (true or false), one of the `echo` statements will print:

```
if ($a <= $b) {
echo "<P>TEST 6: \$a is less than or equal to \$b</P>";
} else {
echo "<P>TEST 6: \$a is not less than or equal to \$b</P>";
}
```

10. Close your PHP block:

```
?>
```

11. Add some more HTML so that the document is valid:

```
</BODY>
</HTML>
```

12. Save the file with the name comparisonscript.php.

13. Place this file in the document root of your Web server.

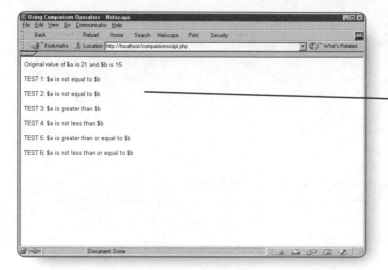

14. Open your Web browser and type **http://localhost/comparisonscript.php**.

The original values, as well as the results of the various comparisons, will be printed to the screen.

The last type of operators you'll tackle are logical operators, which are also used frequently inside blocks of code.

Logical Operators

Logical operators allow your script to determine the status of conditions (such as the comparisons in the preceding section). In the context of your if...else or while statements, logical operators execute certain code based on which conditions are true and which are false.

For now, focus on the && (and) and || (or) operators to determine the validity of a few comparisons.

1. Open a new file in your text editor.

2. Type the following HTML:

```
<HTML>
<HEAD>
<TITLE>Using Logical Operators</TITLE>
</HEAD>
<BODY>
```

3. Start a PHP block and create two variables with values. The comparisons in this script will be based on these two variables:

```
$degrees = "95";
$hot = "yes";
```

4. Within an `if[...]else` statement, test whether `$degrees` is greater than 100 or if the value of `$hot` is "yes". Depending on the result of the two comparisons, one of the echo statements will print:

> **NOTE**
> Since your expression is actually made up of two smaller expressions, an extra set of parentheses surrounds it.

```
if (($degrees > 100) || ($hot == "yes")) {
echo "<P>TEST 1: It's <strong>really</strong>
hot!</P>";
} else {
echo "<P>TEST 1:It's bearable.</P>";
}
```

5. Within an `if...else` statement, test whether `$degrees` is greater than 80 and whether the value of `$hot` is "yes". Depending on the result of the two comparisons, one of the echo statements will print:

```
if (($degrees > 80) && ($hot == "yes")) {
echo "<P>TEST 2: It's <strong>really</strong> hot!</P>";
} else {
echo "<P> TEST 2: It's bearable.</P>";
}
```

6. Close your PHP block:

```
?>
```

7. Add some more HTML so that the document is valid:

```
</BODY>
</HTML>
```

8. Save the file with the name logicalscript.php.

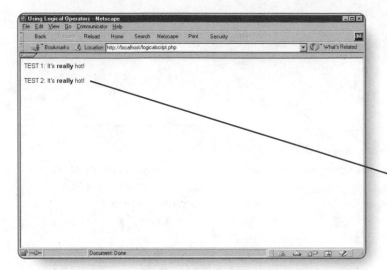

9. Place this file in the document root of your Web server.

10. Open your Web browser and type **http://localhost/ logicalscript.php**.

The text message associated with the comparison result will be printed to the screen.

Both expressions in this example are true. In the first test, only one expression has to be true, and that is satisfied by $hot having a value of "yes". In the second test, both expressions have to be true, and they are; $degrees has a value of 95, which is greater than 80, and $hot has a value of "yes".

Numerous other types of operators are used in PHP. They will be explained as they appear throughout the book. The operators listed in this chapter give you a pretty good head start. In the next chapter, you'll use your newly-acquired knowledge of variables and operators to build scripts that perform more intriguing actions than those explained so far.

6

Using Variables

Now that you know a little bit about variables, it's time to take that knowledge one step further and do more interesting things with them. In this chapter, you'll learn how to do the following:

- Use HTML forms to send variables to your scripts
- Use environment variables

Getting Variables from Forms

HTML forms should contain the following elements:

- A method
- An action
- A submit button

In your HTML code, the first line of a form will look something like this:

```
<FORM METHOD="post" ACTION="yourscript.php">
```

When you click on a submit button in an HTML form, variables are sent to the script specified by the ACTION via the specified METHOD.

The method can be either "post" or "get". Variables passed from a form to a PHP script are placed in the global associative array $HTTP_POST_VARS or $HTTP_GET_VARS, depending on the form method, and are automatically made available to your script. In the next section, you'll see how this works.

NOTE

Enabling variable tracking, or the placement of variables in global arrays, is a configuration option in PHP at installation time.

In the next sections, you'll create an HTML form and accompanying PHP script that perform calculations according to the form input.

Creating a Calculation Form

In this section, you'll create the front end to a calculation script. This form will contain two input fields and a radio button to select the calculation type.

1. Open a new file in your text editor.

2. Type the following HTML:

```
<HTML>
<HEAD>
<TITLE>Calculation Form</TITLE>
</HEAD>
<BODY>
```

3. Begin your form. Assume that the method is post and the action is a script called calculate.php:

```
<FORM METHOD="post" ACTION="calculate.php">
```

4. Create an input field for the first value, with a text label:

```
<P>Value 1: <INPUT TYPE="text" NAME="val1" SIZE=10></P>
```

5. Create an input field for the second value, with a text label:

```
<P>Value 2: <INPUT TYPE="text" NAME="val2" SIZE=10></P>
```

6. Add a submit button:

```
<P><INPUT TYPE="submit" NAME="submit" VALUE="Calculate"></P>
```

7. Close your form:

```
</FORM>
```

8. Add some more HTML so that the document is valid:

```
</BODY>
</HTML>
```

9. Save the file with the name calculate_form.html.

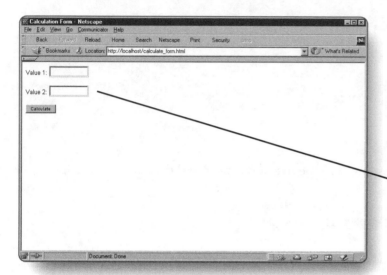

10. Place this file in the document root of your Web server.

11. Open your Web browser and type **http://localhost/ calculate_form.html**

You will see a form containing the Value 1 and Value 2 fields, along with a Calculate button.

Take a moment to examine the HTML form, to understand just how variables will get their names:

```
<HTML>
<HEAD>
<TITLE>Calculation Form</TITLE>
</HEAD>
<BODY>

<FORM METHOD="post" ACTION="calculate.php">

<P>Value 1: <INPUT TYPE="text" NAME="val1" SIZE=10></p>

<P>Value 2: <INPUT TYPE="text" NAME="val2" SIZE=10></p>

<P><INPUT TYPE="submit" NAME="submit" VALUE="Calculate"></p>

</FORM>

</BODY>
</HTML>
```

When submitted, this form will send two variables to your script, $val1 and $val2, because those are the NAMEs used in each text field. The values for those variables will be the values typed in the form fields by the user.

There's one more item to add: a series of radio buttons to determine the type of calculation to perform on the two values.

Adding Radio Buttons to the Forms

1. Open calculate_form.html in your text editor.

2. Add this block before the submit button:

```
<P>Calculation:<br>
<INPUT TYPE="radio" NAME="calc" VALUE="add"> add<br>
<INPUT TYPE="radio" NAME="calc" VALUE="subtract"> subtract<br>
<INPUT TYPE="radio" NAME="calc" VALUE="multiply"> multiply<br>
<INPUT TYPE="radio" NAME="calc" VALUE="divide"> divide</P>
```

3. Save the file.

4. Place this file in the document root of your Web server.

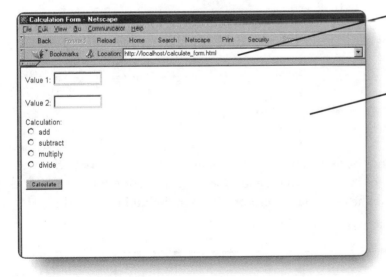

5. Open your Web browser and type **http://localhost/ calculate_form.html**

Your form will now contain the Value 1 and Value 2 fields, a set of radio buttons, and a Calculate button.

Now, in addition to the two values ($val1 and $val2), a variable called $calc will be sent to your script. There's no reason to wait! Move on to the next section and create the calculation script.

Creating the Calculation Script

According to the form action in calculate_form.html, you need a script called calculate.php. The goal of this script is to accept the two values ($val1 and $val2) and perform a calculation depending on the value of $calc.

1. Open a new file in your text editor.

2. Start a PHP block and prepare an if statement that checks for the presence of the three values:

```
<?
if (($val1 == "") || ($val2 == "") || ($calc =="")) {
        // more code goes here
}
```

What this statement actually says is "If any of these three variables do not have a value, do something else."

3. Replace the "more code goes here" with the following two lines:

```
header("Location: http://localhost/calculate_form.html");
exit;
```

The first of these two lines outputs a header statement—in this case, printing a new location: the URL of the form. The second line exits the script. If any of the three variables do not have a value, the user will be redirected back to the original form.

NOTE

Be sure that there are no line breaks, spaces, or any other text before your PHP block starts. You cannot use the header() function if output has already been sent to the browser.

---

4. Begin an `if...else` statement to perform the correct calculation, based on the value of $calc, starting with a value of "add":

```
if ($calc == "add") {
      $result = $val1 + $val2;
}
```

5. Continue the statement for the remaining three calculation types:

```
else if ($calc == "subtract") {
      $result = $val1 - $val2;
}
else if ($calc == "multiply") {
      $result = $val1 * $val2;
}
else if ($calc == "divide") {
      $result = $val1 / $val2;
}
```

6. Close your PHP block:

```
?>
```

7. Start the HTML output:

```
<HTML>
<HEAD>
<TITLE>Calculation Result</TITLE>
</HEAD>
<BODY>
```

8. Using HTML mingled with PHP code, display the value of $result:

```
<P>The result of the calculation is: <? echo "$result"; ?></P>
```

9. Add some more HTML so that the document is valid:

```
</BODY>
</HTML>
```

```
<?
if (($val1 == "") || ($val2 == "") || ($calc =="")) {
        header("Location: http://localhost/calculate_form.html");
        exit;
}

if ($calc == "add") {
        $result = $val1 + $val2;
} else if ($calc == "subtract") {
        $result = $val1 - $val2;
} else if ($calc == "multiply") {
        $result = $val1 * $val2;
} else if ($calc == "divide") {
        $result = $val1 / $val2;
}

?>

<HTML>
<HEAD>
<TITLE>Calculation Result</TITLE>
</HEAD>
<BODY>

<P>The result of the calculation is: <? echo "$result"; ?></p>

</BODY>
</HTML>
```

10. Save the file with the name calculate.php.

11. Place this file in the document root of your Web server.

Your code should look something like this.

In the next section, you'll submit the form and even try to break it! Just a bit of good, healthy debugging.

Submitting Your Form and Getting Results

Now that you've created both the front end (form) and the back end (script), it's time to hold your breath and test it.

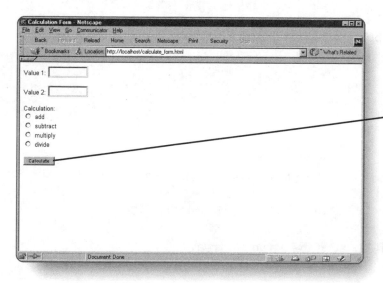

1. Open your Web browser and type **http://localhost/calculate_form.html.** You should see the calculation form.

2. Click on the Calculate button without typing anything in the form fields. Your Web browser will reload the page, because you didn't enter any values for the three required fields.

3. Enter a value for Value 1, but not for Value 2, and do not select a calculation option. After you click on Calculate, the page should reload.

4. Enter a value for Value 2, but not for Value 1, and do not select a calculation option. After you click on Calculate, the page should reload.

5. Enter a value for Value 1 and for Value 2, but do not select a calculation option. After you click on Calculate, the page should reload.

6. Select a calculation option, but do not enter any values for Value 1 or Value 2. After you click on Calculate, the page should reload.

Now that you've debugged the script by attempting to bypass your validation routine, try some calculations.

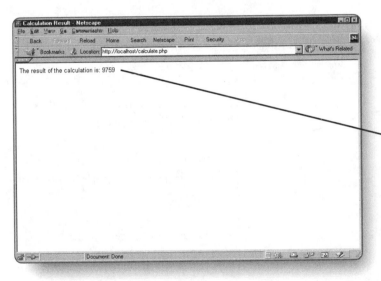

1. Enter 9732 for Value 1 and 27 for Value 2.

2. Select "add" and click on the Calculate button.

The result of the addition calculation will be printed to the screen.

3. Use the Back button to return to the form.

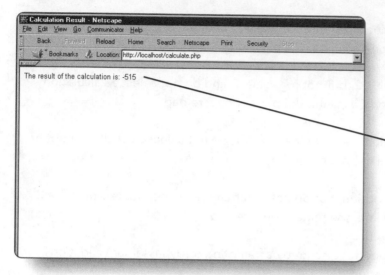

4. Enter 432 for Value 1, and 947 for Value 2.

5. Select "subtract" and click on the Calculate button.

The result of the subtraction calculation will be printed to the screen.

6. Use the Back button to return to the form.

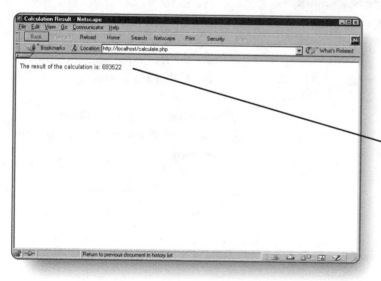

7. Enter 8562 for Value 1, and 81 for Value 2.

8. Select "multiply" and click on the Calculate button.

The result of the multiplication calculation will be printed to the screen.

9. Use the Back button to return to the form.

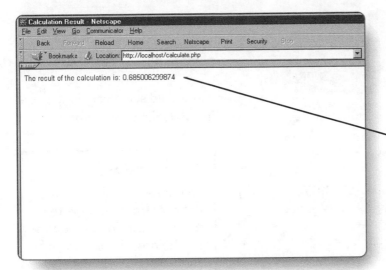

10. Enter 4893 for Value 1, and 7143 for Value 2.

11. Select "divide" and click on the Calculate button.

The result of the division calculation will be printed to the screen.

Knock yourself out by trying all sorts of number calculations!

HTTP Environment Variables

When a Web browser makes a request of a Web server, it sends along with the request a list of extra variables. These are called *environment variables*, and they can be very useful for displaying dynamic content or authorizing users.

The phpinfo() function displays a wealth of information about your Web server software, the version of PHP you are running, and the basic HTTP environment. Let's see what you have.

1. Open a new file in your text editor.

2. Type the following line of PHP code:

```
<? phpinfo(); ?>
```

3. Save the file with the name phpinfo.php.

4. Place this file in the document root of your Web server.

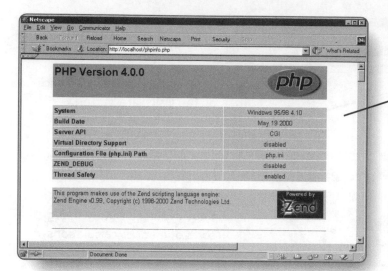

5. Open your Web browser and type **http://localhost/phpinfo.php**.

You should see a very long page full of useful information.

> **NOTE**
>
> Your information will differ, not only from machine to machine, but from platform to platform. These screen shots were taken on a Windows development machine.

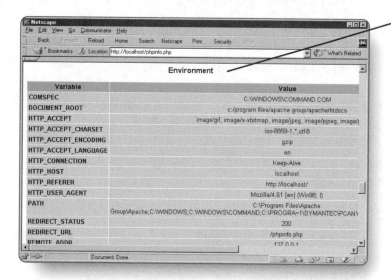

As you scroll down, look for a section titled "Environment."

In the next sections, you'll learn how to use two environment variables: REMOTE_ADDR and HTTP_USER_AGENT. For an explanation of some of the HTTP environment variables shown in the phpinfo() output, visit http://hoohoo.ncsa.uiuc.edu/cgi/env.html.

Retrieving and Using REMOTE_ADDR

By default, environment variables are available to PHP scripts as $VAR_NAME. For example, the REMOTE_ADDR environment variable is already contained as $REMOTE_ADDR. However, to be absolutely sure that you're reading the correct value, use the getenv() function to assign a value to a variable of your choice.

The REMOTE_ADDR environment variable contains the IP address of the machine making the request. Let's get the value of your REMOTE_ADDR.

1. Open a new file in your text editor.

2. Open a PHP block:

```
<?
```

3. Use getenv() to place the value of REMOTE_ADDR in a variable called $address:

```
$address = getenv("REMOTE_ADDR");
```

4. Print the value of $address to the screen:

```
echo "Your IP address is $address.";
```

5. Close your PHP block:

```
?>
```

6. Save the file with the name remoteaddress.php.

7. Place this file in the document root of your Web server.

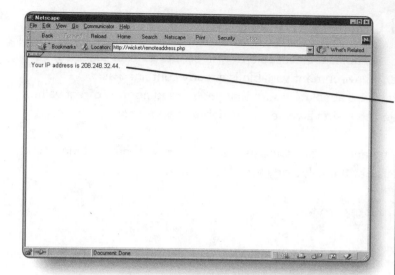

8. Open your Web browser and type **http://localhost/remoteaddress.php**.

Your current IP address will be printed to the screen.

NOTE

Your IP address will differ from that shown in the figure, as that's one of my own IP addresses.

In the next section, you'll get the value of another handy environment variable, HTTP_USER_AGENT (Web browser).

Retrieving and Using HTTP_USER_AGENT

The HTTP_USER_AGENT variable contains the browser type, browser version, language encoding, and platform. For example, the following value string refers to the Netscape (Mozilla) browser, version 4.61, in English, on the Windows 98 platform:

Mozilla/4.61 – (Win98; I)

Here are some other HTTP_USER_AGENT values, for my own browser library:

Mozilla/4.0 (compatible; MSIE 5.0; Windows 98)

This value refers to Microsoft Internet Explorer (MSIE) version 5.0 on Windows 98. Sometimes you will see MSIE return an HTTP_USER_AGENT value that looks like a Netscape value, until you notice that the value says it's "compatible" and is actually "MSIE 5.0."

Don't count out the text-only browsers! A Lynx HTTP_USER_AGENT value looks like this:

Lynx/2.8rel.3 libwww-FM/2.14

Let's find your HTTP_USER_AGENT.

1. Open a new file in your text editor.

2. Open a PHP block:

```
<?
```

3. Use getenv() to place the value of HTTP_USER_AGENT in a variable called $agent:

```
$agent = getenv("HTTP_USER_AGENT");
```

4. Print the value of $agent to the screen:

```
echo " You are using $agent.";
```

5. Close your PHP block:

```
?>
```

6. Save the file with the name useragent.php.

7. Place this file in the document root of your Web server.

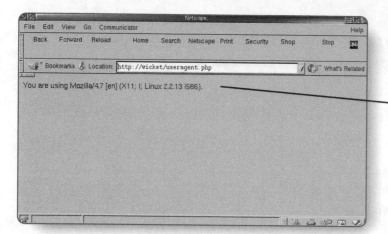

8. Open your Web browser and type **http://localhost/ useragent.php**.

Your current HTTP_USER_AGENT value will be printed to the screen.

> ## NOTE
> Your user agent string might be different than the one shown, unless you're using Netscape 4.7 on Linux.

In the next chapter, you'll learn many of the basic tasks for Web developers, including displaying dynamic content, sending e-mail, and working with your filesystem.

PART III

Start with the Simple Stuff

7

Displaying Dynamic Content

The Web is a dynamic environment, so why not use your programming skills to display dynamic content? Dynamic content can be as simple or as complex as you want it to be. In this chapter, you'll learn how to do the following:

- Display browser-specific HTML
- Display platform-specific HTML
- Use PHP string functions on HTML form input
- Create a redirection menu using an HTML form and the header() function

Displaying Browser-Specific HTML

In the previous chapter, you learned to retrieve and print the HTTP_USER_AGENT environment variable to the screen. In this chapter, you'll do something a bit more interesting with the value of HTTP_USER_AGENT: print browser-specific HTML.

However, having seen some of the possible values of HTTP_USER_AGENT in the last chapter, you can imagine that there are hundreds of slightly different values. So, it's time to learn some basic pattern matching.

You'll use the preg_match() function to perform this task. This function needs two arguments: what you're looking for, and where you're looking:

```
preg_match("/[what you're looking for]/", "[where you're looking]");
```

This function will return a value of true or false, which you can use in an if...else block to do whatever you want. The goal of the first script is to determine if a Web browser is Microsoft Internet Explorer, Netscape, or something else. This can be a little tricky, but not because of PHP.

Within the value of HTTP_USER_AGENT, Netscape always uses the string "Mozilla" to identify itself. Unfortunately, the value of HTTP_USER_AGENT for Microsoft Internet Explorer also uses "Mozilla" to show that it's compatible. Luckily, it also uses the string "MSIE", so you can search for that. If the value of HTTP_USER_AGENT doesn't contain either "Mozilla" or "MSIE", chances are very good that it's not one of those Web browsers.

1. Open a new file in your text editor.

2. Open a PHP block:

```
<?
```

3. Use getenv() to place the value of HTTP_USER_AGENT in a variable called $agent:

```
$agent = getenv("HTTP_USER_AGENT");
```

4. Start an `if...else` statement to find which of the `preg_match()` functions is true, starting with the search for "MSIE":

```
if (preg_match("/MSIE/i", "$agent")) {
    $result = "You are using Microsoft Internet Explorer.";
}
```

5. Continue the statement, testing for "Mozilla":

```
else if (preg_match("/Mozilla/i", "$agent")) {
    $result = "You are using Netscape.";
}
```

6. Finish the statement by defining a default:

```
else {
    $result = "You are using $agent";
}
```

> **NOTE**
>
> The `i` in the `preg_match()` function performs a case-insensitive search.

7. Close your PHP block:

```
?>
```

8. Type the following HTML:

```
<IITML>
<HEAD>
<TITLE>Browser Match Results</TITLE>
</HEAD>
<BODY>
```

9. Type the following PHP code to print the result of the `if...else` statement:

```
<? echo "<P>$result</P>"; ?>
```

10. Add some more HTML so that the document is valid:

```
</BODY>
</HTML>
```

11. Save the file with the name browsermatch.php.

12. Place this file in the document root of your Web server.

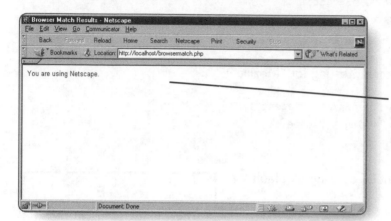

13. Open your Web browser and type **http://localhost/browsermatch.php**

Depending on the Web browser you use, you might see a result such as this,

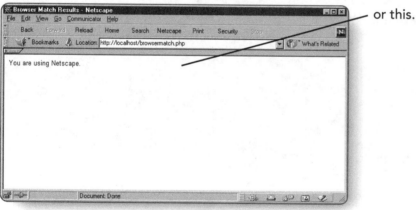

or this.

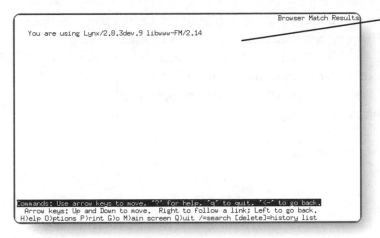

```
                                      Browser Match Results

You are using Lynx/2.8.3dev.9 libwww-FM/2.14
```

```
Commands: Use arrow keys to move. '?' for help. 'q' to quit. '<-' to go back.
  Arrow keys: Up and Down to move.  Right to follow a link; Left to go back.
 H)elp O)ptions P)rint G)o M)ain screen Q)uit /=search [delete]=history list
```

If you're using neither Netscape nor Microsoft Internet Explorer, the actual value of HTTP_USER_AGENT will be printed.

The Browser War rages on! No one Web browser is used by a vast majority of Web surfers. Various flavors of Microsoft Internet Explorer (MSIE) account for approximately 69% of Web browsers in use, while versions of Netscape (NS) assume about 21%. Throw in the die-hard Lynx, Opera, and WebTV users to reach 100%.

Although a 70/30 split might seem like a majority, if 150 million people have access to the Internet, 45 million non-Microsoft users is a huge number of users to consider when developing a good Web site.

HotWired maintains a browser reference at http://www.hotwired.com/webmonkey/ reference/browser_chart/. It shows you some of the differences between the major browsers. In the next section, you'll see that all platforms are not created equal, and in fact do not display HTML the same way either.

Displaying Platform-Specific HTML

There are differences not only between browsers, but also between platforms. This difference is most clear with regards to fonts and font sizes. In the Windows world, you have fonts such as Times New Roman and Courier New. Slight variations of these fonts appear on the Macintosh and Linux/UNIX platforms; they are called Times and Courier. It doesn't end there—the font sizes all display differently. A 10-point font on Macintosh or Linux is sometimes barely legible, but if you bump it up to 11- or 12-point, you're in business. If that same 12-point font is viewed on Windows, however, it might look like your text is trying to take over the world.

So, what to do? Use your new pattern-matching skills to extract the platform from the HTTP_USER_AGENT string, and then display platform-specific HTML. As with matching on a keyword—which you did in the previous section—you need to know what you're looking for to nail down the platform. In the next script, you'll check for the keywords "Win" and "Linux" and print an appropriate stylesheet block in your HTML result page.

1. Open a new file in your text editor.

2. Open a PHP block:

```
<?
```

3. Use getenv() to place the value of HTTP_USER_AGENT in a variable called $agent:

```
$agent = getenv("HTTP_USER_AGENT");
```

4. Start an if...else statement to find which of the preg_match() functions is true, starting with the search for "Win":

```
if (preg_match("/Win/i", "$agent")) {
      $style = "win";
}
```

5. Continue the statement, testing for "Linux":

```
else if (preg_match("/Linux/i", "$agent")) {
      $style = "linux";
}
```

6. Create a basic stylesheet block for Windows users:

```
$win_style = "
<style type=\"text/css\">\n
p, ul, ol, li  {font-family:Arial;font-size:10pt;font-weight:normal;}\n
h1             {font-family:Arial;font-size:16pt;font-weight:bold;}\n
h2             {font-family:Arial;font-size:14pt;font-weight:bold;}\n
strong         {font-family:Arial;font-size:10pt;font-weight:bold;}\n
em             {font-family:Arial;font-size:10pt;font-style:italic;}\n
</style>
";
```

> **NOTE**
>
> When you use quotation marks inside other quotation marks, the inner pair must be delineated from the outside pair using the escape (\) character (also known as a backslash).

7. Create a basic stylesheet block for Linux users:

```
$linux_style = "
<style type=\"text/css\">\n
p, ul, ol, li   {font-family:Times;font-size:12pt;font-weight:normal;}\n
h1              {font-family:Times;font-size:18pt;font-weight:bold;}\n
h2              {font-family:Times;font-size:16pt;font-weight:bold;}\n
strong          {font-family:Times;font-size:12pt;font-weight:bold;}\n
em              {font-family:Times;font-size:12pt;font-style:italic;}\n
</style>
";
```

> **NOTE**
>
> The use of the newline (\n) character will ensure that your code will print on multiple lines. This is helpful when you are viewing your HTML source.

8. Close your PHP block:

```
?>
```

9. Type the following HTML:

```
<HTML>
<HEAD>
<TITLE>Platform Matching</TITLE>
```

10. Type the following PHP code, creating an `if...else` statement used to print the correct stylesheet block:

```
<?
if ($style == "win") {
        echo "$win_style";
} else if ($style == "linux") {
        echo "$linux_style";
}
?>
```

11. Close the top section of your HTML and start the body:

```
</HEAD>
<BODY>
```

12. Type the following HTML to show the use of your stylesheet:

```
<h1 align=center>This is a level 1 heading</h1>
<h2 align=center>Look! A level 2 heading</h2>
<P align=center>This is a simple paragraph with some <strong>bold</strong> and
<em>emphasized</em> text.</P>
```

13. Add some more HTML so that the document is valid:

```
</BODY>
</HTML>
```

14. Save the file with the name platformmatch.php

15. Place this file in the document root of your Web server.

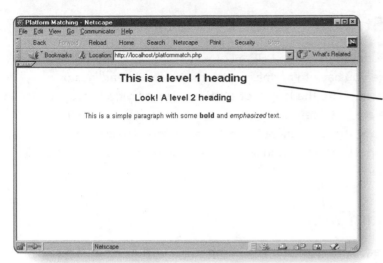

16. Open your Web browser and type **http://localhost/platformmatch.php**

Depending on the Web browser you use, you might see a result such as this,

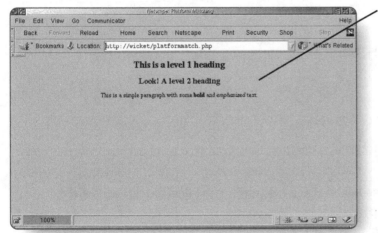

or this.

You can see that the proper stylesheet block was printed, based on the result of the platform match. In the next section, you'll move away from pattern matching and work with some of the string functions in PHP to modify form input before displaying it back to the browser.

Working with String Functions

Numerous string functions are built into PHP, all of which are designed to make your life easier. Suppose you have to normalize strings for news headlines or product ID numbers, or calculate the length of a string before trying to stuff it into a database field. Those are just a few of the string functions you'll learn about in the next section. For more string functions, take a look at the PHP Manual at http://www.php.net/manual/. The function list seems to grow daily as more people contribute to the language.

Creating an Input Form

In this section, you'll create the front end to a string modification script. This form will contain one text area and several radio buttons. The radio buttons will determine the string function to use.

1. Open a new file in your text editor.

2. Type the following HTML:

```
<HTML>
<HEAD>
<TITLE>Generic Input Form</TITLE>
</HEAD>
<BODY>
```

3. Begin your form. Assume that the method is post and the action is a script called display_input.php:

```
<FORM METHOD="post" ACTION="display_input.php">
```

4. Create a text area with a text label:

```
<P><strong>Text Field:</strong><br>
<TEXTAREA NAME="text1" COLS=45 ROWS=5 WRAP=virtual></TEXTAREA></P>
```

5. Add this block of radio buttons:

```
<P><strong>String Function:</strong><br>
<INPUT TYPE="radio" NAME="func" VALUE="md5" checked> get md5<br>
<INPUT TYPE="radio" NAME="func" VALUE="strlen"> get length of string<br>
<INPUT TYPE="radio" NAME="func" VALUE="strrev"> reverse the string<br>
<INPUT TYPE="radio" NAME="func" VALUE="strtoupper"> make string uppercase<br>
<INPUT TYPE="radio" NAME="func" VALUE="strtolower"> make string lowercase<br>
<INPUT TYPE="radio" NAME="func" VALUE="ucwords"> make first letter of all
words uppercase</P>
```

NOTE

The value for each radio button is its exact PHP function name. This will make the back-end script very simple to create, as you'll see in the next section.

---

6. Add a submit button:

```
<P><INPUT TYPE="submit" NAME="submit" VALUE="Do Something With the
String"></P>
```

7. Close your form and add some more HTML so that the document is valid:

```
</FORM>
</BODY>
</HTML>
```

8. Save the file with the name generic_form.html.

9. Place this file in the document root of your Web server.

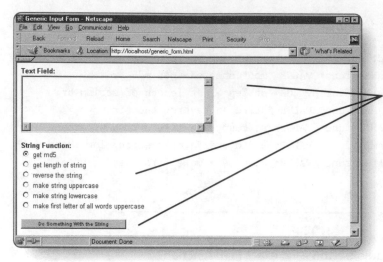

10. Open your Web browser and type **http://localhost/ generic_form.html**

You'll see a form with a text area and several radio buttons, along with a Do Something With the String form submission button.

In the next section, you'll create the back-end script. That script will expect two variables: $text1 and $func.

Creating a Script to Display Form Values

According to the form action in generic_form.html, you need a script called display_input.php. The goal of this script is to accept the text in $text1 and use a particular string function (the value of $func) to get a new result ($result).

1. Open a new file in your text editor.

2. Type the following PHP:

```
<? $result = $func($text1); ?>
```

3. Start the HTML output:

```
<HTML>
<HEAD>
<TITLE>Generic Input Results</TITLE>
</HEAD>
<BODY>
```

4. Display the value of `$result`:

```
<? echo "$result"; ?>
```

5. Add a link back to the form:

```
<p><a href="generic_form.html">Go again!</a></P>
```

6. Add some more HTML so that the document is valid:

```
</BODY>
</HTML>
```

7. Save the file with the name display_input.php.

```
<? $result = $func($text1); ?>

<HTML>
<HEAD>
<TITLE>Generic Input Results</TITLE>
</HEAD>
<BODY>

<? echo "$result"; ?>

<p><a href="generic_form.html">Go again!</a></p>

</BODY>
</HTML>
```

8. Place this file in the document root of your Web server.

Your code should look something like this.

In the next section, you'll submit the form and see all these different types of string functions at work.

Submitting Your Form and Getting Results

Now that you've created both a front-end form and a back-end script, it's time to try them out.

1. Open your Web browser and type **http://localhost/ generic_form.html**

2. Type the following text in the text area:

```
I think PHP is just the coolest server-side scripting language around! Who
knew it would be this simple?
```

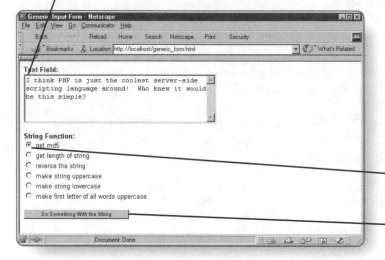

3. Select the "get md5" radio button.

4. Click on the "Do Something With the String" button.

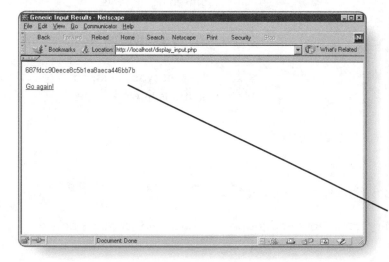

You should see a hash of the string, along with a link back to the form.

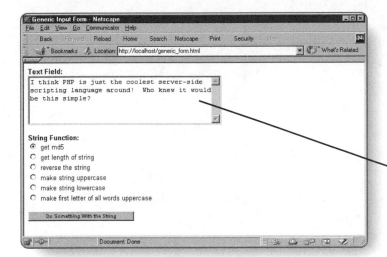

Next, use the `strlen()` function to find the length of the string, including white space and all characters.

1. Click on the Go again! link. The front-end form will appear.

2. Enter the same text in the text area:

```
I think PHP is just the
coolest server-side scripting
language around! Who knew it
would be this simple?
```

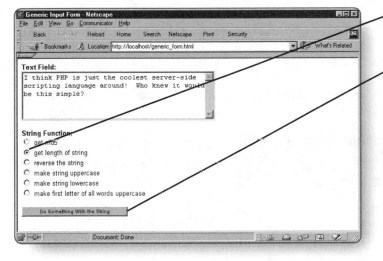

3. Select the "get length of string" radio button.

4. Click on the "Do Something With the String" button.

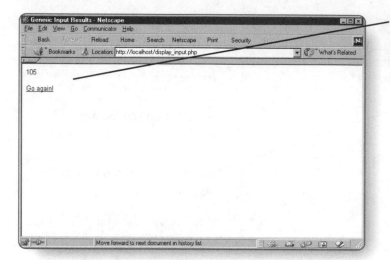

You should see a number representing the character length of the string, along with a link back to the form.

Next, use the `strrev()` function to return the original string, completely reversed.

1. Click on the Go again! link. The front-end form will appear.

2. Enter the same text in the text area:

I think PHP is just the coolest server-side scripting language around! Who knew it would be this simple?

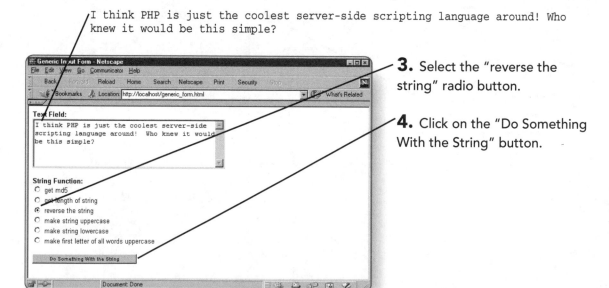

3. Select the "reverse the string" radio button.

4. Click on the "Do Something With the String" button.

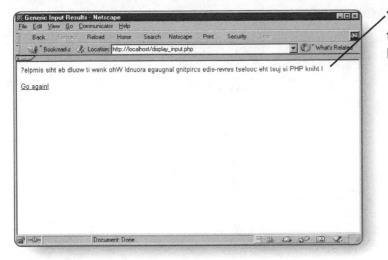

You should see the reverse of the original string, along with a link back to the form.

Next, use the strtoupper() function to return the string with all letters in uppercase.

1. Click on the Go again! link. The front-end form will appear.

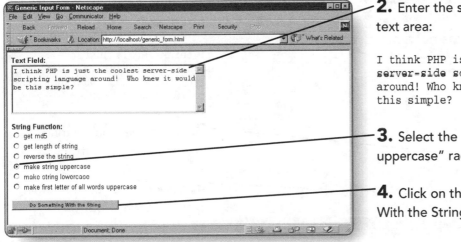

2. Enter the same text in the text area:

I think PHP is just the coolest server-side scripting language around! Who knew it would be this simple?

3. Select the "make string uppercase" radio button.

4. Click on the "Do Something With the String" button.

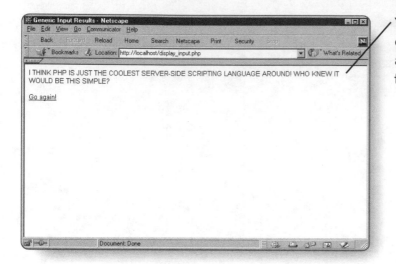

You should see the string completely in uppercase letters, along with a link back to the form.

Next, use the `strtolower()` function to return the string with all letters in lowercase.

1. Click on the Go again! link. The front-end form will appear.

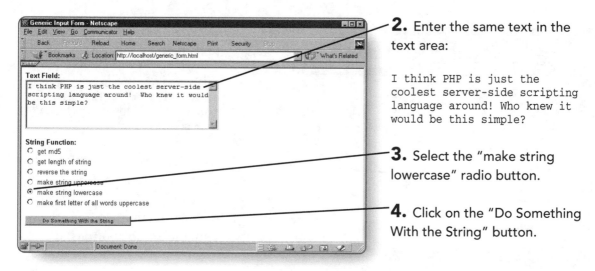

2. Enter the same text in the text area:

```
I think PHP is just the
coolest server-side scripting
language around! Who knew it
would be this simple?
```

3. Select the "make string lowercase" radio button.

4. Click on the "Do Something With the String" button.

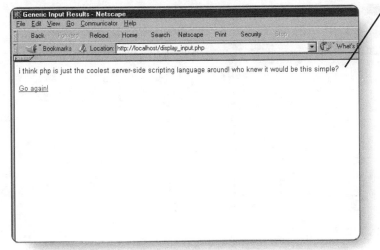

You should see the string completely in lowercase letters, along with a link back to the form.

Next, use the `ucwords()` function to return the string with the first letter of each word in uppercase.

1. Click on the Go again! link. The front-end form will appear.

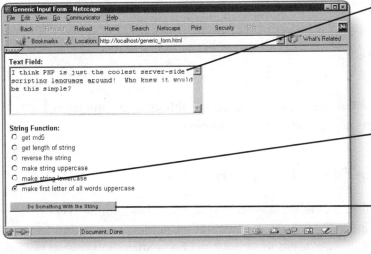

2. Enter the same text in the text area:

I think PHP is just the coolest server-side scripting language around! Who knew it would be this simple?

3. Select the "make first letter of all words uppercase" radio button.

4. Click on the "Do Something With the String" button.

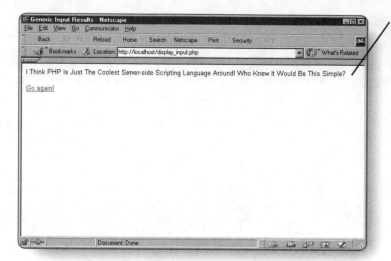

You should see the string, with the first letter of each word capitalized, along with a link back to the form.

To add some error checking to your script, check for the value of $func before any other action occurs. Replace your first block of PHP code with this:

```
<?
if ($func == "") {
        header("Location: http://localhost/generic_form.html");
        exit;
}
$result = $func($text1);
?>
```

Now, if some rogue user directly accesses the script without using the form, he'll be redirected back to the form, and no errors will occur.

Redirecting to a New Location

Redirecting a user to a new location means that your script has sent an HTTP header to the browser, indicating a new location. HTTP headers of any kind (authentication, redirection, cookies, and so on) must be sent to the browser before anything else, including white space, line breaks, and any characters.

In the next section, you'll create a redirection menu and a redirection form. The goal is to have the user select a new location from the menu and then have the script automatically send him there.

Creating a Redirection Form

In this section, you'll create the front end to a redirection script. This form will contain a drop-down list of the names of various Web sites. The value for each option is the Web site's URL.

1. Open a new file in your text editor.

2. Type the following HTML:

```
<HTML>
<HEAD>
<TITLE> Redirection Menu</TITLE>
</HEAD>
<BODY>
```

3. Begin your form. Assume that the method is post and the action is a script called do_redirect.php:

```
<FORM METHOD="post" ACTION="do_redirect.php">
```

4. Add this drop-down list:

```
<P>Send me to:
<SELECT name="location">
        <OPTION value="http://www.prima-tech.com/">Prima-Tech</OPTION>
        <OPTION value="http://www.thickbook.com/">thickbook.com</OPTION>
        <OPTION value="http://www.php.net/">PHP.net</OPTION>
        <OPTION value="http://www.zend.com/">Zend Technologies</OPTION>
        <OPTION
value="http://hotwired.lycos.com/webmonkey/">Webmonkey</OPTION>
        <OPTION value="http://www.zdnet.com/developer/">ZDNet
Developer</OPTION>
</SELECT>
```

5. Add a submit button:

```
<P><INPUT TYPE="submit" NAME="submit" VALUE="Go!"></P>
```

6. Close your form and add some more HTML so that the document is valid:

```
</FORM>
</BODY>
</HTML>
```

7. Save the file with the name redirect_form.html

8. Place this file in the document root of your Web server.

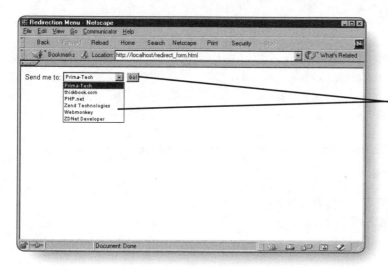

9. Open your Web browser and type **http://localhost/ redirect_form.html**

You should see a drop-down menu containing the names of various Web sites, along with a Go! button.

In the next section, you'll create the back-end script. That script will expect one variable: `$location`.

Creating the Redirection Script and Testing It

According to the form action in redirect_form.html, you need a script called do_redirect.php. The goal of this script is to accept the value of $location and print that value within the header() function so that the user is redirected to the chosen location.

1. Open a new file in your text editor.

2. Type the following PHP to create the proper redirection header:

```
<?
header( "Location: $location");
exit;
?>
```

3. Save the file with the name do_redirect.php.

4. Place this file in the document root of your Web server.

5. Open your Web browser and type **http://localhost/redirect_form.html**

6. Select Prima-Tech from the drop-down list.

7. Click on the Go! button.

Users will now be redirected to the Prima-Tech Web site.

To add some error checking to your script, check for the value of $location before trying to do the redirection. Replace your PHP code with this:

```
<?
if ($location == "") {
        header("Location: http://localhost/redirect_form.html");
        exit;
} else {
        header("Location: $location");
        exit;
}
?>
```

Now, if a user directly accesses the script, he'll be redirected back to the form, and no errors will occur.

8

Sending E-mail

Using PHP to send the contents of a form to a specified e-mail address is so easy that you'll wonder why people don't do it every day. In this chapter, you'll learn how to do the following:

- Create and send a simple feedback form
- Use the $PHP_SELF variable to create a feedback form with custom error messages

Windows Users: Check Your php.ini File

If you're using PHP4 on Windows, look for the following lines in your php.ini file:

```
[mail function]
SMTP              =         ;for win32 only
sendmail_from     =         ;for win32 only
```

You'll need to modify the last two lines so that the `mail()` function works properly.

1. For the SMTP entry, use "localhost" or the name of the outgoing mail server you use in your e-mail client.

2. For the sendmail_from entry, enter your e-mail address.

For example, my php.ini file on Windows contains this:

```
[mail function]
SMTP              =         localhost
sendmail_from     =         julie@thickbook.com
```

A Simple Feedback Form

A simple feedback form contains fields for the user's name and e-mail address, and a text area for some sort of message. In this section, you'll create two files: one for the feedback form, and one for the PHP script to process the form, send the mail, and return a response to the browser.

Creating the Feedback Form

1. Open a new file in your text editor.

2. Type the following HTML:

```
<HTML>
<HEAD>
```

```
<TITLE>Simple Feedback Form</TITLE>
</HEAD>
<BODY>
```

3. Begin your form. Assume that the method is post and the action is a script called send_simpleform.php:

```
<FORM METHOD="post" ACTION="send_simpleform.php">
```

4. Create an input field for the user's name, with a text label:

```
<P><strong>Your Name:</strong><br>
<INPUT type="text" NAME="sender_name" SIZE=30></P>
```

5. Create an input field for the user's e-mail address, with a text label:

```
<P><strong>Your E-Mail Address:</strong><br>
<INPUT type="text" NAME="sender_email" SIZE=30></P>
```

6. Create a text area to hold the message, with a text label:

```
<P><strong>Message:</strong><br>
<TEXTAREA NAME="message" COLS=30 ROWS=5 WRAP=virtual></TEXTAREA></P>
```

7. Add a submit button:

```
<P><INPUT TYPE="submit" NAME="submit" VALUE="Send This Form"></P>
```

8. Close your form and add some more HTML so that the document is valid:

```
</FORM>
</BODY>
</HTML>
```

9. Save the file with the name simple_form.html.

10. Place this file in the document root of your Web server.

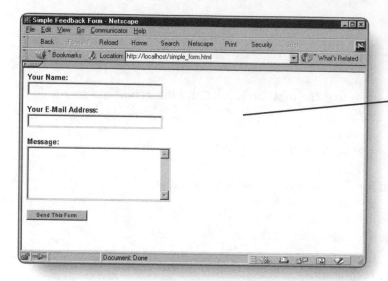

11. Open your Web browser and type **http://localhost/simple_form.html**

You will see a form containing a text field for the person's name, a text field for the person's e-mail address, a text area for the message, and a Send This Form button.

In the next section, you'll create the back-end script. That script will expect three variables: $sender_name, $sender_email, and $message.

Creating a Script to Mail Your Form

According to the form action in simple_form.html, you need a script called send_simpleform.php. The goals of this script are to accept the text in $sender_name, $sender_email, and $message format and send an e-mail; and to display a confirmation to the Web browser.

1. Open a new file in your text editor.

2. Begin a PHP block:

```
<?
```

3. Start building a message string:

```
$msg = "E-MAIL SENT FROM WWW SITE\n";
```

4. Continue building the message string by adding an entry for the sender's name:

```
$msg .= "Sender's Name:\t$sender_name\n";
```

> **NOTE**
> The next few steps will continue building the message string by concatenating smaller strings to form one long message string. "Concatenating" is a fancy word for "smashing together." The concatenation operator (.=) is used.

5. Continue building the message string by adding an entry for the sender's e-mail address:

```
$msg .= "Sender's E-Mail:\t$sender_email\n";
```

6. Continue building the message string by adding an entry for the message:

```
$msg .= "Message:\t$message\n\n";
```

The final line contains two newline characters "\n\n" to add additional white space at the end of the string.

7. Create a variable to hold the recipient's e-mail address (substitute your own):

```
$to = "you@youremail.com";
```

8. Create a variable to hold the subject of the e-mail:

```
$subject = "Web Site Feedback";
```

9. Create a variable to hold additional mailheaders:

```
$mailheaders = "From: My Web Site <> \n";
```

10. Add to the `$mailheaders` variable:

```
$mailheaders .= "Reply-To: $sender_email\n\n";
```

11. Add the `mail()` function:

```
mail($to, $subject, $msg, $mailheaders);
```

```
<?
$msg = "E-MAIL SENT FROM WWW SITE\n";
$msg .= "Sender's Name:\t$sender_name\n";
$msg .= "Sender's E-Mail:\t$sender_email\n";
$msg .= "Message:\t$message\n\n";

$to = "you@youremail.com";
$subject = "Web Site Feedback";
$mailheaders = "From: My Web Site <> \n";
$mailheaders .= "Reply-To: $sender_email\n\n";

mail($to, $subject, $msg, $mailheaders);

?>
```

12. Close your PHP block:

```
?>
```

You're not done yet, but your code should look something like this.

Creating a Confirmation Message

Although this code will send the mail, you should return something to the user's screen so that he knows the form has been sent. Otherwise, he might sit there and continually click the Send This Form button.

1. Start the HTML output:

```
<HTML>
<HEAD>
<TITLE>Simple Feedback Form Sent</TITLE>
</HEAD>
<BODY>
```

2. Add some information to tell the user what has happened:

```
<H1>The following e-mail has been sent:</H1>
```

3. Add the text label for the Your Name field:

```
<P><strong>Your Name:</strong><br>
```

4. Display the user's input:

```
<? echo "$sender_name"; ?>
```

5. Add the text label for the Your E-Mail Address field:

```
<P><strong>Your E-Mail Address:</strong><br>
```

6. Display the user's input:

```
<? echo "$sender_email"; ?>
```

7. Add the text label for the Message field:

```
<P><strong>Message:</strong><br>
```

8. Display the user's input:

```
<? echo "$message"; ?>
```

9. Add some more HTML so that the document is valid:

```
</BODY>
</HTML>
```

10. Save the file with the name send_simpleform.php.

```
<?
$msg = "E-MAIL SENT FROM WWW SITE\n";
$msg .= "Sender's Name:\t$sender_name\n";
$msg .= "Sender's E-Mail:\t$sender_email\n";
$msg .= "Message:\t$message\n\n";

$to = "you@youremail.com";
$subject = "Web Site Feedback";
$mailheaders = "From: My Web Site <> \n";
$mailheaders .= "Reply-To: $sender_email\n\n";

mail($to, $subject, $msg, $mailheaders);

?>
<HTML>
<HEAD>
<TITLE>Simple Feedback Form Sent</TITLE>
</HEAD>
<BODY>

<H1>The following e-mail has been sent:</H1>

<P><strong>Your Name:</strong><br>
<? echo "$sender_name"; ?>

<P><strong>Your E-Mail Address:</strong><br>
<? echo "$sender_email"; ?>

<P><strong>Message:</strong><br>
<? echo "$message"; ?>


</BODY>
</HTML>
```

11. Place this file in the document root of your Web server.

Your code should look something like this.

In the next section, you'll submit the form and see all these different types of string functions at work.

Submitting Your Form and Getting Results

Now that you've created both a front-end form and a back-end script, it's time to try them out.

1. Open your Web browser and type **http://localhost/simple_form.html**

2. Type your name in the Your Name field.

3. Type your e-mail address in the Your E-Mail Address field.

4. Type the following message in the Message field:

PHP is so cool!

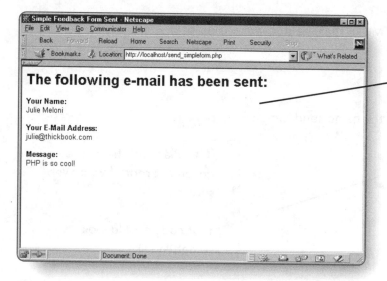

5. Click on the Send This Form button.

The information you entered, along with a confirmation that your e-mail has been sent, will appear.

Now check your e-mail, and see if a message is waiting for you.

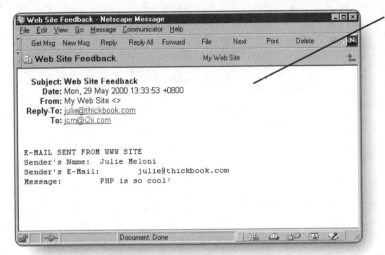

An e-mail sent through this form will look something like this.

Justifying E-mail Text

If it drives you crazy that the tabbed text doesn't line up properly, you can insert as much white space as you'd like in the message string.

1. Open send_simpleform.php in your text editor.

2. Modify the string containing Sender's Name by replacing the tab character (\t) with two spaces:

```
$msg .= "Sender's Name:  $sender_name\n";
```

3. Modify the string containing Sender's E-Mail by replacing the tab character (\t) with four spaces:

```
$msg .= "Sender's E-Mail:    $sender_email\n";
```

4. Modify the string containing Message by replacing the tab character (\t) with 10 spaces:

```
$msg .= "Message:          $message\n\n";
```

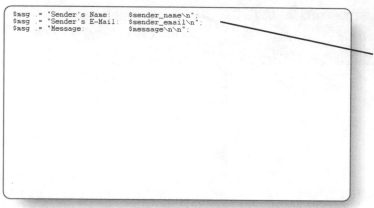

```
$msg .= "Sender's Name:     $sender_name\n";
$msg .= "Sender's E-Mail:   $sender_email\n";
$msg .= "Message:           $message\n\n";
```

5. Save the file.

This new section of code should look like this.

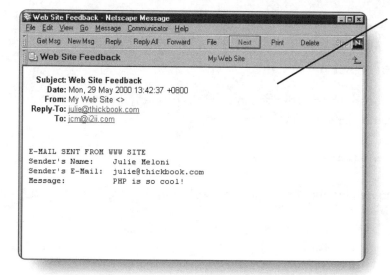

Submit the form again. This time when you receive the e-mail it should all line up.

Just like previous scripts in this book, you should add some error checking to send_simpleform.php. Check that $sender_name, $sender_email, and $message all have values before you perform any other actions. Add this after the first open PHP tag:

```
if (($sender_name == "") || ($sender_email == "") || ($message == "")) {
        header("Location: http://localhost/simple_form.html");
        exit;
}
```

In the next section, you'll create custom error messages for when fields are blank, and you'll streamline the two-step process of sending mail into one cohesive script.

A Feedback Form with Custom Error Messages

In the previous section, you created two separate files. One file contained the front end (form), and the other contained the back end (script). In this section, you'll learn how to use the $PHP_SELF variable in a form action to create a single file that holds both form and script, and how to create custom error messages when required fields are not completed.

Creating the Initial Script

1. Open a new file in your text editor.

2. Type the following HTML:

```
<HTML>
<HEAD>
<TITLE>All-In-One Feedback Form</TITLE>
</HEAD>
<BODY>
```

3. Start a PHP block:

```
<?
```

4. Create a variable called $form_block, which will hold the entire form. Start with the form action, and assume that the method is post and the action is $PHP_SELF:

```
$form_block = "
<FORM METHOD=\"post\" ACTION=\"$PHP_SELF\">
```

> **TIP**
> Since you're putting a long string inside a variable, chances are good that you'll have a quotation mark or two. Remember to escape all your quotation marks with a backslash!

5. Create an input field for the user's name with a text label:

```
<P><strong>Your Name:</strong><br>
<INPUT type=\"text\" NAME=\"sender_name\" SIZE=30></P>
```

6. Create an input field for the user's e-mail address with a text label:

```
<P><strong>Your E-Mail Address:</strong><br>
<INPUT type=\"text\" NAME=\"sender_email\" SIZE=30></P>
```

7. Create a text area to hold the message with a text label:

```
<P><strong>Message:</strong><br>
<TEXTAREA NAME=\"message\" COLS=30 ROWS=5 WRAP=virtual></TEXTAREA></P>
```

8. Add a submit button:

```
<P><INPUT TYPE=\"submit\" NAME=\"submit\" VALUE=\"Send This Form\"></P>
```

9. Close the form and then add the ending quotation marks and instruction terminator (semicolon):

```
</FORM>
";
```

10. Close the PHP block:

```
?>
```

11. Add some more HTML so that the document is valid:

```
</BODY>
</HTML>
```

```
<HTML>
<HEAD>
<TITLE>All-In-One Feedback Form</TITLE>
</HEAD>
<BODY>

<?

$form_block = "

<FORM METHOD=\"post\" ACTION=\"$PHP_SELF\">

<P><strong>Your Name:</strong><br>
<INPUT type=\"text\" NAME=\"sender_name\" SIZE=30></p>

<P><strong>Your E-Mail Address:</strong><br>
<INPUT type=\"text\" NAME=\"sender_email\" SIZE=30></p>

<P><strong>Message:</strong><br>
<TEXTAREA NAME=\"message\" COLS=30 ROWS=5 WRAP=virtual></TEXTAREA></p>

<P><INPUT TYPE=\"submit\" NAME=\"submit\" VALUE=\"Send This Form\"></p>

</FORM>

";

?>

</BODY>
</HTML>
```

12. Save the file with the name allinone_form.php.

You're not done yet, but your code should look something like this.

If you looked at this code in your Web browser, you'd only see a title in the title bar. The burning question should be: "Why do we need all that HTML in a variable called $form_block?" In the next section, you'll add to the script so that it displays particular chunks of code based on certain actions. The string in $form_block is one of those chunks.

Adding Error Checking to the Script

The plan is to use the global variable $PHP_SELF, which has a value of the script's current name. So really, $PHP_SELF will have a value of allinone_form.php in this instance. When you use $PHP_SELF as a form action, you're saying "When the submit button is clicked, reload this script and do something" instead of "When the submit button is clicked, go find another script and do something."

Now that you have a shell of a script, think about what this all-in-one script must do:

- Display the form.
- Submit the form.
- Check for errors.
- Print error messages without sending the form.
- Send the form if no errors are found.

1. Open allinone_form.php in your text editor.

2. Inside the `$form_block` variable, before the HTML code for the submit button, add this line:

```
<INPUT type=\"hidden\" name=\"op\" value=\"ds\">
```

This line creates a hidden variable called $op, which has a value of "ds". The "op" stands for "operation," and "ds" stands for "do something." I made these names up; they have nothing to do with any programming language. You can call them whatever you want, as long as you understand what they do (which you'll soon see).

The $op variable will be present only if the form has been submitted. So, if the value of $op is not "ds", the user hasn't seen the form. If the user hasn't seen the form, we need to show it.

3. Add the following `if...else` statement before the end of the PHP block:

```
if ($op != "ds") {
// they need to see the form
echo "$form_block";
}
```

```
<HTML>
<HEAD>
<TITLE>All-In-One Feedback Form</TITLE>
</HEAD>
<BODY>

<?

$form_block = "

<FORM METHOD=\"post\" ACTION=\"$PHP_SELF\">

<P><strong>Your Name:</strong><br>
<INPUT type=\"text\" NAME=\"sender_name\" SIZE=30></p>

<P><strong>Your E-Mail Address:</strong><br>
<INPUT type=\"text\" NAME=\"sender_email\" SIZE=30></p>

<P><strong>Message:</strong><br>
<TEXTAREA NAME=\"message\" COLS=30 ROWS=5 WRAP=virtual></TEXTAREA></p>
<INPUT type=\"hidden\" name=\"op\" value=\"ds\">
<P><INPUT TYPE=\"submit\" NAME=\"submit\" VALUE=\"Send This Form\"></p>

</FORM>

";

if ($op != "ds") {
        // they need to see the form
        echo "$form_block";
}

?>
</BODY>
</HTML>
```

4. Save the file.

You're not done yet, but your code should now look something like this.

You'll make a few more modifications in the next steps, to add your error messages. If the form is submitted, the value of $op will be "ds", and now you must account for that. Assume that all the form fields are required; after checking for the value of $op, you'll check for a value in all the fields.

1. Open allinone_form.php in your text editor.

2. Continue the `if...else` statement:

```
else if ($op == "ds") {
```

3. Add an if statement within the parent statement to check for values. Start with `$sender_name`:

```
if ($sender_name == "") {
```

4. Create an error message for `$sender_name` called `$name_err`:

```
$name_err = "<font color=red>Please enter your name!</font><br>";
```

5. Set the value of `$send` to "no":

```
$send = "no";
```

6. Create a similar if statement for `$sender_email`:

```
if ($sender_email == "") {
$email_err = "<font color=red>Please enter your e-mail address!</font><br>";
$send = "no";
}
```

7. Create a similar if statement for `$message`:

```
if ($message == "") {
$message_err = "<font color=red>Please enter a message!</font><br>";
$send = "no";
}
```

8. Start an `if...else` statement to handle the value of `$send`:

```
if ($send != "no") {
    // it's ok to send!
```

9. Create a variable to hold the recipient's e-mail address (substitute your own):

```
$to = "you@youremail.com";
```

10. Create a variable to hold the subject of the e-mail:

```
$subject = "All-in-One Web Site Feedback";
```

11. Create a variable to hold additional mail headers:

```
$mailheaders = "From: My Web Site <> \n";
```

12. Add to the $mailheaders variable:

```
$mailheaders .= "Reply-To: $sender_email\n\n";
```

13. Build the message string:

```
$msg = "E-MAIL SENT FROM WWW SITE\n";
$msg .= "Sender's Name:     $sender_name\n";
$msg .= "Sender's E-Mail:  $sender_email\n";
$msg .= "Message:            $message\n\n";
```

14. Add the mail() function:

```
mail($to, $subject, $msg, $mailheaders);
```

15. Add a simple statement to let the user know the mail has been sent, and close the if statement:

```
echo "<P>Mail has been sent!</p>";
}
```

16. Continue the if...else statement to deal with a value of "no" for $send:

```
else if ($send == "no") {
```

17. Print the error messages:

```
echo "$name_err";
echo "$email_err";
echo "$message_err";
```

18. Print the form again:

```
echo "$form_block";
```

19. Close the current `if...else` block:

```
}
```

20. Close the parent `if...else` block:

```
}
```

21. Save the file.

The entire code should look like this:

```
<HTML>
<HEAD>
<TITLE>All-In-One Feedback Form</TITLE>
</HEAD>
<BODY>

<?
$form_block = "
<FORM METHOD=\"post\" ACTION=\"$PHP_SELF\">

<P><strong>Your Name:</strong><br>
<INPUT type=\"text\" NAME=\"sender_name\"  SIZE=30></P>

<P><strong>Your E-Mail Address:</strong><br>
<INPUT type=\"text\" NAME=\"sender_email\"  SIZE=30></P>

<P><strong>Message:</strong><br>
<TEXTAREA NAME=\"message\" COLS=30 ROWS=5 WRAP=virtual></TEXTAREA></P>

<INPUT type=\"hidden\" name=\"op\" value=\"ds\">

<P><INPUT TYPE=\"submit\" NAME=\"submit\" VALUE=\"Send This Form\"></p>
```

```
</FORM>
";

if ($op != "ds") {
    // they need to see the form
    echo "$form_block";

} else if ($op == "ds") {

    if ($sender_name == "") {
        $name_err = "<font color=red>Please enter your name!</font><br>";
        $send = "no";
    }

    if ($sender_email == "") {

        $email_err = "<font color=red>Please enter your e-mail
address!</font><br>";
        $send = "no";
    }

    if ($message == "") {
        $message_err = "<font color=red>Please enter a message!</font><br>";
        $send = "no";
    }

    if ($send != "no") {

        // it's ok to send!
        $msg = "E-MAIL SENT FROM WWW SITE\n";
        $msg .= "Sender's Name:     $sender_name\n";
        $msg .= "Sender's E-Mail:  $sender_email\n";
        $msg .= "Message:          $message\n\n";

        $to = "you@yourdomain.com";
        $subject = "All-in-One Web Site Feedback";
        $mailheaders = "From: My Web Site <> \n";
        $mailheaders .= "Reply-To: $sender_email\n\n";
```

```
            mail($to, $subject, $msg, $mailheaders);
            echo "<P>Mail has been sent!</p>";

        } else if ($send == "no") {

            echo "$name_err";
            echo "$email_err";
            echo "$message_err";
            echo "$form_block";
        }
    }
    ?>
    </BODY>
    </HTML>
```

Submitting Your Form and Getting Results

Now that you've created both a front-end form and a back-end script, it's time to try them out.

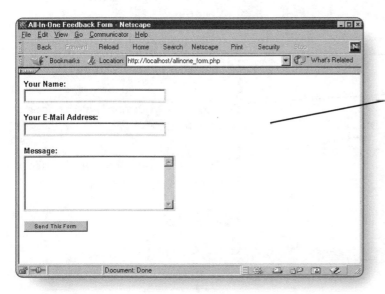

1. Open your Web browser and type **http://localhost/ allinone_form.php**

You will see a form containing a text field for the person's name, a text field for the person's e-mail address, a text area for the message, and a Send This Form button.

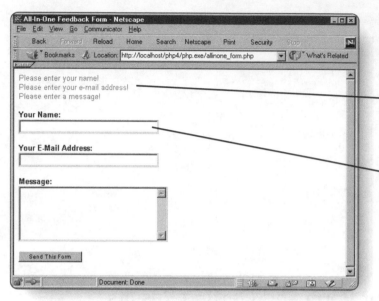

2. Click on the Send This Form button without typing anything in any of the fields.

The form, with all three error messages at the top, will appear in your browser window.

3. Type your name in the Your Name field.

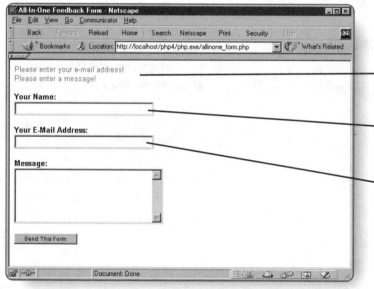

4. Click on the Send This Form button.

The form will reappear, without the Name error message.

5. Type your name in the Your Name field.

6. Type your e-mail address in the Your E-Mail Address field.

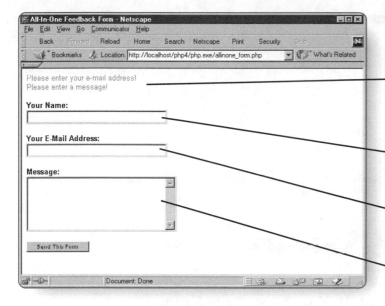

7. Click on the Send This Form button.

The form will reappear again, this time with only the Message error.

8. Type your name in the Your Name field.

9. Type your e-mail address in the Your E-Mail Address field.

10. Type the following in the message text area:

```
This all-in-one thing is
pretty cool!
```

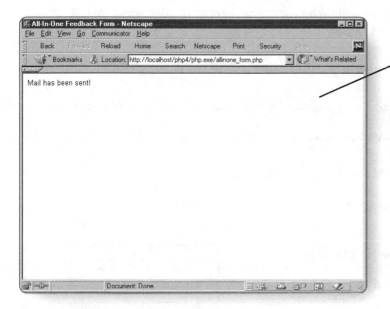

11. Submit the form.

You will see a confirmation that your message has been sent.

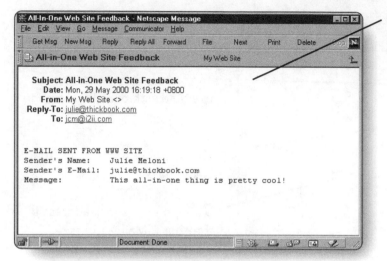

Check your e-mail, and see if a message is waiting for you.

Saving the Values If You Make an Error

One thing you probably noticed in the original script is that if you made an error, the form was reset and you lost the values you had entered. A simple modification to the original $form_block will take care of that problem. Just add a VALUE attribute to the form field to hold any previous value for the given variable.

1. Open allinone_form.php in your text editor.

2. Inside the $form_block variable, modify the input field for Your Name:

```
<INPUT type=\"text\" NAME=\"sender_name\" VALUE=\"$sender_name\" SIZE=30></P>
```

3. Modify the input field for Your E-Mail Address:

```
<INPUT type=\"text\" NAME=\"sender_email\" VALUE=\"$sender_email\"
SIZE=30></P>
```

4. Modify the text area for Message:

```
<TEXTAREA NAME=\"message\" COLS=30 ROWS=5
WRAP=virtual>$message</TEXTAREA></P>
```

5. Save the file.

NOTE

There's no VALUE attribute for TEXTAREA. Instead, the value goes between the start and end tags.

6. Open your Web browser and type **http://localhost/allinone_form.php**

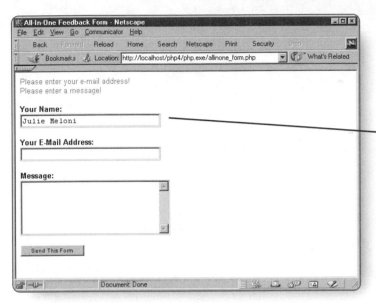

7. Type your name in the Your Name field.

8. Click on the Send This Form button.

The form, complete with error messages, will appear. This time, though, your name has been saved!

9. Type your e-mail address in the Your E-Mail Address field.

10. Click on the Submit This Form button.

The form will reappear, with your name and e-mail address saved.

11. Type the following in the Message text area:

This all-in-one thing is pretty cool!

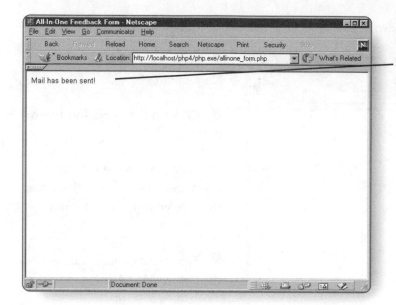

12. Submit the form.

You will see a confirmation that your message has been sent.

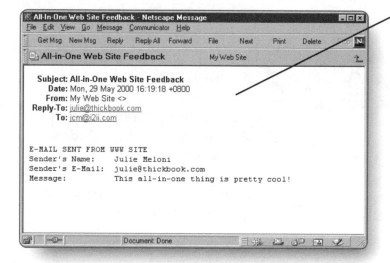

Check your e-mail, and see if a message is waiting for you.

9

Using Your Filesystem

By using simple PHP scripts, you can do anything with your filesystem—after all, it's yours! In this chapter, you'll learn how to do the following:

- Display the contents of a directory
- Create a new file
- Open an existing file and append data to it
- Copy, rename, and delete files

A Note Regarding File Paths

The scripts used in these chapters can be executed on both Windows and Linux/UNIX operating systems. On Windows, you can use both the forward slash (/) and the backslash (\) in file paths, whereas other operating systems use only the forward slash. The scripts in this chapter use the forward slash method in all instances. This method works even if you don't specify a drive letter. For example:

```
$path = "/Program Files/Apache Group/Apache/htdocs";
```

This path, on Windows, is assumed to be on the current drive (in my case, C:/). If you need to specify a drive letter, do so:

```
$path = "K:/Program Files/Apache Group/Apache/htdocs/";
```

You'll have to modify file paths to fit your own directory structure, but you shouldn't have to do more than that.

Displaying Directory Contents

Believe it or not, this script will be the most complicated in this chapter, and it has only 32 lines! The goal is to open a directory, find the names of all the files in the directory, and print the results in a bullet list.

1. Open a new file in your text editor.

2. Start a PHP block:

```
<?
```

3. Create a variable to hold the full path name of a directory:

```
$dir_name = "/windows/desktop/My Downloads/";
```

> **NOTE**
>
> This directory is one that exists on my own machine. Substitute your own directory name so that this works for you.

4. Create a handle and use the `opendir()` function to open the directory specified in step 3:

```
$dir = opendir($dir_name);
```

5. You'll eventually place the results in a bullet list inside a string called `$file_list`. Start that bullet list now:

```
$file_list = "<ul>";
```

6. Start a `while` loop that uses the `readdir()` function to determine when to stop and start the loop. The `readdir()` function returns the name of the next file in the directory, and in this case assigns the value to a variable called `$file_name`:

```
while ($file_name = readdir($dir)) {
```

7. Get rid of those "." and ".." file names using an `if` statement:

```
if (($file_name != ".") && ($file_name != "..")) {
```

8. If `$file_name` is neither of the "dot" file names, add it to `$file_list` using the concatenation assignment operator:

```
$file_list .= "<li>$file_name";
```

9. Close the `if` statement:

```
}
```

10. Close the `while` loop:

```
}
```

11. Add the closing tag to the bullet list:

```
$file_list .= "</ul>";
```

> **NOTE**
>
> The term "handle" will be used to refer to the open directory in subsequent directory-related functions.

12. Close the open directory:

```
closedir($dir);
```

13. Close your PHP block:

```
?>
```

14. Add this HTML:

```
<HTML>
<HEAD>
<TITLE>Directory Listing</TITLE>
</HEAD>
<BODY>
```

15. Mingle some HTML and PHP to print the name of the directory you just read:

```
<P>Files in: <? echo "$dir_name"; ?></P>
```

16. Print the file list:

```
<? echo "$file_list"; ?>
```

```
<?
$dir_name = "/windows/desktop/My Downloads/";

$dir = opendir($dir_name);

$file_list = "<ul>";

while ($file_name = readdir($dir)) {
    if (($file_name != ".") && ($file_name != "..")) {
        $file_list .= "<li>$file_name";
    }
}

$file_list .= "</ul>";

closedir($dir);

?>
<HTML>
<HEAD>
<TITLE>Directory Listing</TITLE>
</HEAD>
<BODY>

<P>Files in: <? echo "$dir_name"; ?></p>

<? echo "$file_list"; ?>

</BODY>
</HTML>
```

17. Add some more HTML so that the document is valid:

```
</BODY>
</HTML>
```

18. Save the file with the name listfiles.php.

Your code should look something like this.

Let's see if it works.

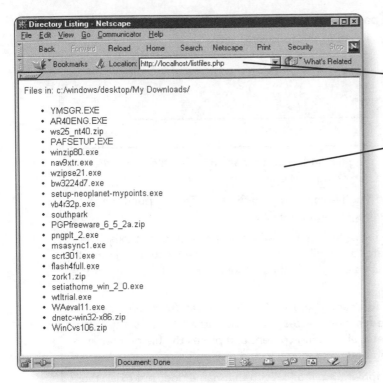

Files in: c:/windows/desktop/My Downloads/

- YMSGR.EXE
- AR40ENG.EXE
- ws25_nt40.zip
- PAFSETUP.EXE
- winzip80.exe
- nav9xtr.exe
- wzipse21.exe
- bw3224d7.exe
- setup-neoplanet-mypoints.exe
- vb4r32p.exe
- southpark
- PGPfreeware_6_5_2a.zip
- pngplt_2.exe
- msasync1.exe
- scrt301.exe
- flash4full.exe
- zork1.zip
- setiathome_win_2_0.exe
- wtltrial.exe
- WAeval11.exe
- dnetc-win32-x86.zip
- WinCvs106.zip

19. Place this file in the document root of your Web server.

20. Open your Web browser and type **http://localhost/ listfiles.php**

You should see a bulleted list, displaying the files within the directory provided in $dir_name. The results shown here show the files in one of my own directories; your list will differ.

Assuming that this worked, try it for other directories on your system. If a directory doesn't exist, the script won't return an error—it just won't have any results.

In the next section, you'll work with the fopen() and fclose() functions to open and close specific files.

Working with fopen() and fclose()

Before you jump headfirst into working with files, you need to learn a bit about the fopen() function, which is used to open files. This function requires a file name and mode, and it returns a file pointer. A file pointer provides information about the file and is used as a reference.

The file name is the full path to the file you want to create or open, and the mode can be any of the modes listed in the following table.

Modes Used with fopen()

Mode	Usage
r	Opens an existing file and reads data from it. The file pointer is placed at the beginning of the file.
r+	Opens an existing file for reading or writing. The file pointer is placed at the beginning of the file.
w	Opens a file for writing. If a file with that name does not exist, the function creates a new file. If the file exists, the function deletes all existing contents and places the file pointer at the beginning of the file.
w+	Opens a file for reading and writing. If a file with that name does not exist, the function creates a new file. If the file exists, the function deletes all existing content and places the file pointer at the beginning of the file.
a	Opens a file for writing. If a file with that name does not exist, the function creates a new file. If the file exists, the function places the file pointer at the end of the file.
a+	Opens a file for reading and writing. If a file with that name does not exist, the function attempts to create a new file. If the file exists, the function places the file pointer at the end of the file.

Creating a New File

Compared to the first section of this chapter, this next task will be a piece of cake. The goal is simply to create a new, empty file in a specified location.

1. Open a new file in your text editor.

2. Start a PHP block:

```
<?
```

3. Create a variable to hold the full path name to a file:

```
$filename = "/Apache/mydata.txt";
```

4. Create a file pointer and use the `fopen()` function to open the file specified in step 3 for reading and writing. The `die()` function will cause the script to end and a message to display if the file doesn't open properly.

```
$newfile = fopen($filename, "w+") or
die("Couldn't create file.");
```

5. Close the file pointer:

```
fclose($newfile);
```

6. Create a message to print upon success:

```
$msg = "<P>File created!</P>";
```

7. Close your PHP block:

```
?>
```

8. Add this HTML:

```
<HTML>
<HEAD>
<TITLE>Creating a New File</TITLE>
</HEAD>
<BODY>
```

9. Print the message:

```
<? echo "$msg"; ?>
```

> **NOTE**
>
> This directory is one that exists on my own machine. Substitute your own directory name so that this works for you.

> **NOTE**
>
> The term "file pointer" will be used to refer to the open file in subsequent file-related functions.

10. Add some more HTML so that the document is valid:

```
</BODY>
</HTML>
```

11. Save the file with the name newfile.php.

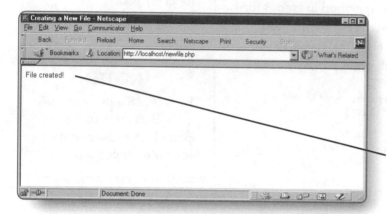

12. Place this file in the document root of your Web server.

13. Open your Web browser and type **http://localhost/newfile.php**

If the file creation was successful, you should see the success message.

However, if your file creation failed, you will see a nasty parse error. You can force an error by using an invalid value for $filename, such as this:

```
$filename = "/bozo/mydata.txt";
```

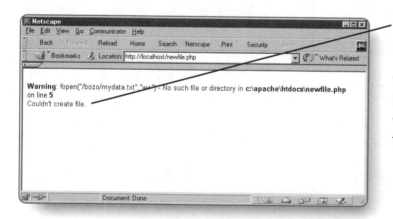

When you run your script, you'll see something like this.

You can prevent this nastiness by suppressing errors and warnings using the @ sign in front of functions.

Change this line:

```
$newfile = fopen($filename, "w+") or die("Couldn't create file.");
```

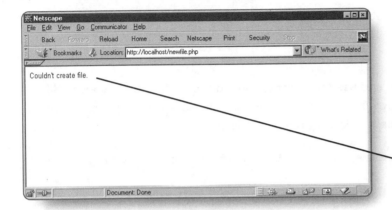

to this:

```
$newfile = @fopen($filename,
"w+") or die("Couldn't create
file.");
```

Save the file and access the
script via your Web browser.

You'll now see just the message
from the die() function, and no
other warnings.

Checking Whether a File Already Exists

To avoid any possible housekeeping errors when running around your filesystem,
you can use the file_exists() function to check whether a file already exists
before you create it. This next script will do just that and will print a message one
way or the other.

1. Open a new file in your text editor.

2. Start a PHP block:

```
<?
```

3. Create a variable to hold the full path name
to a file (use your own file path):

```
$filename = "/Apache/mydata.txt";
```

4. Start an if...else statement that checks
for a true/false result to the file_exists()
function:

```
if (file_exists($filename)) {
```

> **NOTE**
>
> Yes, this is the same file
> you probably created in
> the previous section.
> That's fine, because it can
> trip the error checking!

5. Create a variable to hold a message regarding the file's existence:

```
$msg = "<P>File already exists.</Pp>";
```

6. Continue the `else` statement, to do something if the file doesn't exist:

```
} else {
```

7. Create a file pointer and use the `fopen()` function to open the file specified in step 3 for reading and writing. The `die()` function will cause the script to end and a message to display if the file doesn't open properly.

```
$newfile = @fopen($filename, "w+") or die("Couldn't create file.");
```

8. Create a variable to hold a success message:

```
$msg = "<P>File created!</P>";
```

9. Close the file pointer:

```
fclose($newfile);
```

10. Close the `if...else` statement:

```
}
```

11. Close your PHP block:

```
?>
```

12. Add this HTML:

```
<HTML>
<HEAD>
<TITLE>Creating a New File</TITLE>
</HEAD>
<BODY>
```

13. Print the message:

```
<? echo "$msg"; ?>
```

14. Add some more HTML so that the document is valid:

```
</BODY>
</HTML>
```

15. Save the file with the name newfile_checkfirst.php.

16. Place this file in the document root of your Web server.

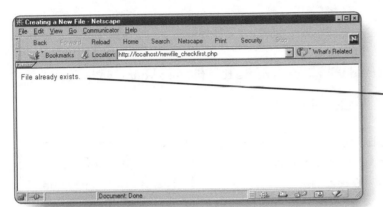

17. Open your Web browser and type **http://localhost/ newfile_checkfirst.php**

Assuming that you used the filename of a previously-created file, you should see the failure message.

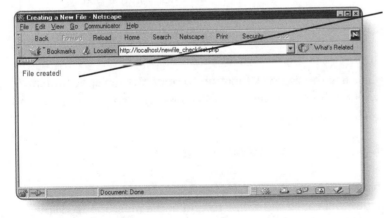

If you change the value of $filename to a file that doesn't exist and then access the script again, you'll see the success message.

Just creating a file is boring. In the next section you'll learn to write data to the file.

Appending Data to a File

The goal of the next script is to append data to a file. If the file exists, the script will just write data into it. If the file doesn't exist, it will be created before data is written to it.

1. Open a new file in your text editor.

2. Start a PHP block:

```
<?
```

3. Create a variable to hold the full path name to a file (use your own file path):

```
$filename = "/Apache/textfile.txt";
```

4. Create a variable called $newstring to hold the string you want to write to the file. Populate that string with this very exciting message:

```
$newstring = "
Check it out!\n
I've created a new file and stuck all this text
into it!
";
```

> **NOTE**
>
> The use of the newline character causes a line break to occur at that point in the text.

5. Create a file pointer and use the fopen() function to open the file specified in step 4 for reading and writing. The die() function will cause the script to end and a message to display if the file doesn't open properly.

```
$myfile = @fopen($filename, "w+") or die("Couldn't open file.");
```

6. Use the fwrite() function to place the text ($newstring) inside the file ($myfile). The die() function will cause the script to end and a message to display if the fwrite() function fails.

```
@fwrite($myfile, $newstring) or die("Couldn't write to file.");
```

7. Create a variable to hold a success message:

```
$msg = "<P>File has data in it now...</p>";
```

8. Close the file pointer:

```
fclose($myfile);
```

9. Close your PHP block:

```
?>
```

10. Add this HTML:

```
<HTML>
<HEAD>
<TITLE>Adding Data to a File</TITLE>
</HEAD>
<BODY>
```

11. Print the message:

```
<? echo "$msg"; ?>
```

12. Add some more HTML so that the document is valid:

```
</BODY>
</HTML>
```

13. Save the file with the name writedata.php.

14. Place this file in the document root of your Web server.

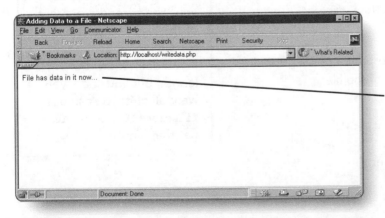

15. Open your Web browser and type **http://localhost/writedata.php**

You should see a success message printed on the screen.

In the next section, you'll read the data from the text file created in this script.

Reading Data from a File

You'll now create a script to read the data from the file you created in the previous section. You could just open that file in a text editor, but where's the fun in that? PHP has a handy function called `fread()` that does the job for you.

1. Open a new file in your text editor.

2. Start a PHP block:

```
<?
```

3. Create a variable to hold the full path name to the file you created in the previous section (use your own path):

```
$filename = "/Apache/textfile.txt";
```

4. Create a file pointer and use the `fopen()` function to open the file specified in step 3 for reading only. The `die()` function will cause the script to end and a message to display if the file doesn't open properly.

```
$whattoread = @fopen($filename, "r") or die("Couldn't open file");
```

5. Create a variable called `$file_contents`, and use the `fread()` function to read all the lines from the open file pointer (`$whattoread`) for as long as there are lines in the file:

```
$file_contents = fread($whattoread,
filesize($filename));
```

6. Create a variable to print a message, including the contents of the file:

```
$msg = "The file
contains:<br>$file_contents";
```

7. Close the file pointer:

```
fclose($whattoread);
```

> **NOTE**
>
> Using the `filesize()` function on an existing file lets PHP do the work for you. The second argument of the `fread()` function is for the length of the file. If you don't know the length, but you know you want all of it, you can use `filesize($filename)` to get that length.

8. Close your PHP block:

```
?>
```

9. Add this HTML:

```
<HTML>
<HEAD>
<TITLE>Reading Data From a File</TITLE>
</HEAD>
<BODY>
```

10. Print the message:

```
<? echo "$msg"; ?>
```

11. Add some more HTML so that the document is valid:

```
</BODY>
</HTML>
```

12. Save the file with the name readdata.php.

13. Place this file in the document root of your Web server.

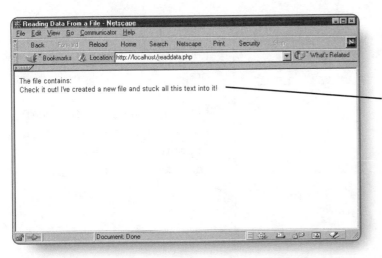

14. Open your Web browser and type **http://localhost/ readdata.php**

You should see the contents of the file you just read printed on the screen.

That's definitely the string written to the file, but what happened to that line break? The newline character means nothing to a Web browser, which renders only HTML. Luckily, the PHP Development Team had great forethought and created the nl2br() function (newline-to-break; get it?). Make some slight adjustments to the readdata.php script:

15. Add this line after the line containing the fread() function:

```
$new_file_contents = nl2br($file_contents);
```

```
<?
$filename = "/Apache/textfile.txt";
$whattoread = @fopen($filename, "r") or die("Couldn't open file");
$file_contents = fread($whattoread, filesize($filename));
$new_file_contents = nl2br($file_contents);
$msg = "The file contains:<br>$new_file_contents";
fclose($whattoread);
?>
<HTML>
<HEAD>
<TITLE>Reading Data From a File</TITLE>
</HEAD>
<BODY>

<? echo "$msg"; ?>

</BODY>
</HTML>
```

16. Modify the $msg string so that it looks like this:

```
$msg = "The file contains:<br>
$new_file_contents";
```

17. Save the file.

Your modified code should look something like this.

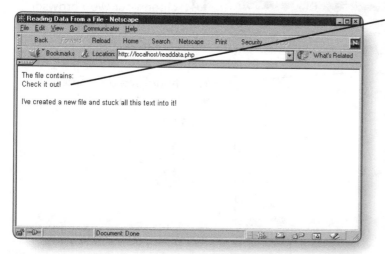

Now open this file in your Web browser, and notice the line break.

In the next section, you'll read the same message, but instead of printing it on the screen, you'll send it via e-mail.

Sending File Contents Via E-Mail

If you're saving the results of HTML forms to a plain text file, which you want to read only at specific times, you can write a little script that mails the contents of the file to you on demand.

1. Open a new file in your text editor.

2. Start a PHP block:

```
<?
```

3. Create a variable to hold the full path name to the file containing the data (use your own path):

```
$filename = "/Apache/textfile.txt";
```

4. Create a file pointer and use the `fopen()` function to open the file specified in step 3 for reading only. The `die()` function will cause the script to end and a message to display if the file doesn't open properly.

```
$whattoread = @fopen($filename, "r") or die("Couldn't open file");
```

5. Create a variable called `$file_contents`, and use the `fread()` function to read all the lines from the open file pointer (`$whattoread`) for as long as there are lines in the file:

```
$file_contents = fread($whattoread, filesize($filename));
```

6. Create a variable to hold your e-mail address:

```
$to = "you@yourdomain.com";
```

7. Create a variable for the subject of the e-mail:

```
$subject = "File Contents";
```

8. Create a variable for additional mail headers:

```
$mailheaders = "From: My Web Site <> \n";
```

9. Populate the `mail()` function using the `$file_contents` string as the third argument (the message):

```
mail($to, $subject, $file_contents, $mailheaders);
```

10. Create a variable to print a message to the screen:

```
$msg = "<P>Check your mail!</P>";
```

11. Close the file pointer:

```
fclose($whattoread);
```

12. Close your PHP block:

```
?>
```

13. Add this HTML:

```
<HTML>
<HEAD>
<TITLE>Mailing Data From a File</TITLE>
</HEAD>
<BODY>
```

14. Print the message:

```
<? echo "$msg"; ?>
```

15. Add some more HTML so that the document is valid:

```
</BODY>
</HTML>
```

16. Save the file with the name mailcontents.php.

17. Place this file in the document root of your Web server.

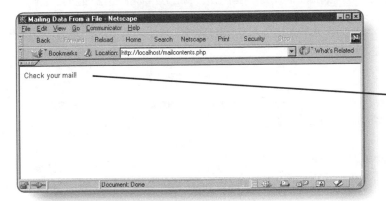

18. Open your Web browser and type **http://localhost/ mailcontents.php**

You should see a message printed on the screen telling you to check your mail.

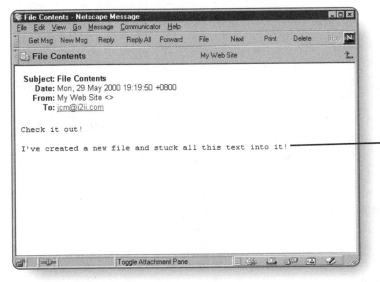

Like the message says, go check your mail. Unlike with the previous script you didn't need to use the `nl2br()` function, since you weren't displaying text in a Web browser window.

The plain text e-mail will keep the original line break.

Filesystem Housekeeping

The next series of scripts will help you perform very basic filesystem tasks, such as copying, renaming, and deleting files. Remember that you can perform filesystem functions only if the proper permissions are in place for the PHP user.

Copying Files

The `copy()` function is very simple: It needs to know the original filename and a new filename—and that's all there is to it.

1. Open a new file in your text editor.

2. Start a PHP block:

```
<?
```

3. Create a variable to hold the full path name to the original file (use your own path):

```
$orig_filename = "/Apache/textfile.txt";
```

4. Create a variable to hold the full path name to the new file (use your own path):

```
$new_filename = "/Apache/textfile.bak";
```

5. Create a variable to hold the true/false result of the function. Suppress warnings by using the @ in front of the function, and use `die()` to print a message if the function fails:

```
$success = @copy($orig_filename, $new_filename) or die("Couldn't copy file.");
```

6. Start an `if...else` statement to print the proper message based on the outcome of the function:

```
if ($success) {
```

7. The message string, if successful, should print a confirmation of the copy:

```
$msg = "Copied $orig_filename to
$new_filename";
```

8. Continue the statement for a failure:

```
} else {
        $msg = "Could not copy file.";
}
```

9. Close your PHP block:

```
?>
```

10. Add this HTML:

```
<HTML>
<HEAD>
<TITLE>Copy a File</TITLE>
</HEAD>
<BODY>
```

11. Print the message:

```
<? echo "$msg"; ?>
```

12. Add some more HTML so that the document is valid:

```
</BODY>
</HTML>
```

13. Save the file with the name copyfile.php.

14. Place this file in the document root of your Web server.

> **NOTE**
>
> The use of the `else` statement in this case is actually unnecessary, but it's good practice for providing a default result. If the `copy()` function fails, the `die()` function will exit the script and print the error before even getting to the `if...else` part of the script.

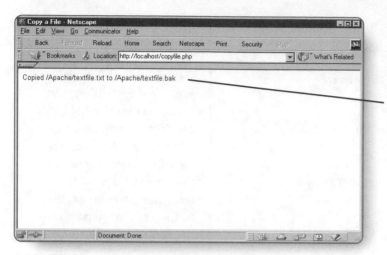

15. Open your Web browser and type **http://localhost/ copyfile.php**

You should see a confirmation of the file copying procedure, stating the old and new names of the file that was renamed.

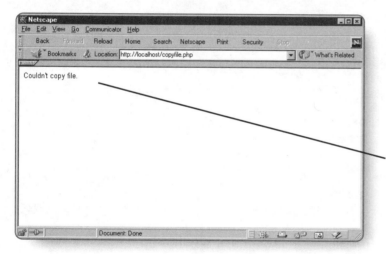

See if your error handling works by changing the value of $new_filename to something that doesn't exist:

```
$new_filename =
"/bozo/textfile.bak";
```

Access the script via your Web browser, and you should see something like this.

Next, move on to renaming files. The script is remarkably similar!

Renaming Files

Like the copy() function, the rename() function just needs to know the original filename and a new filename. In this case you're just renaming the original, not copying it.

1. Open a new file in your text editor.

2. Start a PHP block:

```
<?
```

3. Create a variable to hold the full path name to the original file (use your own path):

```
$orig_filename = "/Apache/textfile.bak";
```

4. Create a variable to hold the full path name to the new file (use your own path):

```
$new_filename = "/Apache/textfile.old";
```

5. Create a variable to hold the true/false result of the function. Suppress warnings by using the @ in front of the function, and use die() to print a message if the function fails:

```
$success = @rename($orig_filename, $new_filename) or die("Couldn't rename
file.");
```

6. Start an if...else statement to print the proper message based on the outcome of the function:

```
if ($success) {
```

7. The message string, if successful, should print a confirmation of the renaming function:

```
$msg = "Renamed $orig_filename to
$new_filename";
```

8. Continue the statement for a failure:

```
} else {
        $msg = "Could not rename file.";
}
```

9. Close your PHP block:

```
?>
```

> **NOTE**
>
> The use of the else statement in this case is actually unnecessary, but it's good practice for providing a default result. If the rename() function fails, the die() function will exit the script and print the error before even getting to the if...else part of the script.

10. Add this HTML:

```
<HTML>
<HEAD>
<TITLE>Rename a File</TITLE>
</HEAD>
<BODY>
```

11. Print the message:

```
<? echo "$msg"; ?>
```

12. Add some more HTML so that the document is valid:

```
</BODY>
</HTML>
```

13. Save the file with the name renamefile.php.

14. Place this file in the document root of your Web server.

15. Open your Web browser and type **http://localhost/renamefile.php**

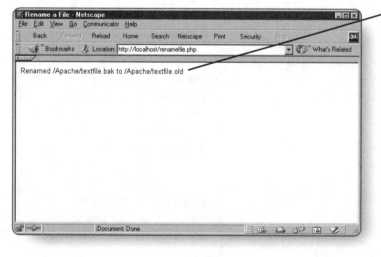

You should see a confirmation of the file copying procedure, stating the name of the original file as well as the name of the new file.

See if your error handling works by changing the value of $new_filename to something that doesn't exist:

```
$new_filename =
"/bozo/textfile.bak";
```

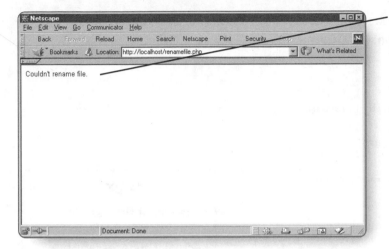

Access the script via your Web browser, and you should see this.

There's one more housekeeping function in the next section: deleting a file.

Deleting Files

Be very careful when using the unlink() function, because once you've deleted a file, it's gone for good.

1. Open a new file in your text editor.

2. Start a PHP block:

```
<?
```

3. Create a variable to hold the full path name to the file you want to delete (use your own path):

```
$filename = "/Apache/textfile.old";
```

4. Create a variable to hold the true/false result of the function. Suppress warnings by using the @ in front of the function, and use die() to print a message if the function fails:

```
$success = @unlink($filename) or die("Couldn't delete file.");
```

5. Start an `if...else` statement to print the proper message based on the outcome of the function:

```
if ($success) {
```

6. The message string, if successful, should print a confirmation of the deletion:

```
$msg = "Deleted $filename";
```

7. Continue the statement for a failure:

```
} else {
    $msg = "Could not delete file.";
}
```

8. Close your PHP block:

```
?>
```

> **NOTE**
>
> The use of the `else` statement in this case is actually unnecessary, but it's good practice for providing a default result. If the `unlink()` function fails, the `die()` function will exit the script and print the error before even getting to the `if[...]else` part of the script.

9. Add this HTML:

```
<HTML>
<HEAD>
<TITLE>Delete a File</TITLE>
</HEAD>
<BODY>
```

10. Print the message:

```
<? echo "$msg"; ?>
```

11. Add some more HTML so that the document is valid:

```
</BODY>
</HTML>
```

12. Save the file with the name deletefile.php.

13. Place this file in the document root of your Web server.

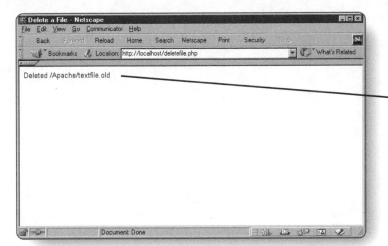

14. Open your Web browser and type **http://localhost/ deletefile.php**

You should see a confirmation of the file deletion process, stating the name of the file that was deleted.

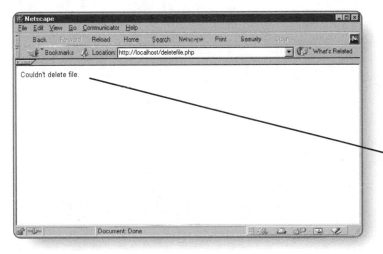

See if your error handling works, by changing the value of $filename to something that doesn't exist:

```
$filename =
"/bozo/textfile.old";
```

Access the script via your Web browser, and you should see this.

In the next chapter, you'll create a two-step process (front-end form and back-end script) to initiate file uploads from a Web browser to your filesystem.

10

Uploading Files to Your Web Site

If you need a quick interface for uploading files to your Web site from a remote location, you can create a two-step form and script interface with PHP. In this chapter, you'll learn how to do the following:

- Create an HTML form for file uploads
- Create a PHP script to handle file uploads

Check Your php.ini File

Before you start uploading files, check a few values in your php.ini file. Look for these two lines:

```
;upload_tmp_dir         =                  ; temporary directory for HTTP uploaded
                                            files
upload_max_filesize   = 2097152         ; 2 Meg default limit on file uploads
```

You'll need to modify these lines so that the file upload process will work smoothly.

1. Uncomment the `upload_tmp_dir` line by deleting the initial semicolon.

2. Enter a directory name after the = for `upload_tmp_dir`.

3. If you want to allow larger uploads, change the number of bytes for `upload_max_filesize`.

For example, my php.ini file on Windows contains this:

```
upload_tmp_dir        = c:/Windows/temp    ; temporary directory for HTTP
                                             uploaded files
upload_max_filesize   = 2097152            ; 2 Meg default limit on file
                                             uploads
```

Understanding the Process

The process of uploading a file to a Web server through an HTML form interface puzzles a lot of people. Take a moment to understand the process you'll create in the sections following this one.

To start and finish this process, you'll need the following:

- An HTML form
- A file to upload
- A place to put the file
- A script to put it there

The process itself goes something like this:

1. The user accesses the HTML form and sees a text field and the Browse button in his Web browser.

2. The user browses his hard drive for the file he wants to upload and then selects a file.

3. The full file path and file name appear in the text field.

4. The user clicks the Submit button.

5. The selected file goes out and lands at the Web server and sits around in a temporary directory.

6. The PHP script used in the form action checks that a file was sent and executes a copy command on the temporary file to move it to a real directory on the Web server.

7. The PHP script confirms the action for the user.

Start with simply creating the HTML form interface in the next section.

> **NOTE**
>
> The PHP user (the user under which PHP runs, such as "nobody" or "www" or "joe") must have write permissions in the temporary directory as well as the target directory for the file.

Creating the Form

Start out by creating a one-field form. You can create a form to upload as many files as you like after you get this sequence to work with one file.

1. Open a new file in your text editor.

2. Type the following HTML:

```
<HTML>
<HEAD>
<TITLE>Upload a File</TITLE>
</HEAD>
<BODY>
<H1>Upload a File</H1>
```

3. Begin your form. Assume that the method is post and the action is a script called do_upload.php. Because you'll be sending more than just text, use the ENCTYPE attribute.

```
<FORM METHOD="post" ACTION=" do_upload.php" ENCTYPE="multipart/form-data">
```

4. Create an input field for the file with a text label. Assume that you'll be uploading an image file, and name the input field img1:

```
<p><strong>File to Upload:</strong><br>
<INPUT TYPE="file" NAME="img1" SIZE="30"></P>
```

5. Add a submit button:

```
<P><INPUT TYPE="submit" NAME="submit"
VALUE="Upload File"></P>
```

> **NOTE**
> The TYPE="file" attribute in the form field will display an input field with a Browse button. The Browse button launches a file manager through which you select the file to upload.

6. Close your form and add some more HTML so that the document is valid:

```
</FORM>
</BODY>
</HTML>
```

7. Save the file with the name upload_form.html.

8. Place this file in the document root of your Web server.

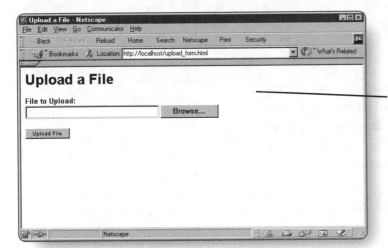

9. Open your Web browser and type **http://localhost/ upload_form.html**

You should see the file upload form, with a text field, a browse button, and a submit button.

In the next section, you'll create the script that handles the file upload.

Creating the Upload Script

Take a moment to commit the following list to memory—it contains the variables created automatically after a successful file upload. The base of img1 comes from the name of the input field in the original form.

- **$img1.** The value refers to the temporary file on the Web server.
- **$img1_name.** The value is the actual name of the file that was uploaded. For example, if the name of the file was me.jpg, the value of $img1_name is me.jpg.
- **$img1_size.** The size of the uploaded file, in bytes.
- **$img1_type.** The mime type of the uploaded file, such as image/jpg.

The goal of this script is to take the uploaded file and copy it to the document root of the Web server and return a confirmation to the user containing values for all the variables in the preceding list.

1. Open a new file in your text editor.

2. Start a PHP block:

```
<?
```

3. Create an `if...else` statement that checks for a value in `$img1_name`:

```
if ($img1_name != "") {
```

4. If `$img1_name` is not empty, execute the copy function. Use @ before the function name to suppress warnings, and use the `die()` function to cause the script to end and a message to display if the `copy()` function fails.

```
@copy("$img1", "/usr/local/apache_1.3.12/
htdocs/$img1_name") or die("Couldn't copy the
file.");
```

> **NOTE**
>
> If the document root of your Web server is not /usr/local/apache_1.3.12/htdocs/ as shown in step 4, change the path to match your own system. For example, a Windows user might use /Apache/htdocs/.

5. Continue the `else` statement to handle the lack of a file for upload:

```
} else {
        die("No input file specified");
```

6. Close the `if...else` statement:

```
}
```

7. Close your PHP block:

```
?>
```

8. Add this HTML:

```
<HTML>
<HEAD>
<TITLE>Successful File Upload</TITLE>
</HEAD>
<BODY>
<H1>Success!</H1>
```

9. Mingle HTML and PHP, printing a line that displays values for the various elements of the uploaded file (name, size, type):

```
<P>You sent: <? echo "$img1_name"; ?>, a <? echo "$img1_size"; ?>
byte file with a mime type of <? echo "$img1_type"; ?>.</P>
```

```
<?

if ($img1_name != "") {

        @copy("$img1", "/Apache/htdocs/$img1_name")
             or die("Couldn't copy the file.");

} else {

        die("No input file specified");

}

?>

<HTML>
<HEAD>
<TITLE>Successful File Upload</TITLE>
</HEAD>
<BODY>

<H1>Success!</H1>

<P>You sent: <? echo "$img1_name"; ?>, a <? echo "$img1_size"; ?>
byte file with a mime type of <? echo "$img1_type"; ?>.</P>

</BODY>
</HTML>
```

10. Add some more HTML so that the document is valid:

```
</BODY>
</HTML>
```

11. Save the file with the name do_upload.php.

The code should look something like this.

In the next section, you'll finally get to upload a file!

Uploading a File Using Your Form and Script

This is the moment of truth, where you hold your breath and test the script.

1. Open your Web browser and type **http://localhost/upload_form.html**

2. Use the Browse button to locate a file you want to upload.

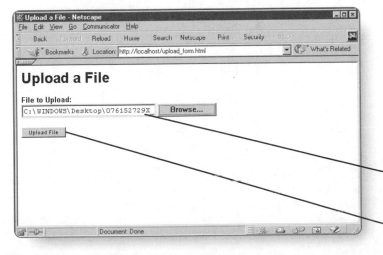

Upload a File

File to Upload:

C:\WINDOWS\Desktop\076152729X   Browse...

Upload File

NOTE

This example uses a file on my own machine, so the figures won't look quite the same as your results.

The full path to the file should appear in the form field.

3. Click the Upload File button.

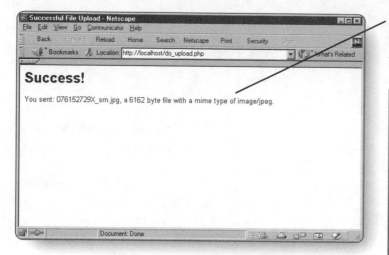

The result screen should appear, providing information about the file you just uploaded.

Just to be sure, use the File, Open Page menu item in your Web browser to navigate through your filesystem and find the file you just uploaded.

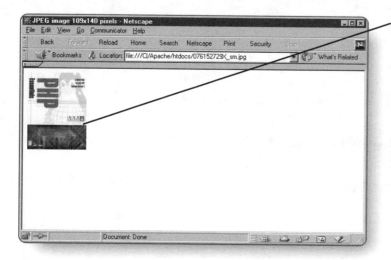

Here is the result of the file I uploaded through the file upload form.

There's nothing to it! You're now a filesystem wizard. In the next section, you'll become a database wizard as well.

PART IV

Getting to Know Your Database

11

Establishing a Connection and Getting Started with MySQL

During the process of installing and testing MySQL in Chapter 1, you should have created a sample database and a sample table, and even inserted and selected some data. The next several chapters focus on making the same types of connections and queries, using PHP scripts for the front end. In this chapter, you'll learn how to do the following:

- Connect to MySQL
- List all databases on the localhost
- List all tables in a database
- Create a database
- Drop (delete) a database

Creating a Username and Password

When you installed the MySQL database in Chapter 1, you were working as the anonymous or root user. Before you begin working with databases on a regular basis, you should create a real user with a real password. There are two simple commands to issue, using the MySQL monitor and the `mysqladmin` program.

NOTE

These commands are exactly the same for MySQL on Windows and Linux/UNIX platforms.

1. Start the MySQL monitor.

2. Select the database called `mysql` by typing **Use mysql** at the `mysql>` prompt:

3. Type the following SQL statement, substituting your own username and password:

```
insert into user (host, user, password) values ('localhost', 'sandman',
password('tQ9472b');
```

4. Exit the MySQL monitor by typing `exit` at the mysql> prompt.

5. Issue the `mysqladmin flush-privileges` command to reload the privilege tables using the `mysqladmin` program.

The new user (sandman) will now have access to all databases and tables when using the password tQ9472b.

NOTE

"sandman" will be the sample user in all database connectivity scripts from this point forward. Please substitute your own username and password where appropriate.

Connecting to MySQL

The goal of this script is simply to connect to MySQL, which is running on your machine (localhost).

1. Open a new file in your text editor.

2. Start a PHP block:

```
<?
```

3. Create a variable to hold the result of the `mysql_connect()` function:

```
$connection = mysql_connect("localhost",
"sandman", "tQ9472b")
```

> **NOTE**
>
> The `mysql_connect()` function requires a hostname, username, and password (in that order).

4. Add a `die()` function to the `mysql_connect()` line to cause the script to end and a message to display if the connection fails. The new line should read as follows:

```
$connection = mysql_connect("localhost", "sandman", "tQ9472b") or
die("Couldn't connect.");
```

5. Test the value of `$connection`. If it's true, the connection to MySQL was made, and a variable is created to hold a message:

```
if ($connection) {
    $msg = "success!";
}
```

> **NOTE**
>
> If a connection cannot be made, the script will end with the `die()` function.

6. Close your PHP block:

```
?>
```

7. Add this HTML:

```
<HTML>
<HEAD>
<TITLE>MySQL Connection</TITLE>
</HEAD>
<BODY>
```

8. Print the message string:

```
<? echo "$msg"; ?>
```

9. Add some more HTML so that the document is valid:

```
</BODY>
</HTML>
```

10. Save the file with the name db_connect.php.

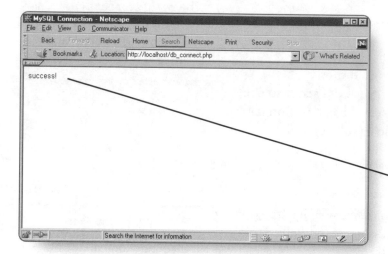

11. Place this file in the document root of your Web server.

12. Open your Web browser and type **http://localhost/ db_connect.php**

If you entered the correct username and password, you should have a successful result.

Breaking Your Connection Script

Anytime you work with databases you will have errors. It's inevitable. That's why I want to show you some common errors and how to handle them fairly gracefully.

You'll make a modification to the db_connect.php script that causes it to fail on connection, simply by changing the username.

1. Change the username to booboo (unless booboo is a real user!) so that the connection line reads as follows:

```
$connection = mysql_connect("localhost", "booboo", "tQ9472b") or die("Couldn't
connect.");
```

2. Save the file.

3. Open your Web browser and type **http://localhost/ db_connect.php**

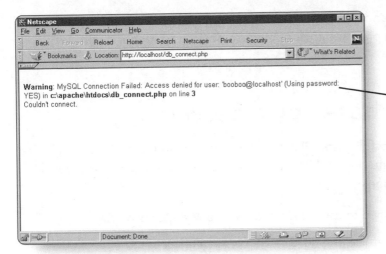

What a nasty response! At least it tells you exactly what is wrong: user "booboo@localhost" couldn't connect to MySQL. After the warning, the message from the `die()` function did indeed print.

You can suppress the ugly warning and just go with the message from the `die()` function by placing the @ before the `mysql_connect()` function name. Try it:

4. Add the @ before the `mysql_connect()` function, keeping the bad username:

```
$connection = @mysql_connect("localhost", "booboo", "tQ9472b") or
die("Couldn't connect.");
```

5. Save the file.

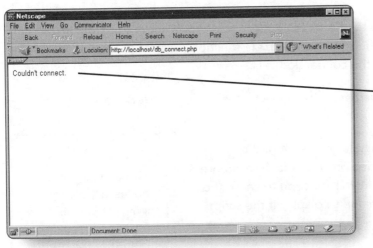

6. Open your Web browser and type **http://localhost/ db_connect.php**

With this change, the warning is suppressed, and only the message from the die() function is displayed.

If you can keep errors and warnings to a minimum, it will make the overall user experience much more pleasant if your database decides to render itself unavailable during peak Web-surfing hours.

Listing Databases on a Server

Now that you've successfully used PHP to make a connection to MySQL, familiarize yourself with some of the built-in MySQL-related functions. In this section, you'll use the following functions:

- `mysql_list_dbs()` Used to list the databases on a MySQL server.

- `mysql_num_rows()` Returns the number of rows in a result set.

- `mysql_tablename()` Despite its name, this function can extract the name of a table or a database from a result.

The goal of this script is to list all the databases on the local MySQL server.

1. Open a new file in your text editor.

2. Start a PHP block:

```
<?
```

3. Create a variable to hold the result of the `mysql_connect()` function. Include the @ to suppress warnings, as well as the `die()` function to cause the script to end and a message to display if the connection fails:

```
$connection = @mysql_connect("localhost", "sandman", "tQ9472b") or
die("Couldn't connect.");
```

4. Create a variable to hold the result of the `mysql_list_dbs()` function. Include the @ to suppress warnings, as well as the `die()` function to cause the script to end and a message to display if the script can't get the list:

```
$dbs = @mysql_list_dbs($connection) or
die("Couldn't list databases.");
```

> **NOTE**
> The only argument necessary for the `mysql_list_dbs()` function is the link identifier for the current connection.

5. You'll be looping through a result and dynamically populating a bullet list. Start that bullet list outside the loop:

```
$db_list = "<ul>";
```

6. Start a counter. You'll need it for your loop:

```
$i = 0;
```

7. Begin a while loop. This loop will continue for as long as the value of $i is less than the number of rows in the $dbs result value:

```
while ($i < mysql_num_rows($dbs)) {
```

8. Once you're within the while loop, get the name of the database reflected in the current row of the result:

```
$db_names[$i] = mysql_tablename($dbs, $i);
```

Counting starts at 0, not 1, so this would reflect the first row in the result. As the counter increments, so does the row number.

9. Add the current database name to the bullet list:

```
$db_list .= "<li>$db_names[$i]";
```

10. Increment your count before you close the while loop:

```
$i++;
```

11. Close the while loop:

```
}
```

12. Close the bullet list:

```
$db_list .= "</ul>";
```

> **NOTE**
>
> The variable $i is replaced by its value, so during the first loop, this line would be something like $db_names[0] = mysql_tablename($dbs, 0);

13. Close your PHP block:

```
?>
```

14. Add the following HTML:

```
<HTML>
<HEAD>
<TITLE>MySQL Databases</TITLE>
</HEAD>
<BODY>
<P><strong>Databases on localhost</strong>:</P>
```

15. Print the message string:

```
<? echo "$db_list"; ?>
```

16. Add some more HTML so that the document is valid:

```
</BODY>
</HTML>
```

```
<?

$connection = @mysql_connect("localhost", "sandman", "tQ9472b")
        or die("Couldn't connect.");

$dbs = @mysql_list_dbs($connection) or die("Couldn't list databases.");

$db_list = "<ul>";

$i = 0;

while ($i < mysql_num_rows($dbs)) {
        $db_names[$i] = mysql_tablename($dbs, $i);
        $db_list .= "<li>$db_names[$i]";
        $i++;
}

$db_list .= "</ul>";

?>

<HTML>
<HEAD>
<TITLE>MySQL Databases</TITLE>
</HEAD>
<BODY>

<P><strong>Databases on localhost</strong>:</p>

<? echo "$db_list"; ?>

</BODY>
</HTML>
```

17. Save the file with the name db_listdb.php.

Your code should look something like this.

Now it's time to see if this script lists the databases on your server.

18. Place this file in the document root of your Web server.

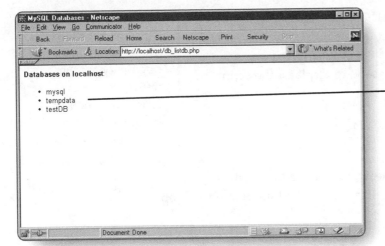

19. Open your Web browser and type **http://localhost/db_listdb.php**

Unless you added or deleted databases on your own, you should see these three databases. Two are MySQL system databases (`mysql` and `tempdata`), and `testDB` was created during installation and testing in Chapter 1.

Next, you'll add another loop to this script to print the tables within each database.

Listing Tables in a Database

A few additions to the db_listdb.php script are all you need to list the tables in the databases as well. The only new function you'll see is `mysql_list_tables()`, which is used to list tables within a MySQL database.

The goal of this script is to list all of the databases, including the tables within those databases, on the local MySQL server.

1. Open a new file in your text editor.

2. Start a PHP block:

```
<?
```

3. Create a variable to hold the result of the `mysql_connect()` function. Include the @ to suppress warnings, as well as the `die()` function to cause the script to end and a message to display if the connection fails:

```
$connection = @mysql_connect("localhost", "sandman", "tQ9472b") or
die("Couldn't connect.");
```

4. Create a variable to hold the result of the `mysql_list_dbs()` function. Include the @ to suppress warnings, as well as the `die()` function to cause the script to end and a message to display if the script can't get the list:

```
$dbs = @mysql_list_dbs($connection) or
die("Couldn't list databases.");
```

> **NOTE**
>
> The only argument necessary for the `mysql_list_dbs()` function is the link identifier for the current connection.

5. You'll be looping through a result and dynamically populating a bullet list. Start that bullet list outside the loop:

```
$db_list = "<ul>";
```

6. Start a counter. You'll need it for your loop:

```
$db_num = 0;
```

7. Begin a `while` loop. This loop will continue for as long as the value of `$db_num` is less than the number of rows in the `$dbs` result value:

```
while ($db_num < mysql_num_rows($dbs)) {
```

> **NOTE**
>
> Use `$db_num` instead of `$i` as the counter, because at one point in this script, you'll have two counters going at the same time.

8. Once you're within the `while` loop, get the name of the database reflected in the current row of the result:

```
$db_names[$db_num] = mysql_tablename($dbs, $db_num);
```

9. Add the current database name to the bullet list:

```
$db_list .= "<li>$db_names[$db_num]";
```

10. Start an `if` statement that checks the name of the current database against the names of the two system tables, `mysql` and `tempdata`:

```
if (($db_names[$db_num] != "mysql") &&
($db_names[$db_num] != "tempdata")) {
```

> **NOTE**
>
> Only the root user has access to the tables within the `mysql` and `tempdata` databases, so attempting to get a list of tables on these databases will automatically produce an error.

11. Create a variable to hold the result of the `mysql_list_tables()` function. Include the @ to suppress warnings, as well as the `die()` function to cause the script to end and a message to display if the script can't get the list:

```
$tables = @mysql_list_dbs($db_names[$db_num])
or die("Couldn't list databases.");
```

> **NOTE**
>
> The only argument necessary for the `mysql_list_tables()` function is the name of the current database.

12. You'll be looping through a result and dynamically populating a bullet list. Start that bullet list outside the loop:

```
$table_list = "<ul>";
```

13. Start a counter. You'll need it for your second loop:

```
$table_num = 0;
```

14. Begin a `while` loop. This loop will continue for as long as the value of `$table_num` is less than the number of rows in the `$tables_result` value.

```
while ($table_num < mysql_num_rows($tables)) {
```

15. Once you're within the `while` loop, get the name of the table reflected in the current row of the result:

```
$table_names[$table_num] = mysql_tablename($tables, $table_num);
```

16. Add the current table name to the bullet list:

```
$table_list .= "<li>$table_names[$table_num]";
```

17. Increment your count before you close the while loop:

```
$table_num++;
```

18. Close the inner while loop:

```
}
```

19. Close the bullet list of tables:

```
$table_list .= "</ul>";
```

20. Close the `if` statement:

```
}
```

21. Add the value of `$table_list` to `$db_list`, and then increment your count before you close the outer `while` loop:

```
$db_list .= "$table_list";
$db_num++;
```

22. Close the outer `while` loop:

```
}
```

23. Close the bullet list of databases:

```
$db_list .= "</ul>";
```

24. Close your PHP block:

```
?>
```

25. Add this HTML:

```
<HTML>
<HEAD>
<TITLE>MySQL Tables</TITLE>
</HEAD>
<BODY>
<P><strong>Databases and tables on localhost</strong>:</P>
```

26. Print the message string:

```
<? echo "$db_list"; ?>
```

27. Add some more HTML so that the document is valid:

```
</BODY>
</HTML>
```

28. Save the file with the name db_listtables.php.

29. Place this file in the document root of your Web server.

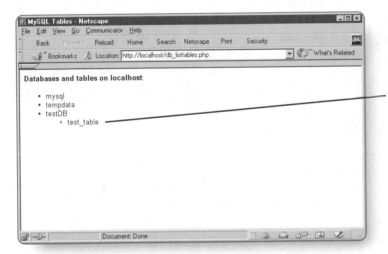

30. Open your Web browser and type **http://localhost/ db_listtables.php**

Unless you added or deleted tables within the testDB database, you should see one table (test_table) listed under testDB.

In the next section, you'll attempt to create new databases on your server.

Creating a New Database

The complex elements of the previous scripts are nowhere to be found in this next script. The goal of this script is to create a new database on the MySQL server.

1. Open a new file in your text editor.

2. Start a PHP block:

```
<?
```

3. Create a variable to hold the name of the new database:

```
$new_db = "testDB2";
```

4. Create a variable to hold the result of the `mysql_connect()` function. Include the @ to suppress warnings, as well as the `die()` function to cause the script to end and a message to display if the connection fails:

```
$connection = @mysql_connect("localhost", "sandman", "tQ9472b") or
die("Couldn't connect.");
```

5. Create a variable to hold the result of the `mysql_create_db()` function. Include the @ to suppress warnings, as well as the `die()` function to cause the script to end and a message to display if the creation of the database fails:

```
$result = @mysql_create_db($new_db,
$connection) or die("Couldn't create
database.");
```

> **NOTE**
> The `mysql_create_db()` function requires a database name and the link identifier for the current connection.

6. Test the value of `$result`. If it's true, the database was created, and a variable is created to hold a message:

```
if ($result) {
    $msg = "<P>Database has been
created!</P>";
}
```

> **NOTE**
> If the database cannot be created, the script will end with the `die()` function.

7. Close your PHP block:

```
?>
```

8. Add this HTML:

```
<HTML>
<HEAD>
<TITLE>Create a MySQL Database</TITLE>
</HEAD>
<BODY>
```

9. Print the message string:

```
<? echo "$msg"; ?>
```

10. Add some more HTML so that the document is valid:

```
</BODY>
</HTML>
```

11. Save the file with the name db_createdb.php.

12. Place this file in the document root of your Web server.

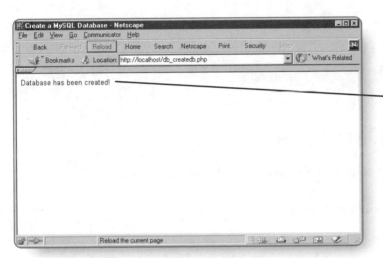

13. Open your Web browser and type **http://localhost/ db_createdb.php**

If the database creation was successful, you'll see this message.

If you reload the script, you're issuing the same database creation command.

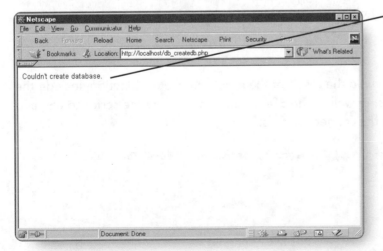

Since the database was already created, and you can't have two databases with the same name on the same server, you should get an error. Try it!

Verify that the new database is present by opening your Web browser to http://localhost/ db_listdb.php.

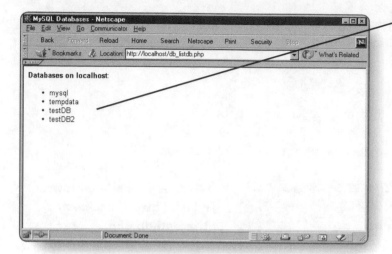

You should see these databases in the list.

In the next section, you'll drop (delete) the database you just created.

Deleting a Database

The goal of this script is to delete a database on the MySQL server.

1. Open a new file in your text editor.

2. Start a PHP block:

```
<?
```

3. Create a variable to hold the name of the database you want to delete:

```
$drop_db = "testDB2";
```

4. Create a variable to hold the result of the mysql_connect() function. Include the @ to suppress warnings, as well as the die() function to cause the script to end and a message to display if the connection fails:

```
$connection = @mysql_connect("localhost", "sandman", "tQ9472b") or
die("Couldn't connect.");
```

5. Create a variable to hold the result of the `mysql_drop_db()` function. Include the @ to suppress warnings, as well as the `die()` function to cause the script to end and a message to display if the deletion of the database fails:

```
$result = @mysql_drop_db($drop_db,
$connection) or die("Couldn't delete
database.");
```

6. Test the value of `$result`. If it's true, the database was deleted, and a variable is created to hold a message:

```
if ($result) {
        $msg = "<P>Database has been
dropped!</P>";
}
```

7. Close your PHP block:

```
?>
```

8. Add this HTML:

```
<HTML>
<HEAD>
<TITLE>Drop a MySQL Database</TITLE>
</HEAD>
<BODY>
```

9. Print the message string:

```
<? echo "$msg"; ?>
```

10. Add some more HTML so that the document is valid:

```
</BODY>
</HTML>
```

NOTE

The `mysql_drop_db()` function requires a database name and the link identifier for the current connection.

NOTE

If the database cannot be deleted, the script will end with the `die()` function.

11. Save the file with the name db_dropdb.php.

12. Place this file in the document root of your Web server.

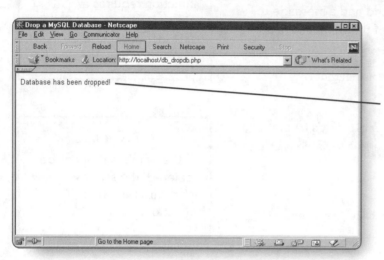

13. Open your Web browser and type **http://localhost/db_dropdb.php**

If the database deletion was successful, you'll see this message.

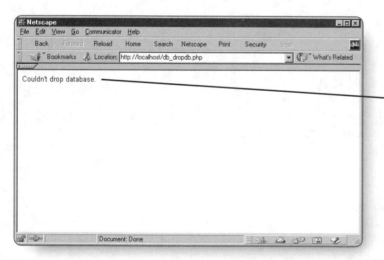

If you reload the script, you're issuing the same database deletion command.

Since the database was deleted when you ran the script the first time, you should get an error. Try it!

In the next chapter, you'll create a database table for keeps, and you'll eventually populate that table with some data.

12

Creating a Database Table

You have this great database server and nothing but a table called test_table sitting in a database called testDB. Where's the fun in that? In this chapter, you'll learn how to do the following:

- Plan for a database table
- Recognize the pitfalls of certain datatypes
- Recognize the importance of unique fields
- Follow a two-step process for table creation
- Create a table to hold your personal music catalog

Planning Your Fields

Creating a table is easy—it's the planning that takes some brain power. To create a simple table, you only need to give it a name. But that would make for a boring table, since it wouldn't contain any columns (fields) and couldn't hold any data. So, besides the name, you should know the number of fields and the types of fields you'd like to have in your table.

The overall goal of this chapter is to create a table to hold data from your own personal music collection. Take a moment to think about the kinds of things you'd want to know: the title and artist, obviously, and maybe the record label, the date it was acquired, and your own personal notes regarding the recording.

I thought about what I wanted for my own table, which I've decided to call my_music. The table below shows the fields I want it to contain.

Field Name	Description
id	A unique ID number for the entry
format	Is it a CD, cassette, or even an LP?
title	The title of the recording
artist_fn	The artist's first name
artist_ln	The artist's last name, or the name of the group
rec_label	The record label
my_notes	My own thoughts about the recording
date_acq	Date acquired

In the next section, you'll create a sequence of forms that will take your table information and send it to your MySQL database. In the first step, you'll submit the name of the table and the number of fields you want to include. The second step will display additional form fields so that you can define the properties of your table columns. A third step will send the request to MySQL, verify that the table was created, and display a "Success!" message.

Before getting into all that, take a moment to read about datatypes and unique fields.

A Word about Datatypes

All fields in table are given a particular datatype definition. The datatype defines the type of data that's allowed in the field. With some datatype definitions, you must also define the maximum length allowed in the field, but others are assumed to have no particular length.

It's very important to define fields appropriately. For example, if you have a 50-character varchar field to hold the name of a recording, and you try to stuff a 100-character string into the field, your string will truncate at 50 characters.

Not only is it important to define the fields correctly so that the data fits inside the fields, it is also important to define the fields with the correct SQL syntax—otherwise, the table won't be created, period. For example, if you want to use the text datatype for the my_notes field, you cannot specify a length; it's automatically assumed to have a particular length.

The following table shows a brief list of common datatypes, their descriptions, and how to define the length. A larger list can be found at www.thickbook.com in the "Extra" section.

Datatype	Description	Define the Length?
INT	A normal-sized integer, between 0 and 4294967295	Not required; defaults to 11
FLOAT	A floating-point number (such as money)	Not required; defaults to 10,2 where 2 is the number of decimals
DATE	A date, in YYYY-MM-DD format, between 1000-01-01 and 9999-12-31	No
CHAR	A fixed-length string between 1 and 255 characters	Not required; defaults to 1
VARCHAR	A variable-length string between 1 and 255 characters	Yes
TEXT	A field with a maximum length of 65535 characters	No

The Importance of Unique Fields

Using unique ID numbers helps you keep track of your data, and it will also help you down the road, as you attempt to establish relationships between multiple tables. In the my_music table, there will be an id field. Using this field as the unique field, instead of the title field, will allow you to have two recordings in your table that have the same name. For example, if you own the album *Strange Fire* by Indigo Girls, you could have two entries in your table: one for the version released in 1987 and one for the version rereleased in 1989.

If you didn't use a unique identifier, you would have to pick only one version to put in your table, and your table wouldn't be very accurate. I hope this simple example conveys the importance of having a unique identifier in each record in your table. The usage of the unique identifier will become more apparent throughout the remainder of this book, as you create more database-driven elements.

A Two-Step Form Sequence

A two-step form sequence for creating a database table might seem like overkill. After all, you saw a basic table-creation SQL statement in Chapter 1, "Installing and Configuring MySQL," when you created test_table:

```
create table test_table (test_id int, test_note text);
```

When you use a PHP script to create a table, all you're doing is sending the exact same query to MySQL. However, you can tie a pretty ribbon around the process (creating a form-based interface) and call it an "administrative interface"!

In the process of creating the administrative interface, you'll start with an HTML form, then create a PHP script that takes information from that form and dynamically creates another form. Finally, you'll create a script that sends the actual SQL query.

Step 1: Number of Fields

This HTML form will contain two input fields: one for the name of the table and one for the number of fields your table will contain.

1. Open a new file in your text editor.

2. Type the following HTML:

```
<HTML>
<HEAD>
<TITLE>Create a Database Table: Step 1</TITLE>
</HEAD>
<BODY>
<H1>Step 1: Name and Number</H1>
```

3. Begin your form. Assume that the method is post and the action is a script called do_showfielddef.php:

```
<FORM METHOD="post" ACTION="do_showfielddef.php">
```

4. Create an input field for the table name with a text label:

```
<P><strong>Table Name:</strong><br>
<INPUT TYPE="text" NAME="table_name" SIZE=30></P>
```

5. Create an input field for the number of fields in the table with a text label:

```
<P><strong>Number of Fields:</strong><br>
<INPUT TYPE="text" NAME="num_fields" SIZE=5></P>
```

6. Add a submit button:

```
<P><INPUT TYPE="submit" NAME="submit" VALUE="Go to Step 2"></P>
```

7. Close your form and add some more HTML so that the document is valid:

```
</FORM>
</BODY>
</HTML>
```

8. Save the file with the name show_createtable.html.

9. Place this file in the document root of your Web server.

10. Open your Web browser and type **http://localhost/show_createtable.html**

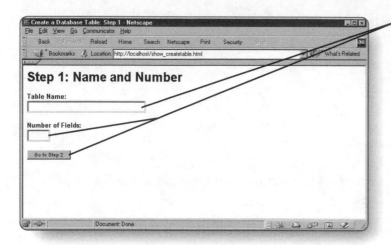

You will see a form containing two input fields, one for the table name and one for the number of fields, as well as a submit button.

In the next section, you'll follow step 2 of the process, and create the script that dynamically creates another form based on the values of $table_name and $num_fields.

Step 2: Defining Your Fields

In step 1, you created variables to hold the name of the table ($table_name) and the number of fields you want to place in the table ($num_fields). In this step, you'll create a PHP script to display additional form elements needed for further definition of the fields: name, type, and length.

1. Open a new file in your text editor.

2. Start a PHP block:

```
<?
```

3. Check that values were actually entered for $table_name and $num_fields. If they weren't, direct the user back to the form and exit the script:

```
if ((!$table_name) || (!$num_fields)) {
    header( "Location: http://localhost/show_createtable.html");
    exit;
}
```

4. Start building a string called `$form_block`, beginning with the form action and method. Assume that the method is post and the action is a script called do_createtable.php. Remember to escape your quotation marks!

```
$form_block = "
<FORM METHOD=\"POST\"
ACTION=\"do_createtable.php\">
```

NOTE

Since the script is creating the next form on-the-fly (dynamically), build one big string so that you can echo just the string after the complicated parsing has taken place. This way, you won't be stuck with a half-built page that won't display if an error occurs.

5. Add a hidden field to hold the value of `$table_name`, which you'll use at the end of the sequence just to show the user that the proper table has been created:

```
<INPUT TYPE=\"hidden\" NAME=\"table_name\" VALUE=\"$table_name\">
```

6. Display your form in an HTML table so that fields line up nicely. Start with a row of column headings, and close the `$form_block` string for now:

```
<TABLE CELLSPACING=5 CELLPADDING=5>
<TR>
<TH>FIELD NAME</TH><TH>FIELD TYPE</TH><TH>FIELD LENGTH</TH></TR>
";
```

7. Start a `for` loop to handle the creation of the form fields. Like a `while` loop, a `for` loop continues for as long as a condition is true. In this case, the `for` loop starts out with the variable `$i` having a value of 0, and it continues for as long as `$i` is less than the value of `$num_fields`. After each loop, `$i` is incremented by 1:

```
for ($i = 0; $i < $num_fields; $i++) {
```

8. Within the `for` loop, add to the original `$form_block`. Add one row for each field you want to have in your database table. Start with the table row tag and a table data cell containing an input type for the field name:

```
$form_block .= "
<TR>
<TD ALIGN=CENTER><INPUT TYPE=\"text\" NAME=\"field_name[]\" SIZE=\"30\"></TD>
```

NOTE

The use of brackets ([]) after `field_name` in your input field indicates an array. For each field you define in this form, you'll be adding a value to the `$field_name` array.

An array holds many variables in numbered slots, beginning with 0. Slots are added automatically as the array grows. For example, if you are creating a database table with six fields, the `$field_name` array will be made up of six field name variables: `$field_name[0]`, `$field_name[1]`, `$field_name[2]`, `$field_name[3]`, `$field_name[4]`, and `$field_name[5]`.

---

9. In the next table data cell, create a drop-down list containing common field types:

```
<TD ALIGN=CENTER>
<SELECT NAME=\"field_type[]\">
        <OPTION VALUE=\"char\">char</OPTION>
        <OPTION VALUE=\"date\">date</OPTION>
        <OPTION VALUE=\"float\">float</OPTION>
        <OPTION VALUE=\"int\">int</OPTION>
        <OPTION VALUE=\"text\">text</OPTION>
        <OPTION VALUE=\"varchar\">varchar</OPTION>
</SELECT>
</TD>
```

10. In the final table data cell, create a text field for the length of the field, and close your table row. Also close the `$form_block` string, because you're done with it for now:

```
<TD ALIGN=CENTER><INPUT TYPE=\"text\" NAME=\"field_length[]\" SIZE=\"5\"></TD>
</TR>
";
```

11. Close the `for` loop:

```
}
```

12. Add the final chunk of HTML to the `$form_block` string. You'll add one row that holds the submit button and then close your table and form:

```
$form_block .= "
<TR>
<TD ALIGN=CENTER COLSPAN=3><INPUT TYPE=\"submit\" VALUE=\"Create Table\"></TD>
</TR>
</TABLE>
</FORM>
";
```

13. Close the PHP block:

```
?>
```

14. Type the following HTML:

```
<HTML>
<HEAD>
<TITLE>Create a Database Table: Step 2</TITLE>
</HEAD>
<BODY>
```

15. Add a nice heading so that the user knows what he's viewing. Mingle HTML and PHP to include the value of the `$table_name` variable:

```
<H1>Define fields for <? echo "$table name"; ?></H1>
```

16. Display the contents of `$form_block`:

```
<? echo "$form_block"; ?>
```

17. Add some more HTML so that the document is valid:

```
</BODY>
</HTML>
```

18. Save the file with the name do_showfielddef.php.

19. Place this file in the document root of your Web server.

In the next section, you'll go from step 1 to step 2, as you prepare to create the table.

Starting the Table Creation Process

You should be able to go from step 1 (naming the table and providing the number of fields) to step 2 (defining the fields) without any problems. Let's try it out.

1. Open your Web browser and type **http://localhost/show_createtable.html**

2. In the Table Name field, type **my_music**.

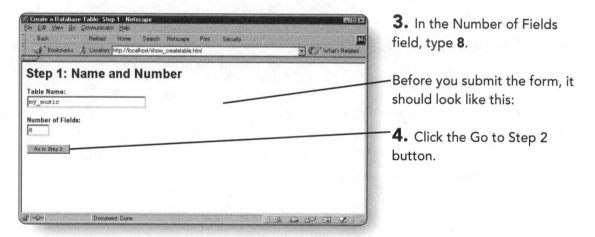

3. In the Number of Fields field, type **8**.

Before you submit the form, it should look like this:

4. Click the Go to Step 2 button.

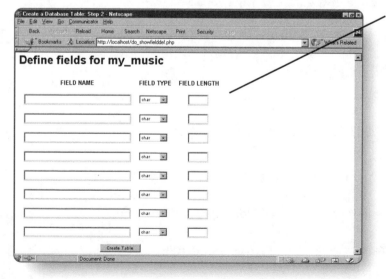

You should see a form like this.

There are eight rows, corresponding to the eight fields you want to create in the my_music table. Populate those fields, but hold off on pressing the Create Table button, since you haven't created the script yet!

5. In the first row, type **id** for the Field Name, select int from the Field Type drop-down menu, and specify a Field Length of **5**.

6. In the second row, type **format** for the Field Name, select char from the Field Type drop-down menu, and specify a Field Length of **2**.

7. In the third row, type **title** for the Field Name, select varchar from the Field Type drop-down menu, and specify a Field Length of **150**.

8. In the fourth row, type **artist_fn** for the Field Name, select varchar from the Field Type drop-down menu, and specify a Field Length of **100**.

9. In the fifth row, type **artist_ln** for the Field Name, select varchar from the Field Type drop-down menu, and specify a Field Length of **100**.

10. In the sixth row, type **rec_label** for the Field Name, select varchar from the Field Type drop-down menu, and specify a Field Length of **50**.

11. In the seventh row, type **my_notes** for the Field Name and select text from the Field Type drop-down menu.

12. In the eighth row, type **date_acq** for the Field Name and select date from the Field Type drop-down menu.

The completed form should look like this.

In the next section, you'll create the back-end script for this form so that you can click that button and create the table.

Creating the Table-Creation Script

This script will build a SQL statement and then send it to MySQL to create the my_music table.

1. Open a new file in your text editor.

2. Start a PHP block:

```
<?
```

3. Create a variable to hold the name of the database on which the table should reside:

```
$db_name = "testDB";
```

4. Create a variable to hold the result of the mysql_connect() function. Include the @ to suppress warnings, as well as the die() function to cause the script to end and a message to display if the connection fails:

```
$connection = @mysql_connect("localhost", "sandman", "tQ9472b") or
die("Couldn't connect.");
```

5. Create a variable to hold the result of the mysql_select_db() function. Include the @ to suppress warnings, as well as the die() function to cause the script to end and a message to display if the selection of the database fails:

```
$db = @mysql_select_db($db_name, $connection)
or die("Couldn't select database.");
```

> **NOTE**
> The mysql_select_db() function requires a database name and the link identifier for the current connection.

6. Start building the query by placing the initial syntax in a variable called $sql:

```
$sql = "CREATE TABLE $table_name (";
```

7. Create a for loop to create the remainder of the SQL statement. The loop should repeat for the number of fields contained as elements in the $field_name array:

```
for ($i = 0; $i < count($field_name); $i++) {
```

> **NOTE**
> The count() function counts the number of elements in an array.

8. For each new field, you'll need to add the field name and type to the SQL statement:

```
$sql .= "$field_name[$i] $field_type[$i]";
```

9. Since some field definitions will have a specific length and others will not, start an if...else block to handle this aspect. If a length is present, it must go inside parentheses, followed by a comma, to start the next field definition:

```
if ($field_length[$i] != "") {
    $sql .= " ($field_length[$i]),";
```

10. If no length is present, just print the comma to separate the field definitions. Then close the if...else block:

```
} else {
    $sql .= ",";
}
```

11. Close the for loop:

```
}
```

12. The SQL statement held in $sql still needs some help: It should have an extraneous comma at the end of it, and the parentheses must be closed. Use the substr() function to return the entire string, with the exception of the last character:

```
$sql = substr($sql, 0, -1);
```

> **NOTE**
>
> The 0 in the substr() argument list tells the function to begin at the first character, and the -1 tells the function to stop at the next-to-last character.

13. Close the parentheses:

```
$sql .= ")";
```

14. Create a variable to hold the result of the mysql_query() function. Include the @ to suppress warnings, as well as the die() function to cause the script to end and a message to display if the query fails:

> **NOTE**
>
> The mysql_query() function requires a SQL statement and the link identifier for the current connection.

```
$result = mysql_query($sql,$connection) or die("Couldn't execute query.");
```

15. Test the value of $result. If it's true, the query was successful, and a variable is created to hold a message:

```
if ($result) {
    $msg = "<P>$table_name has been
created!</P>";
}
```

> **NOTE**
>
> If a connection cannot be made, the script will end with the die() function.

16. Close your PHP block:

```
?>
```

17. Add this HTML:

```
<HTML>
<HEAD>
<TITLE>Create a Database Table: Step 3</TITLE>
</HEAD>
<BODY>
```

18. Add a heading so that the user knows what he's viewing. Mingle HTML and PHP to include the value of the $db_name variable:

```
<h1>Adding table to <? echo "$db_name"; ?>...</h1>
```

19. Print the message string:

```
<? echo "$msg"; ?>
```

20. Add some more HTML so that the document is valid:

```
</BODY>
</HTML>
```

21. Save the file with the name db_createtable.php.

22. Place this file in the document root of your Web server.

Go on to the next step, where you get to click a button and create a table.

Create That Table!

You should still have your Web browser opened to the field definition form, with the fields complete and ready for submission. Go ahead and click the Create Table button.

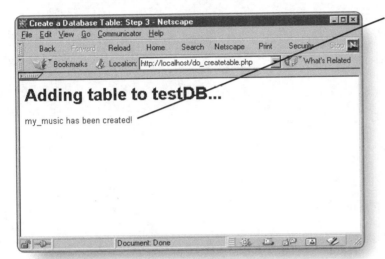

If everything goes smoothly, you'll see this response.

To prove that the my_music table has really been created on the testDB database, access the db_listtables.php script you created in the previous chapter.

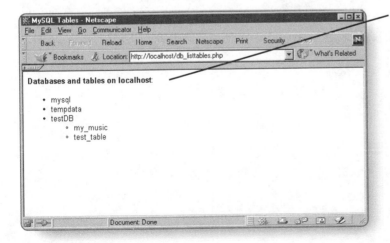

You should see this.

In the next chapter, you'll create an HTML form interface to a script that adds entries to the my_music table.

13

Inserting Data into the Table

The my_music database table is waiting for you to add information about your music collection. In this chapter, you'll learn how to do the following:

- Create an administrative interface for adding a record
- Create a script to insert the record into your table

Creating the Record Addition Form

The HTML form will contain an input field for each column in the my_music database table. In the previous chapter, you created eight fields, which corresponds to eight columns. Your record addition interface should have a space for each of these fields.

1. Open a new file in your text editor.

2. Type the following HTML:

```
<HTML>
<HEAD>
<TITLE>Add a Record</TITLE>
</HEAD>
<BODY>
<H1>Adding a Record to my_music</H1>
```

> **NOTE**
> Use the database field names as the value of the NAME attribute in the HTML form fields. Also, where appropriate, use the size of the database field as the value of the MAXLENGTH attribute in the HTML form fields.

3. Begin your form. Assume that the method is post and the action is a script called do_addrecord.php:

```
<FORM METHOD="post" ACTION="do_addrecord.php">
```

4. Begin an HTML table to assist in layout. Start a new table row and table data cell, and then create an input field for the ID, with a text label:

```
<TABLE CELLSPACING=3 CELLPADDING=3>
<TR>
<TD VALIGN=TOP>
<P><STRONG>ID:</STRONG><BR>
<INPUT TYPE="text" NAME="id" SIZE=5 MAXLENGTH=5></P>
```

5. Create an input field for the date acquired with a text label. Close the table data cell after the input field:

```
<P><STRONG>Date Acquired (YYYY-MM-
DD):</STRONG><BR>
<INPUT TYPE="text" NAME="date_acq" SIZE=10
MAXLENGTH=10></P>
</TD>
```

> **NOTE**
> The date type used in MySQL uses the YYYY-MM-DD format. An example of a date using this format is 2000-05-31 (May 31, 2000).

6. In a new table data cell, create a set of radio buttons to select the format of the recording. Close the table data cell and the table row after the set of radio buttons:

```
<TD VALIGN=TOP>
<P><STRONG>Format:</STRONG><BR>
<INPUT TYPE="radio" NAME="format" VALUE="CD" checked> CD
<INPUT TYPE="radio" NAME="format" VALUE="CS"> cassette
<INPUT TYPE="radio" NAME="format" VALUE="LP"> LP
</P>
</TD>
</TR>
```

7. Start a new table row and table data cell, and then create an input field for the title with a text label. Close the table data cell after the input field:

```
<TR>
<TD VALIGN=TOP>
<P><STRONG>Title:</STRONG><BR>
<INPUT TYPE="text" NAME="title" SIZE=35 MAXLENGTH=150></P>
</TD>
```

8. In a new table data cell, create an input field for the record label information with a text label. Close the table data cell and the table row after the input field:

```
<TD VALIGN=TOP>
<P><STRONG>Record Label:</STRONG><BR>
<INPUT TYPE="text" NAME="rec_label" SIZE=35 MAXLENGTH=50></P>
</TD>
</TR>
```

9. Start a new table row and table data cell, and then create an input field for the artist's first name with a text label. Close the table data cell after the input field:

```
<TR>
<TD VALIGN=TOP>
<P><STRONG>Artist's First Name:</STRONG><BR>
<INPUT TYPE="text" NAME="artist_fn" SIZE=35 MAXLENGTH=100></P>
</TD>
```

10. In a new table data cell, create an input field for the artist's last name (or group name) with a text label. Close the table data cell and the table row after the input field:

```
<TD VALIGN=TOP>
<P><STRONG>Artist's Last Name (or Group Name):</STRONG><BR>
<INPUT TYPE="text" NAME="artist_ln" SIZE=35 MAXLENGTH=100></P>
</TD>
</TR>
```

11. Start a new table row and a table data cell that spans two columns. Create a text area with a text label to hold your notes regarding the recording:

```
<TR>
<TD VALIGN=TOP COLSPAN=2 ALIGN=CENTER>
<P><STRONG>My Notes:</STRONG><BR>
<TEXTAREA NAME="my_notes" COLS=35 ROWS=5 WRAP=virtual></TEXTAREA></P>
```

12. Add a submit button, and then close the table data cell, the table row, and the table itself:

```
<P><INPUT TYPE="SUBMIT" NAME="submit" VALUE="Add Record"></P>
</TD>
</TR>
</TABLE>
```

13. Close your form and add some more HTML so that the document is valid:

```
</FORM>
</BODY>
</HTML>
```

14. Save the file with the name show_addrecord.html.

15. Place this file in the document root of your Web server.

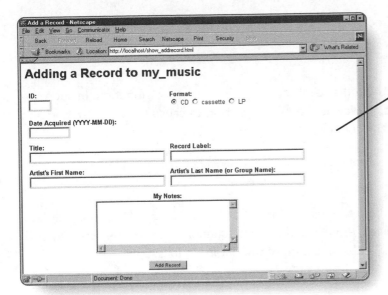

16. Open your Web browser and type **http://localhost/ show_addrecord.html**

You will see the complete form used to add data to the my_music table.

In the next section, you'll create the script that takes the form input, creates a SQL statement, and adds the record to the database table.

Creating the Record Addition Script

The script you'll create for a record addition is a lot simpler than the script for table creation!

1. Open a new file in your text editor.

2. Start a PHP block:

```
<?
```

3. Check that values were actually entered for $id, $format, and $title. If they weren't, direct the user back to the form and exit the script:

```
if ((!$id) || (!$format) || (!$title)) {
    header( "Location:
http://localhost/show_addrecord.html");
    exit;
}
```

> **NOTE**
>
> You can have as many (or as few) required fields as you'd like.

4. Create a variable to hold the name of the database on which the table resides:

```
$db_name = "testDB";
```

5. Create a variable to hold the name of the table you're populating with this script:

```
$table_name = "my_music";
```

6. Create a variable to hold the result of the `mysql_connect()` function. Include the @ to suppress warnings, as well as the `die()` function to cause the script to end and a message to display if the connection fails:

```
$connection = @mysql_connect("localhost", "sandman", "tQ9472b") or
die("Couldn't connect.");
```

7. Create a variable to hold the result of the `mysql_select_db()` function. Include the @ to suppress warnings, as well as the `die()` function to cause the script to end and a message to display if the selection of the database fails:

```
$db = @mysql_select_db($db_name, $connection) or die("Couldn't select
database.");
```

8. Create the SQL statement. The first parenthetical statement gives the names of the fields to populate (in order), and the second parenthetical statement sends the actual strings:

> **NOTE**
>
> Use escaped quotation marks around the strings you're inserting into the database.

```
$sql = "
INSERT INTO $table_name
(id, format, title, artist_fn, artist_ln, rec_label, my_notes, date_acq)
VALUES
(\"$id\", "$format\",\"$title\",\"$artist_fn\",\"$artist_ln\",
\"$rec_label\",\"$my_notes\",\"$date_acq\")
";
```

9. Create a variable to hold the result of the `mysql_query()` function. Include the @ to suppress warnings, as well as the `die()` function to cause the script to end and a message to display if the query fails:

```
$result = @mysql_query($sql,$connection) or die("Couldn't execute query.");
```

10. Close your PHP block:

```
?>
```

11. Add this HTML:

```
<HTML>
<HEAD>
<TITLE>Add a Record</TITLE>
</HEAD>
<BODY>
```

12. Add a heading so that the user knows what he's viewing. Mingle HTML and PHP to include the value of the $table_name variable:

```
<H1>Adding a Record to <? echo "$table_name"; ?></H1>
```

13. Next, you'll re-create the layout used in show_addrecord.html, only it won't contain form fields. Instead, you'll mingle HTML and PHP to show the values that were entered. Start a new table row and table data cell, and then display a text label and value for ID:

```
<TABLE CELLSPACING=3 CELLPADDING=3>
<TR>
<TD VALIGN=TOP>
<P><STRONG>ID:</STRONG><BR>
<? echo "$id"; ?></P>
```

14. Display a text label and value for the date acquired, and then close the table data cell:

```
<P><STRONG>Date Acquired (YYYY-MM-DD):</STRONG><BR>
<? echo "$date_acq"; ?></P>
</TD>
```

15. Display a text label and the format of the recording, and then close the table data cell and table row:

```
<TD VALIGN=TOP>
<P><STRONG>Format:</STRONG><BR>
<? echo "$format"; ?>
</P>
</TD>
</TR>
```

16. Start a new table row and table data cell, display a text label and value for the title, and close the table data cell:

```
<TR>
<TD VALIGN=TOP>
<P><STRONG>Title:</STRONG><BR>
<? echo "$title"; ?></P>
</TD>
```

17. In a new table data cell, display a text label and value for the record label information, and then close the table data cell and table row:

```
<TD VALIGN=TOP>
<P><STRONG>Record Label:</STRONG><BR>
<? echo "$rec_label"; ?></P>
</TD>
</TR>
```

18. Start a new table row and table data cell, and then create an input field for the artist's first name with a text label. Close the table data cell after the input field:

```
<TR>
<TD VALIGN=TOP>
<P><STRONG>Artist's First Name:</STRONG><BR>
<? echo "$artist_fn"; ?></P>
</TD>
```

19. In a new table data cell, display a text label and value for the artist's last name (or group name), and then close the table data cell and table row:

```
<TD VALIGN=TOP>
<P><STRONG>Artist's Last Name (or Group Name):</STRONG><BR>
<? echo "$artist_ln"; ?></P>
</TD>
</TR>
```

20. Start a new table row and a table data cell that spans two columns. Display a text label and value for your notes regarding the recording:

```
<TR>
<TD VALIGN=TOP COLSPAN=2 ALIGN=CENTER>
<P><STRONG>My Notes:</STRONG><BR>
<? echo stripslashes($my_notes); ?></P>
```

21. Add a link back to the original form, and then close the table data cell, the table row, and the table itself:

```
<P><a href="show_addrecord.html">Add
Another</a></P>
</TD>
</TR>
</TABLE>
```

22. Add some more HTML so that the document is valid:

```
</FORM>
</BODY>
</HTML>
```

23. Save the file with the name do_addrecord.php.

24. Place this file in the document root of your Web server.

Go on to the next section, where you get to click a button and add a record.

> **NOTE**
>
> The `stripslashes()` function will remove any slashes automatically added to your form data. By default, `magic_quotes_gpc` is turned on in your php.ini file. It will add slashes where necessary, to escape special characters such as single quotes and double quotes. You can turn it off by modifying your php.ini file. If you leave it on, it's one less thing you have to worry about.

Populating Your Table

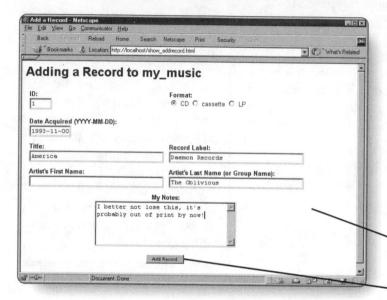

Now the fun begins! If you didn't close your Web browser after the first part of this chapter, show_addrecord.html should still be visible in your browser window. If it's not, open http://localhost/show_addrecord.html now.

Complete the addition form for an album you have lying around.

Here's an example from my collection.

Go ahead and click the Add Record button.

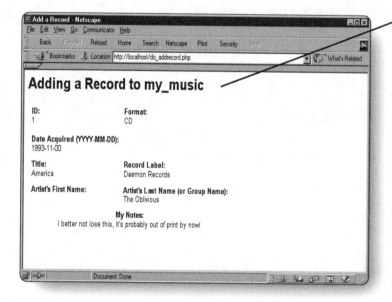

You should see a confirmation screen.

Add several of your own recordings to the database table. Unless you changed the script on your own, the only required fields are ID, format, and title.

NOTE

In later chapters, you'll learn to make modifications to your table so that the ID field really is unique and increments automatically so that you don't have to keep entering a number and hoping it works.

14

Selecting and Displaying Data

By now, you've happily and repeatedly populated the my_music table with all—or at least a few—of the items in your music collection. In this chapter, you'll learn how to do the following:

- Select records from a table using the SQL ORDER BY clause
- Format and display records from a database table

Planning and Creating Your Administrative Menu

You could just write one script that says "Select all of my data; I don't care about the order," but that would be boring. In this chapter, you'll see four ways to select records from the my_music table. To facilitate easy navigation, create an administration menu—fancy words for "a list of links to scripts."

1. Open a new file in your text editor.

2. Type the following HTML:

```
<HTML>
<HEAD>
<TITLE>My Menu</TITLE>
</HEAD>
<BODY>
<H1>My Menu</H1>
<P><strong>My Music</strong></P>
```

3. Start a bullet list and create the first link, to a script called sel_byid.php. This script will display the records, ordered by ID number:

```
<ul>
<li><a href="sel_byid.php">ordered by ID</a>
```

4. Add a link to a script called sel_bydateacq.php. This script will display the records, ordered by date acquired. The most recently acquired item will be listed first:

```
<li><a href="sel_bydateacq.php">ordered by date acquired</a> (most recent first)
```

5. Add a link to a script called sel_bytitle.php. This script will display the records, ordered by title:

```
<li><a href="sel_bytitle.php">ordered by title</a>
```

6. Add a link to a script called sel_byartist.php. This script will display the records, ordered by artist:

```
<li><a href="sel_byartist.php">ordered by artist</a>
```

7. Close the bulleted list, and then add some HTML so that the document is valid:

```
</ul>
</BODY>
</HTML>
```

8. Save the file with the name my_menu.html.

9. Place this file in the document root of your Web server.

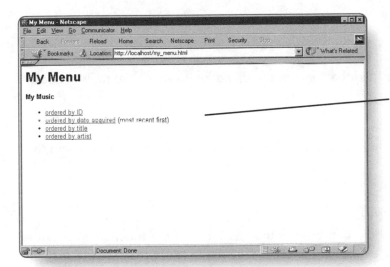

10. Open your Web browser and type **http://localhost/ my_menu.html**

You will see a menu with several options for viewing the records in the my_music table.

In the next sections, you'll create the scripts that do all the aforementioned selecting.

Selecting Data from the my_music Table

The next four sections contain scripts that are variations on a theme: selecting and displaying data. A large portion of the scripts is repeated, but repetition makes perfection, as they say.

The only new function in these scripts is the mysql_fetch_array() function. This function takes the result of a SQL query and places the rows in array format. Using a simple while loop, you can extract and display these elements.

Hang on to your hat, and start with the first script, which just returns the results ordered by their ID number.

Displaying Records Ordered by ID

One of the required fields in the record addition script is ID. In this script, you'll select all the records in the my_music table, ordered by the ID number. The default value of the ORDER BY clause is ASC (ascending), so the records will be returned with ID #1 first, followed by #2, #3, and so on.

1. Open a new file in your text editor.

2. Start a PHP block:

```
<?
```

3. Create a variable to hold the name of the database on which the table resides:

```
$db_name = "testDB";
```

4. Create a variable to hold the name of the table you're selecting from, using this script:

```
$table_name = "my_music";
```

5. Create a variable to hold the result of the `mysql_connect()` function. Include the @ to suppress warnings, as well as the `die()` function to cause the script to end and a message to display if the connection fails:

```
$connection = @mysql_connect("localhost", "sandman", "tQ9472b") or
die("Couldn't connect.");
```

6. Create a variable to hold the result of the `mysql_select_db()` function. Include the @ to suppress warnings, as well as the `die()` function to cause the script to end and a message to display if the selection of the database fails:

```
$db = @mysql_select_db($db_name, $connection) or die("Couldn't select
database.");
```

7. Create the SQL statement:

```
$sql = "
SELECT id, format, title, artist_fn,
artist_ln, rec_label, my_notes, date_acq
FROM $table_name
ORDER BY id
";
```

> **TIP**
>
> Since you're selecting all of the fields, you could use a * in the SQL statement instead of naming all of the fields.

8. Create a variable to hold the result of the `mysql_query()` function. Include the @ to suppress warnings, as well as the `die()` function to cause the script to end and a message to display if the query fails:

```
$result = @mysql_query($sql,$connection) or die("Couldn't execute query.");
```

9. Start the `while` loop. The `while` loop will create an array called `$row` for each record in the result set (`$result`):

```
while ($row = mysql_fetch_array($result)) {
```

10. Get the individual elements of the record, and give them good names:

```
$id = $row['id'];
$format = $row['format'];
$title = $row['title'];
$artist_fn = $row['artist_fn'];
$artist_ln = $row['artist_ln'];
$rec_label = $row['rec_label'];
$my_notes = $row['my_notes'];
$date_acq = $row['date_acq'];
```

11. Do a little formatting with the artists' names. Since some artists have only a first name, some artists use both first and last names, and group names are thrown into the artist_ln field, start an `if...else` block to deal with this. Start by looking for groups:

```
if ($artist_fn != "") {
```

12. Create a variable called `$artist_fullname`, which will contain a string with `$artist_fn`, followed by a space, followed by `$artist_ln`, all within the `trim()` function:

```
$artist_fullname = trim("$artist_fn
$artist_ln");
```

> **NOTE**
>
> The `trim()` function gets rid of extraneous space at the beginning and end of a string.

13. Continue the block, assigning the trimmed value of `$artist_ln` to `$artist_fullname`:

```
} else {
    $artist_fullname = trim("$artist_ln");
}
```

14. Do a little more formatting. If you didn't enter a date in the date_acq field, MySQL will enter a default value of "0000-00-00". Create an `if` block that looks for this value and then replaces it with something more friendly:

```
if ($date_acq == "0000-00-00") {
    $date_acq = "[unknown]";
}
```

15. Create a variable called `$display_block`, to hold all the formatted records. The formatting in this block places the title of the recording in bold, followed by the artist's name in parentheses. Next comes a line break, then your notes, and then an emphasized parenthetical statement that holds the date acquired and format:

```
$display_block .= "
<P><strong>$title</strong> ($artist_fullname)<br>
$my_notes <em>(acquired: $date_acq, format: $format)</em></P>
";
```

16. Close the `while` loop:

```
}
```

17. Close your PHP block:

```
?>
```

18. Add the following HTML:

```
<HTML>
<HEAD>
<TITLE>My Music (Ordered by ID)</TITLE>
</HEAD>
<BODY>
<H1>My Music</H1>
```

19. Display the results:

```
<? echo "$display_block"; ?>
```

20. Add a link back to the main menu, and then add some more HTML to make a valid document:

```
<P><a href="my_menu.html">Return to Menu</a></P>
</BODY>
</HTML>
```

21. Save the file with the name sel_byid.php.

22. Place this file in the document root of your Web server.

23. Open your Web browser and type **http://localhost/my_menu.html**

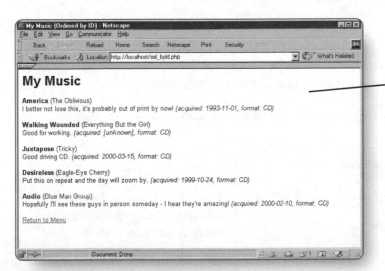

24. Click on the link called "ordered by ID."

Your records will be different from mine, but you should see a screen like this, where the records are ordered by internal ID number.

In the next section, you'll create the script that displays results ordered by date acquired.

Displaying Records Ordered by Date Acquired

Although it isn't a required field, the record addition script has a space for the date on which the recording made its way into your music collection. In this script, you'll select all the records in the my_music table, ordered by this date.

1. Open a new file in your text editor.

2. Start a PHP block:

```
<?
```

3. Create a variable to hold the name of the database on which the table resides:

```
$db_name = "testDB";
```

4. Create a variable to hold the name of the table you're selecting from, using this script:

```
$table_name = "my_music";
```

5. Create a variable to hold the result of the mysql_connect() function. Include the @ to suppress warnings, as well as the die() function to cause the script to end and a message to display if the connection fails:

```
$connection = @mysql_connect("localhost", "sandman", "tQ9472b") or
die("Couldn't connect.");
```

6. Create a variable to hold the result of the mysql_select_db() function. Include the @ to suppress warnings, as well as the die() function to cause the script to end and a message to display if the selection of the database fails:

```
$db = @mysql_select_db($db_name, $connection) or die("Couldn't select
database.");
```

7. Create the SQL statement:

```
$sql = "SELECT * FROM $table_name ORDER
BY date_acq DESC";
```

> **NOTE**
>
> Use DESC (descending) in the ORDER BY clause to return the records starting with the most recently acquired recording.

8. Create a variable to hold the result of the `mysql_query()` function. Include the @ to suppress warnings, as well as the `die()` function to cause the script to end and a message to display if the query fails:

```
$result = @mysql_query($sql,$connection) or die("Couldn't execute query.");
```

9. Start the `while` loop. The `while` loop will create an array called `$row` for each record in the result set (`$result`):

```
while ($row = mysql_fetch_array($result)) {
```

10. Get the individual elements of the record, and give them good names:

```
$id = $row['id'];
$format = $row['format'];
$title = $row['title'];
$artist_fn = $row['artist_fn'];
$artist_ln = $row['artist_ln'];
$rec_label = $row['rec_label'];
$my_notes = $row['my_notes'];
$date_acq = $row['date_acq'];
```

11. Do a little formatting with the artists' names. Since some artists have only a first name, some artists have both first and last names, and group names are thrown into the artist_ln field, start an `if...else` block to deal with this. Start by looking for groups:

```
if ($artist_fn != "") {
```

12. Create a variable called `$artist_fullname`, which will contain a string with `$artist_fn`, followed by a space, followed by `$artist_ln`, all within the `trim()` function:

```
$artist_fullname = trim("$artist_fn $artist_ln");
```

13. Continue the block, assigning the trimmed value of `$artist_ln` to `$artist_fullname`:

```
} else {
    $artist_fullname = trim("$artist_ln");
}
```

14. Do a little more formatting. If you didn't enter a date in the date_acq field, MySQL will enter a default value of "0000-00-00". Create an `if` block that looks for this value and then replaces it with something more friendly:

```
if ($date_acq == "0000-00-00") {
    $date_acq = "[unknown]";
}
```

15. Create a variable called `$display_block` to hold all the formatted records. The formatting in this block places the title of the recording in bold, followed by the artist's name in parentheses. Next comes a line break, then your notes, and then an emphasized parenthetical statement that holds the date acquired and format:

```
$display_block .= "
<P><strong>$title</strong> ($artist_fullname)<br>
$my_notes <em>(acquired: $date_acq, format: $format)</em></P>
";
```

16. Close the `while` loop:

```
}
```

17. Close your PHP block:

```
?>
```

18. Add this HTML:

```
<HTML>
<HEAD>
<TITLE>My Music (Ordered by Date Acquired)</TITLE>
</HEAD>
<BODY>
<H1>My Music</H1>
```

19. Display the results:

```
<? echo "$display_block"; ?>
```

20. Add a link back to the main menu, and then add some more HTML to make a valid document:

```
<P><a href="my_menu.html">Return to Menu</a></P>
</BODY>
</HTML>
```

21. Save the file with the name sel_bydateacq.php.

22. Place this file in the document root of your Web server.

23. Open your Web browser and type **http://localhost/my_menu.html**

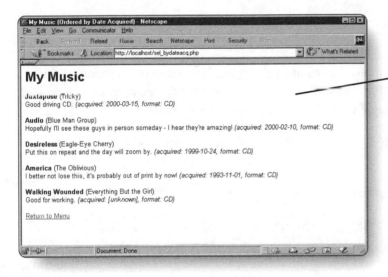

24. Click on the link called "ordered by date acquired."

Your records will be different from mine, but you should see a screen like this, where the records are ordered by the date the recordings were acquired. Those without dates are at the end of the list.

In the next section, you'll create the script that displays results ordered by title.

Displaying Records Ordered by Title

As you might imagine, the recording title is a required field in the record addition script. In this script, you'll select all the records in the my_music table, ordered alphabetically by title.

1. Open a new file in your text editor.

2. Start a PHP block:

```
<?
```

3. Create a variable to hold the name of the database on which the table resides:

```
$db_name = "testDB";
```

4. Create a variable to hold the name of the table you're selecting from, using this script:

```
$table_name = "my_music";
```

5. Create a variable to hold the result of the `mysql_connect()` function. Include the @ to suppress warnings, as well as the `die()` function to cause the script to end and a message to display if the connection fails:

```
$connection = @mysql_connect("localhost", "sandman", "tQ9472b") or
die("Couldn't connect.");
```

6. Create a variable to hold the result of the `mysql_select_db()` function. Include the @ to suppress warnings, as well as the `die()` function to cause the script to end and a message to display if the selection of the database fails:

```
$db = @mysql_select_db($db_name, $connection) or die("Couldn't select
database.");
```

7. Create the SQL statement:

```
$sql = "SELECT * FROM $table_name ORDER BY title";
```

8. Create a variable to hold the result of the `mysql_query()` function. Include the "@" to suppress warnings, as well as the `die()` function, to cause the script to end and a message to display if the query fails:

```
$result = @mysql_query($sql,$connection) or die("Couldn't execute query.");
```

9. Start the `while` loop. The `while` loop will create an array called $row for each record in the result set ($result):

```
while ($row = mysql_fetch_array($result)) {
```

10. Get the individual elements of the record, and give them good names:

```
$id = $row['id'];
$format = $row['format'];
$title = $row['title'];
$artist_fn = $row['artist_fn'];
$artist_ln = $row['artist_ln'];
$rec_label = $row['rec_label'];
$my_notes = $row['my_notes'];
$date_acq = $row['date_acq'];
```

11. Do a little formatting with the artists' names. Since some artists have only a first name, some artists have both first and last names, and group names are thrown into the artist_ln field, start an `if...else` block to deal with this. Start by looking for groups:

```
if ($artist_fn != "") {
```

12. Create a variable called `$artist_fullname`, which will contain a string with `$artist_fn`, followed by a space, followed by `$artist_ln`, all within the `trim()` function:

```
$artist_fullname = trim("$artist_fn $artist_ln");
```

13. Continue the block, assigning the trimmed value of `$artist_ln` to `$artist fullname`:

```
} else {
    $artist_fullname = trim("$artist_ln");
}
```

14. Do a little more formatting. If you didn't enter a date in the date_acq field, MySQL will enter a default value of "0000-00-00". Create an if block that looks for this value and then replaces it with something more friendly:

```
if ($date_acq == "0000-00-00") {
    $date_acq = "[unknown]";
}
```

15. Create a variable called `$display_block` to hold all the formatted records. The formatting in this block places the title of the recording in bold, followed by the artist's name in parentheses. Next comes a line break, then your notes, and then an emphasized parenthetical statement that holds the date acquired and format:

```
$display_block .= "
<P><strong>$title</strong> ($artist_fullname)<br>
$my_notes <em>(acquired: $date_acq, format: $format)</em></P>
";
```

16. Close the `while` loop:

```
}
```

17. Close your PHP block:

```
?>
```

18. Add the following HTML:

```
<HTML>
<HEAD>
<TITLE>My Music (Ordered by Title)</TITLE>
</HEAD>
<BODY>
<H1>My Music</H1>
```

19. Display the results:

```
<? echo "$display_block"; ?>
```

20. Add a link back to the main menu, and then add some more HTML to make a valid document:

```
<P><a href="my_menu.html">Return to Menu</a></P>
</BODY>
</HTML>
```

21. Save the file with the name sel_bytitle.php.

22. Place this file in the document root of your Web server.

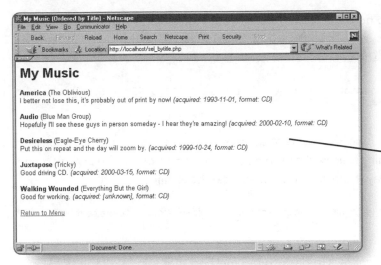

23. Open your Web browser and type
http://localhost/my_menu.html

24. Click on the link called "ordered by title."

Your records will be different from mine, but you should see a screen like this, where the records are ordered by title of the recording.

In the next section, you'll create the script that displays results ordered by artist name.

Displaying Records Ordered by Artist

This script is a bit trickier, because you have to take into consideration issues associated with artist names: Some have only a first name, some have first and last names, and group names are thrown into the artist_ln field as well. In this script, you'll select all the records in the my_music table, ordered alphabetically by the full name of the artist.

1. Open a new file in your text editor.

2. Start a PHP block:

```
<?
```

3. Create a variable to hold the name of the database on which the table resides:

```
$db_name = "testDB";
```

4. Create a variable to hold the name of the table you're selecting from, using this script:

```
$table_name = "my_music";
```

5. Create a variable to hold the result of the mysql_connect() function. Include the @ to suppress warnings, as well as the die() function to cause the script to end and a message to display if the connection fails:

```
$connection = @mysql_connect("localhost", "sandman", "tQ9472b") or
die("Couldn't connect.");
```

6. Create a variable to hold the result of the mysql_select_db() function. Include the @ to suppress warnings, as well as the die() function to cause the script to end and a message to display if the selection of the database fails:

```
$db = @mysql_select_db($db_name, $connection) or die("Couldn't select
database.");
```

7. Create the SQL statement. Go back to the method that names all the fields in the SELECT statement:

```
$sql = "SELECT
id, format, title, trim(concat(artist_fn,' ',artist_ln)) as artist_fullname,
rec_label, my_notes, date_acq
FROM $table_name ORDER BY artist_fullname";
```

> ## NOTE
>
> Within this SQL statement, you're essentially creating a new field from two fields that already exist, using the concat() function (a MySQL string function) to combine artist_fn and artist_ln, with a space in between. Using "as artist_fullname" assigns this new value to a field called artist_fullname.
>
> The trim() function still strips the white space. The phrase "trim(concat(artist_fn,' ',artist_ln)) as artist_fullname" replaces the if...else block usually seen within the while loop in previous scripts.

8. Create a variable to hold the result of the mysql_query() function. Include the @ to suppress warnings, as well as the die() function to cause the script to end and a message to display if the query fails:

```
$result = @mysql_query($sql,$connection) or die("Couldn't execute query.");
```

9. Start the `while` loop. The `while` loop will create an array called `$row` for each record in the result set (`$result`):

```
while ($row = mysql_fetch_array($result)) {
```

10. Get the individual elements of the record, and give them good names:

```
$id = $row['id'];
$format = $row['format'];
$title = $row['title'];
$artist_fullname = $row['artist_fullname'];
$rec_label = $row['rec_label'];
$my_notes = $row['my_notes'];
$date_acq = $row['date_acq'];
```

11. If you didn't enter a date in the date_acq field, MySQL will enter a default value of "0000-00-00". Create an `if` block that looks for this value and then replaces it with something more friendly:

```
if ($date_acq == "0000-00-00") {
        $date_acq = "[unknown]";
}
```

12. Create a variable called `$display_block` to hold all the formatted records. The formatting in this block places the title of the recording in bold, followed by the artist's name in parentheses. Next comes a line break, then your notes, and then an emphasized parenthetical statement that holds the date acquired and format:

```
$display_block .= "
<P><strong>$title</strong> ($artist_fullname)<br>
$my_notes <em>(acquired: $date_acq, format: $format)</em></P>
";
```

13. Close the `while` loop:

```
}
```

14. Close your PHP block:

```
?>
```

15. Add the following HTML:

```
<HTML>
<HEAD>
<TITLE>My Music (Ordered by Artist)</TITLE>
</HEAD>
<BODY>
<H1>My Music</H1>
```

16. Display the results:

```
<? echo "$display_block"; ?>
```

17. Add a link back to the main menu, and then add some more HTML to make a valid document:

```
<P><a href="my_menu.html">Return to Menu</a></P>
</BODY>
</HTML>
```

18. Save the file with the name sel_byartist.php.

19. Place this file in the document root of your Web server.

20. Open your Web browser and type **http://localhost/my_menu.html**

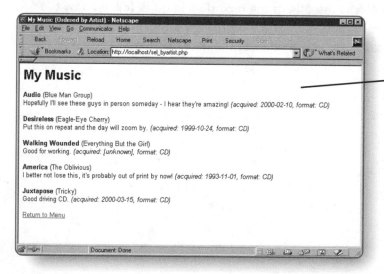

21. Click on the link called "ordered by artist."

Your records will be different from mine, but you should see a screen like this, where the records are ordered by the name of the artist.

The next chapters will give you a break from heavy-duty database work, as you learn a bit about user authentication, cookies, and sessions.

PART V

User Authentication and Tracking

15

Database-Driven User Authentication

Everyone has secrets they don't want to share with the entire world. But some secrets *can* be shared—with certain people. In this chapter, you'll learn how to do the following:

- Create a database table for authorized users
- Create a login form and script sequence that authenticates users before displaying any secrets

Why Authenticate Anyone?

When initially developing a Web site, you might want to restrict access to certain members of your development team. If your corporate Web site contains sensitive financial data, you might want to restrict your financial statements to a particular list of investors. Or maybe you just don't want people poking around your personal things.

A common type of user authentication is *database-driven,* in which usernames and passwords are kept in a database table and accessed via a login form and script. In the next section, you'll create this database table and add some users to it.

Creating the User Table

In Chapter 12, "Creating a Database Table," you followed a two-step table-creation process. You'll be able to use that same process to create the authorized users table.

1. Open your Web browser and type **http://localhost/show_createtable.html**

2. In the Table Name field, type `auth_users`.

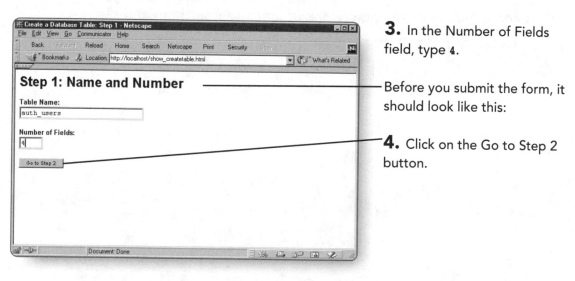

3. In the Number of Fields field, type **4**.

Before you submit the form, it should look like this:

4. Click on the Go to Step 2 button.

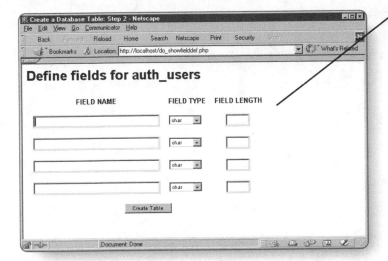

You should see a form like this.

There are four rows, corresponding to the four fields you want to create in the auth_users table. Populate those fields:

5. In the first row, type **f_name** for the Field Name, select varchar from the Field Type drop-down menu, and specify a Field Length of **50**. This field will hold the user's first name.

6. In the second row, type **l_name** for the Field Name, select varchar from the Field Type drop-down menu, and specify a Field Length of **50**. This field will hold the user's last name.

7. In the third row, type **username** for the Field Name, select varchar from the Field Type drop-down menu, and specify a Field Length of **25**. This field will hold the user's username.

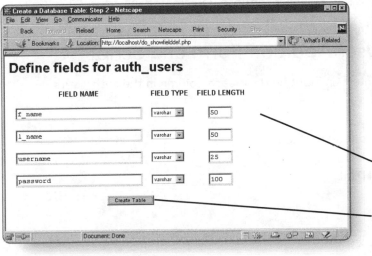

8. In the fourth row, type **password** for the Field Name, select varchar from the Field Type drop-down menu, and specify a Field Length of **100**. This field will hold a hash of the password.

The completed form should look like this:

Click on the Create Table button.

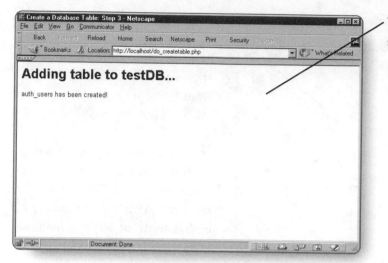

You should see a confirmation screen.

In the next section, you'll create a record addition form and script and add users to the auth_users table.

Adding Users to Your Table

An empty auth_users table does you no good. In this section, you'll create a simple record addition form and script, similar to those you created in Chapter 13.

Creating the User Addition Form and Script

The HTML form will contain an input field for each column in the auth_users database table.

1. Open a new file in your text editor.

2. Type the following HTML:

```
<HTML>
<HEAD>
<TITLE>Add a User</TITLE>
</HEAD>
<BODY>
<H1>Adding a Record to auth_users</H1>
```

3. Begin your form. Assume that the method is post and the action is a script called do_adduser.php:

```
<FORM METHOD="post" ACTION="do_adduser.php">
```

4. Create an input field for the user's first name with a text label:

```
<P><STRONG>First Name:</STRONG><BR>
<INPUT TYPE="text" NAME="f_name" SIZE=25 MAXLENGTH=50></p>
```

5. Create an input field for the user's last name with a text label.

```
<P><STRONG>Last Name:</STRONG><BR>
<INPUT TYPE="text" NAME="l_name" SIZE=25 MAXLENGTH=50></p>
```

6. Create an input field for the username with a text label.

```
<P><STRONG>Username:</STRONG><BR>
<INPUT TYPE="text" NAME="username" SIZE=25 MAXLENGTH=25></p>
```

7. Create an input field for the password with a text label.

```
<P><STRONG>Password:</STRONG><BR>
<INPUT TYPE="text" NAME="password" SIZE=25 MAXLENGTH=25></p>
```

NOTE

The MAXLENGTH of the password form field is 25, while the database field maximum length is 100. This discrepancy in length takes into consideration the encryption that will occur. A 25-character plain-text password, such as that entered in this form field, will be probably be longer than 25 characters when encrypted. Since only the encrypted password is stored in the database, the greater maximum length will handle the extra data.

---

8. Add a submit button:

```
<P><INPUT TYPE="SUBMIT" NAME="submit" VALUE="Add User"></P>
```

9. Close your form and add some more HTML so that the document is valid:

```
</FORM>
</BODY>
</HTML>
```

10. Save the file with the name show_adduser.html.

11. Place this file in the document root of your Web server.

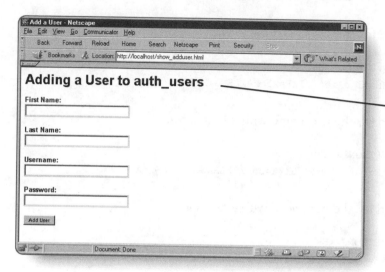

12. Open your Web browser and type **http://localhost/ show_adduser.html**

You will see a form for adding a user, with four fields for name and password information as well as a submit button.

Next, create the back-end script for the record-addition form.

Creating the Back-end Script

1. Open a new file in your text editor.

2. Start a PHP block:

```
<?
```

3. Check that values were actually entered for all four fields. If they weren't, direct the user back to the form and exit the script:

```
if ((!$f_name) || (!$l_name) || (!$username) || (!$password)) {
    header( "Location: http://localhost/show_adduser.html");
    exit;
}
```

4. Create a variable to hold the name of the database on which the table resides:

```
$db_name = "testDB";
```

5. Create a variable to hold the name of the table you're populating with this script:

```
$table_name = "auth_users";
```

6. Create a variable to hold the result of the `mysql_connect()` function. Include the @ to suppress warnings, as well as the `die()` function to cause the script to end and a message to display if the connection fails:

```
$connection = @mysql_connect("localhost", "sandman", "tQ9472b") or
die("Couldn't connect.");
```

7. Create a variable to hold the result of the `mysql_select_db()` function. Include the @ to suppress warnings, as well as the `die()` function to cause the script to end and a message to display if the selection of the database fails:

```
$db = @mysql_select_db($db_name, $connection) or die("Couldn't select
database.");
```

8. Create the SQL statement. The first parenthetical statement gives the names of the fields to populate (in order), and the second parenthetical statement sends the actual strings:

```
$sql = "INSERT INTO $table_name
(f_name, l_name, username, password)
VALUES
(\"$f_name\", \"$l_name\",\"$username\",
password(\"$password\"))
";
```

> **NOTE**
>
> The `PASSWORD()` function inserts a hash of the password, not the password itself. This alleviates the security risk of having plain-text passwords sitting in your database.

9. Create a variable to hold the result of the `mysql_query()` function. Include the @ to suppress warnings, as well as the `die()` function to cause the script to end and a message to display if the query fails:

```
$result = @mysql_query($sql,$connection) or die("Couldn't execute query.");
```

10. Close your PHP block:

```
?>
```

11. Add this HTML:

```
<HTML>
<HEAD>
<TITLE>Add a User</TITLE>
</HEAD>
<BODY>
```

12. Add a heading so that the user knows what he's viewing:

```
<H1>Added to auth_users:</H1>
```

13. Mingle HTML and PHP to show the values entered for each field, starting with the first-name field:

```
<P><STRONG>First Name:</STRONG><BR>
<? echo "$f_name"; ?></p>
```

14. Display a text label and value for the last name:

```
<P><STRONG>Last Name:</STRONG><BR>
<? echo "$l_name"; ?></p>
```

15. Display a text label and value for the username:

```
<P><STRONG>Username:</STRONG><BR>
<? echo "$username"; ?></p>
```

16. Display a text label and value for the password:

```
<P><STRONG>Password:</STRONG><BR>
<? echo "$password"; ?></p>
```

17. Add a link back to the original form:

```
<P><a href="show_adduser.html">Add Another</a></p>
```

18. Add some more HTML so that the document is valid:

```
</BODY>
</HTML>
```

19. Save the file with the name do_adduser.php.

20. Place this file in the document root of your Web server.

Next you'll test this by adding some sample users to your table.

Adding Some Users

The next examples are based on made-up users on my server. Your results will vary, depending on what you enter in your table. To get to the user addition form, open your Web browser and type **http://localhost/show_adduser.html**

In my user addition form, I typed information for a user named Joe Webby, with a username of "joe' and a password of "ilikecheese."

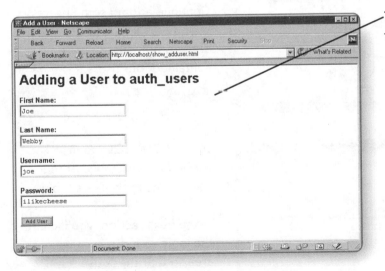

The completed form looks like this.

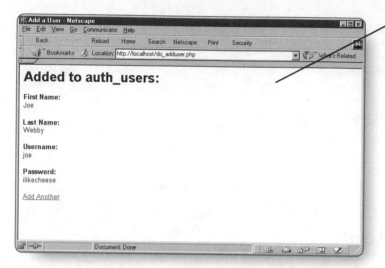

After I clicked on the Add User button, the confirmation screen was displayed.

To see an example of how the password hash is stored, use the command-line interface to the MySQL Monitor to view your record.

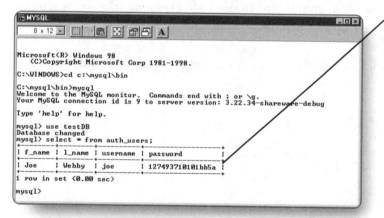

In this example, notice how the password entry says 127493710101bb5a, not ilikecheese.

Continue adding some users on your own. I added three more, until my auth_users table contained four users.

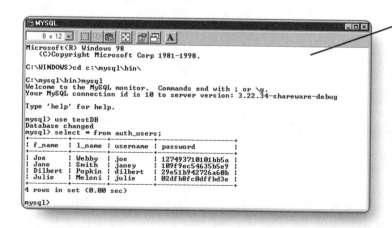

Using the MySQL monitor, I verified the existence of four users in my auth_users table.

In the next section, you'll create the login form for your secret area so that these users will have something to do.

Creating the Login Form

The HTML form will contain just two fields: username and password. Both are required.

1. Open a new file in your text editor.

2. Type the following HTML:

```
<HTML>
<HEAD>
<TITLE>Login</TITLE>
</HEAD>
<BODY>
<H1>Login to Secret Area</H1>
```

3. Begin your form. Assume that the method is post and the action is a script called do_authuser.php:

```
<FORM METHOD="post" ACTION="do_authuser.php">
```

4. Create an input field for the username with a text label:

```
<P><STRONG>Username:</STRONG><BR>
<INPUT TYPE="text" NAME="username" SIZE=25 MAXLENGTH=25></p>
```

5. Create an input field for the password with a text label:

```
<P><STRONG>Password:</STRONG><BR>
<INPUT TYPE="text" NAME="password" SIZE=25 MAXLENGTH=25></p>
```

6. Add a submit button.

```
<P><INPUT TYPE="SUBMIT" NAME="submit" VALUE="Login"></P>
```

7. Close your form and add some more HTML so that the document is valid:

```
</FORM>
</BODY>
</HTML>
```

8. Save the file with the name show_login.html.

9. Place this file in the document root of your Web server.

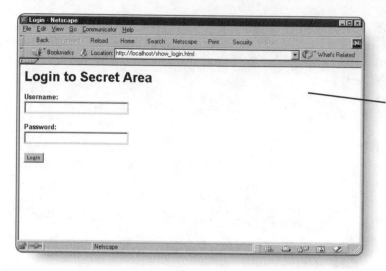

10. Open your Web browser and type **http://localhost/show_login.html**

You will see the login form, with text fields for the username and password as well as a submit button.

Next, you'll create the back-end script for the login form.

Creating the Authentication Script

This goal of this script is to match the username and password entered in the form with a username and password (in the same record) in the auth_users table.

1. Open a new file in your text editor.

2. Start a PHP block:

```
<?
```

3. Check that values were actually entered for both. If they weren't, direct the user back to the form and exit the script:

```
if ((!$username) || (!$password)) {
    header("Location: http://localhost/show_login.html");
    exit;
}
```

4. Create a variable to hold the name of the database on which the table resides:

```
$db_name = "testDB";
```

5. Create a variable to hold the name of the table you're populating with this script:

```
$table_name = "auth_users";
```

6. Create a variable to hold the result of the `mysql_connect()` function. Include the @ to suppress warnings, as well as the `die()` function to cause the script to end and a message to display if the connection fails:

```
$connection = @mysql_connect("localhost", "sandman", "tQ9472b") or
die("Couldn't connect.");
```

7. Create a variable to hold the result of the `mysql_select_db()` function. Include the @ to suppress warnings, as well as the `die()` function to cause the script to end and a message to display if the selection of the database fails:

```
$db = @mysql_select_db($db_name, $connection) or die("Couldn't select
database.");
```

8. Create the SQL statement. The statement is looking for all fields in a record where the username in the table matches the username entered in the form and the password hash in the table matches a hash of the password entered in the form:

```
$sql = "SELECT * FROM $table_name
WHERE username = \"$username\" AND password = password(\"$password\")
";
```

9. Create a variable to hold the result of the `mysql_query()` function. Include the @ to suppress warnings, as well as the `die()` function to cause the script to end and a message to display if the query fails:

```
$result = @mysql_query($sql,$connection) or die("Couldn't execute query.");
```

10. Check for any results from the query by counting the number of rows returned in the result set:

```
$num = mysql_numrows($result);
```

11. Start an `if...else` block to deal with your result. If the number of returned rows is more than 1, a match was found. Create a variable to hold an appropriate message:

```
if ($num != 0) {
$msg = "<P>Congratulations, you're authorized!</p>";
```

12. If the number of returned rows is 0, no matches were found. In that case, direct the user back to the login form, and then close the `if...else` block:

```
} else {
header("Location: http://localhost/show_login.html");
exit;
}
```

13. Close your PHP block:

```
?>
```

14. Add this HTML:

```
<HTML>
<HEAD>
<TITLE>Secret Area</TITLE>
</HEAD>
<BODY>
```

15. Display the message:

```
<? echo "$msg"; ?>
```

16. Add some more HTML so that the document is valid:

```
</BODY>
</HTML>
```

17. Save the file with the name do_authuser.php.

18. Place this file in the document root of your Web server.

Next, you get to test the login form!

Trying to Authenticate Yourself

In this section, you'll attempt to log in as one of the users you added to the auth_users table. Your results will vary, depending on the usernames and passwords you're using. To get to the login form, open your Web browser and type **http://localhost/show_login.html**

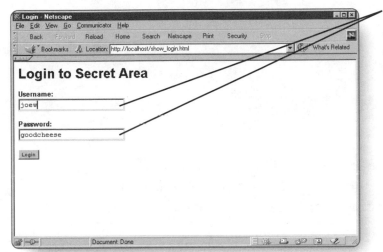

I first tried to break the authentication routine by entering a bad username and a bad password:

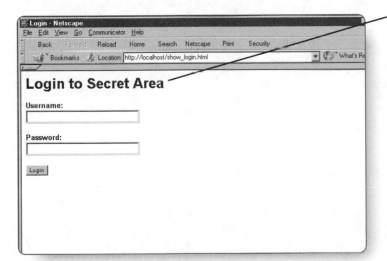

After I clicked on the Login button, I was directed back to the login page, since both the username and password were invalid:

NOTE

Any combination of bad username and bad password will cause the authentication to fail.

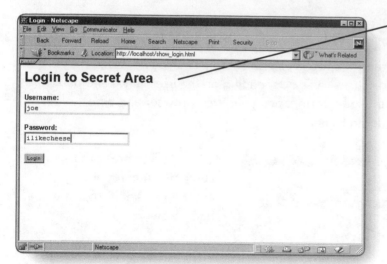

Then I entered correct values in the Username and Password fields:

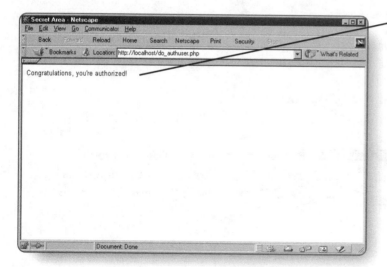

After I clicked on the Login button, I saw the success message.

In the next chapter, you'll be introduced to cookies, and you'll see how to use them in an authentication scheme or just for general user tracking.

16

Using Cookies

Cookies are great little tools, but they get a bad rap in the press when nasty people misuse them. These little bits of text will make your development life much easier if you use them properly. In this chapter, you'll learn how to do the following:

- Set a cookie
- Extract data from a cookie
- Amend your user authentication routines to use a cookie

What's a Cookie?

Cookies are little pieces of text that are sent to a user's Web browser. Cookies can help you create shopping carts, user communities, and personalized sites. It's not recommended that you store sensitive data in a cookie, but you can store a unique identification string that will match a user with data held securely in a database.

Take the shopping example. Suppose you assign an identification variable to a user so that you can track what he does when he visits your site. First, the user logs in, and you send a cookie with variables designed to say, "This is Joe, and Joe is allowed to be here." While Joe is surfing around your site, you can say, "Hello, Joe!" on each and every page. If Joe clicks through your catalog and chooses 14 different items to buy, you can keep track of these items and display them all in a bunch when Joe goes to the checkout area.

Setting Cookies

Before you start setting cookies, determine how you will use them and at what point you will set them. Whatever cookies you decide to set, remember that you absolutely must set a cookie before sending any other content to the browser, because a cookie is actually part of the header information.

```
<HTML>
<HEAD>
<TITLE>Bad Cookie</TITLE>
</HEAD>
<BODY>
<?
setcookie("test", "ok", "", "/" ,".yourdomain.com",0)
?>
<h1>Bad Cookie</h1>
</BODY>
</HTML>
```

If you heed this warning, you won't spend hours wondering why you're getting "Cannot add header information" errors.

This sample code does just that.

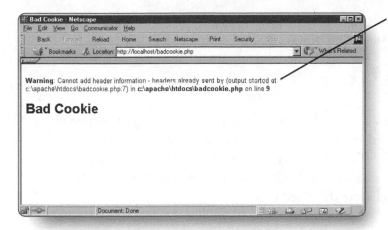

It produces this error.

Anytime you see this error, assume that you've sent *something* to the Web browser. This can include white space, a line break, or text you can actually see.

The `setcookie()` function, used to set one cookie at a time, expects six arguments:

- **Name.** Holds the name of the variable that will be kept in the global `$HTTP_COOKIE_VARS` and will be accessible in subsequent scripts.

- **Value**. The value of the variable passed in the name parameter.

- **Expiration**. Sets a specific time at which the cookie value will no longer be accessible. Cookies without a specific expiration time will expire when the Web browser closes.

- **Path**. Determines for which directories the cookie is valid. If a single slash is in the path parameter, the cookie is valid for all files and directories on the Web server. If a specific directory is named, this cookie is valid only for pages within that directory.

- **Domain**. Cookies are valid only for the host and domain that set them. If no domain is specified, the default value is the host name of the server that generated the cookie. The domain parameter must have at least two periods in the string in order to be valid.

- **Security**. If the security parameter is 1, the cookie will only be transmitted via HTTPS.

This following line is an example of a cookie called `id` with a value of 55sds809892jjsj2. This particular cookie will expire in four hours (the current time plus 14,400 seconds), and it is valid for any page below the document root on the domain yourdomain.com.

```
setcookie("id", "55sds809892jjsj2", time()+14400, "/" ,".yourdomain.com",0);
```

In the next section, I'll give you a cheat sheet for common values of time. Then you'll move into using cookie variables.

Counting Time

If you want to specify an expiration date or time, the easiest way to do that is to tell PHP to count forward for you, and then place a value in the expiration slot within the setcookie() function. This value should be a UNIX time integer (the number of seconds since January 1, 1970), which you can get using the `time()` function, with additional seconds added to it.

The following table shows some common uses of `time()+n` within the `setcookie()` function.

Value	Definition
time()+60	One minute from the current time
time()+900	15 minutes from the current time
time()+1800	30 minutes from the current time
time()+3600	One hour from the current time
time()+14400	Four hours from the current time
time()+43200	12 hours from the current time
time()+86400	24 hours from the current time
time()+259200	Three days from the current time
time()+604800	One week from the current time
time()+2592000	30 days from the current time

Setting a Test Cookie

The goal of this little script is just to set a test cookie and then print a message to the screen. Before you start, modify your Web browser preferences to prompt you before setting cookies. This is the only way to watch a cookie as the server attempts to send it to your browser.

1. Open a new file in your text editor.

2. Start a PHP block:

```
<?
```

3. Create a set of variables called $cookie_name, $cookie_value, $cookie_expire, and $cookie_domain, and give them the following values:

```
$cookie_name = "test_cookie";
$cookie_value = "test string!";
$cookie_expire = time()+86400;
$cookie_domain = ".yourdomain.com";
```

> **NOTE**
> Substitute your own domain name for the value of $cookie_domain.

4. Use the setcookie() function to set this test cookie:

```
setcookie($cookie_name, $cookie_value, $cookie_expire, "/" , $cookie_domain, 0);
```

5. Close the PHP block:

```
?>
```

6. Type the following HTML:

```
<HTML>
<HEAD>
<TITLE>Set Test Cookie</TITLE>
</HEAD>
<BODY>
<h1>Mmmmmmmm...cookie!</h1>
</BODY>
</HTML>
```

7. Save the file with the name setcookie.php.

8. Place this file in the document root of your Web server.

9. Open your Web browser and type **http://localhost/setcookie.php**

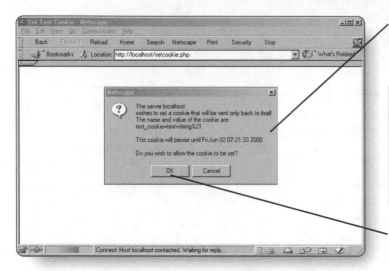

You should see a dialog box prompting you to accept the cookie.

> **NOTE**
>
> Since you set a 24-hour cookie, the date on the confirmation should be 24 hours in the future.

10. Click on OK to accept the cookie.

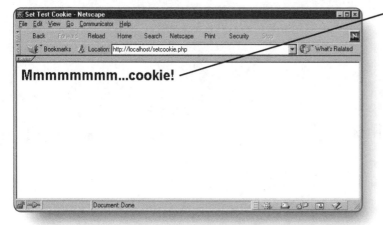

You should see the HTML text.

Using Cookie Variables

There's an element to using cookies that most people forget about until they spend a few hours trying to debug something that isn't even wrong (I've done this). When a Web browser accepts a cookie, you can't extract its value until the next HTTP request is made.

In other words, if you set a cookie called "name" with a value of "Julie" on page 1, you can't extract that value until the user reaches page 2 (or page 5 or page 28—just some other page that isn't the page on which the cookie is initially set).

Using Cookies with Authentication

In the authentication script in the previous chapter, you had a login form and a results page. However, the authentication was valid only for the result page, because it dynamically displayed the secret content (in this case, a "Congratulations!" message). If you want to require authentication for a series of static pages, you have to make some minor adjustments.

1. Open do_authuser.php in your text editor.

2. Scroll down to the if...else block that deals with the result of the authentication. Add a block that sets a cookie:

```
if ($num != 0) {
$cookie_name = "auth";
$cookie_value = "ok";
$cookie_expire = "";
$cookie_domain = "";
setcookie($cookie_name, $cookie_value,
$cookie_expire, "/" , $cookie_domain, 0);
```

> **NOTE**
>
> The setcookie() function will send a cookie called auth with a value of "ok". It will expire at the end of the browser session and will be valid for all directories on localhost.

3. Delete the following line:

```
$msg = "<P>Congratulations, you're authorized!</p>";
```

4. Add this string:

```
$display_block = "
<p><strong>Secret Menu:</strong></p>
<ul>
<li><a href=\"secretA.php\">secret page A</a>
<li><a href=\"secretB.php\">secret page B</a>
</ul>
";
```

> **NOTE**
>
> Don't worry; you'll create these pages soon enough.

5. Scroll until you see the following:

```
<? echo "$msg"; ?>
```

6. Replace it with this:

```
<? echo "$display_block"; ?>
```

7. Save the file.

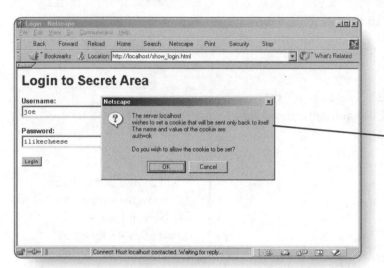

Open your Web browser and type **http://localhost/ show_login.html** to get to the login form, and then enter a valid username and password.

If you still have your preferences set to warn before accepting cookies, you'll see a dialog box like this.

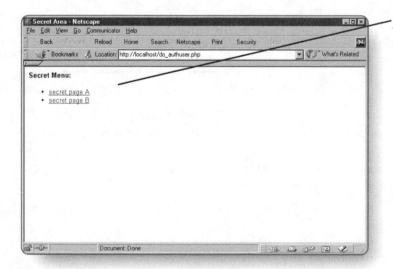

After you click on OK, the new menu will display.

Checking for the Authentication Cookie

The secret menu contains links to two files: secretA.php and secretB.php. By adding a snippet of code to the beginning of these pages, you'll be able to check for an authorized user.

1. Open a new file in your text editor.

2. Start a PHP block:

```
<?
```

3. Start an if...else block to check the value of $auth. The value must be "ok" for the user to be an authorized user:

```
if ($auth == "ok") {
```

4. Create a value to hold a success message:

```
$msg = "<P>Welcome to secret page A, authorized user!</p>";
```

5. Continue the if...else statement to account for an unauthorized visitor. An unauthorized user will be redirected to the login form:

```
} else {
    header( "Location:
http://localhost/show_login.html");
    exit;
}
```

> **NOTE**
>
> A unauthorized visitor is one who attempts to access secretA.php directly without going through the authentication process.

6. Close the PHP block:

```
?>
```

7. Type the following HTML:

```
<HTML>
<HEAD>
<TITLE>Secret Page A</TITLE>
</HEAD>
<BODY>
```

8. Display the message:

```
<? echo "$msg"; ?>
```

9. Add some more HTML so that the document is valid:

```
</BODY>
</HTML>
```

10. Save the file with the name secretA.php.

11. Place this file in the document root of your Web server.

The contents of secretB.php should be nearly identical to secretA.php, so these next instructions should be familiar:

12. Open a new file in your text editor.

13. Start a PHP block:

```
<?
```

14. Start an `if...else` block to check the value of `$auth`. The value must be "ok" for the user to be an authorized user:

```
if ($auth == "ok") {
```

15. Create a value to hold a success message:

```
$msg = "<P>Welcome to secret page B, authorized user!</p>";
```

16. Continue the `if...else` statement to account for an unauthorized visitor. An unauthorized user will be redirected to the login form:

```
} else {
    header( "Location: http://localhost/show_login.html");
    exit;
}
```

17. Close the PHP block:

```
?>
```

18. Type the following HTML:

```
<HTML>
<HEAD>
<TITLE>Secret Page B</TITLE>
</HEAD>
<BODY>
```

19. Display the message:

```
<? echo "$msg"; ?>
```

20. Add some more HTML so that the document is valid:

```
</BODY>
</HTML>
```

21. Save the file with the name secretB.php.

22. Place this file in the document root of your Web server.

It's time for some tests. Unless your browser crashed, you should still be logged in (the auth cookie hasn't expired), and you should have the secret menu in front of you.

Click on the link for secret page A.

> **NOTE**
>
> Using two separate pages will help you understand this example, but if you're in a hurry, you can use just one.

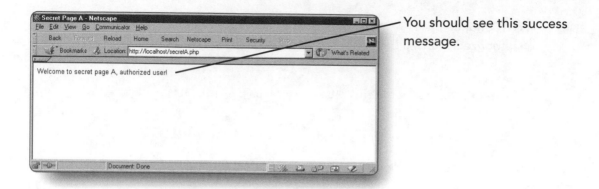

You should see this success message.

Now, exit completely out of your Web browser. This includes closing all browser windows and your mail client (if it's integrated). The auth cookie should now have expired (there's nothing to see; it just goes away).

23. Reopen your Web browser, and attempt to directly access secretB.php by typing **http://localhost/secretB.php**

24. Because you are not an authorized user anymore, you should be redirected to the login screen. Go ahead and log back in as an authorized user, and accept the cookie.

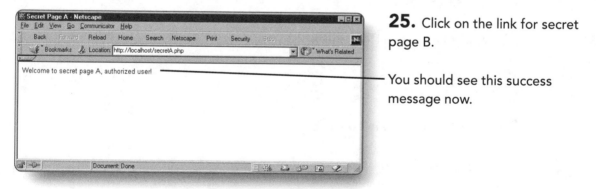

25. Click on the link for secret page B.

You should see this success message now.

Thus concludes this brief introduction to user authentication. Fore more tips, tricks, and techniques, please check the "Extra" section at www.thickbook.com.

17

Session Basics

Sessions are like cookies on steroids. Using sessions, you can maintain user-specific information without setting multiple cookies or even using a database. In this chapter, you'll learn how to do the following:

- Start a session
- Register a session variable
- Enable a per-user access count
- Maintain user preferences throughout multiple pages

Check Your php.ini File

Before you start working with sessions, check a value in your php.ini file. Look for this option:

```
session.save_path    = /tmp     ; argument passed to save_handler
                                 ; in the case of files, this is the
                                 ; path where data files are stored
```

You'll need to modify the value of session.save_path so that the file can be written to a directory that exists. This change primarily affects Windows users, and the modification is simple:

Enter a directory name after the = for session.save_path. For example, my php.ini file on Windows contains this:

```
session.save_path    = /Windows/temp    ; argument passed to save_handler
                                         ; in the case of files, this is the
                                         ; path where data files are stored
```

What's a Session?

In terms of time, a *session* is the amount of time during which a user visits a site. In the programming world, a session is kind of like a big blob that can hold all sorts of variables and values.

- This blob has an identification string, such as 940f8b05a40d5119c030c9c7745aead9.

- This identification string is automatically sent to the user when a session is initiated, in a cookie called PHPSESSID.

- On the server side, a matching temporary file is created with the same name (940f8b05a40d5119c030c9c7745aead9).

Understanding Session Variables

In the temporary session file on the Web server, registered session variables (and their values) are stored. Since these values and variables are not kept in a database, no additional system resources are required to connect to and extract information from database tables.

For example, a temporary session file might contain the following:

```
count|s:7:"76";
valid|s:7:"yes";
```

In this example, count and valid are the names of the registered variables and "76" and "yes" are their respective values. The keyword here is "registered." You have to register a variable within an active session before you can extract the value (using $count or $valid, in this example).

When you attempt to retrieve a registered session variable, the sequence goes something like this (say you're trying to get the value of $count):

1. The PHP parser gets the value of $PHPSESSID from the user cookie.

2. The PHP parser finds a matching temporary session file.

3. Inside the session file, the PHP parser looks for count and then finds its value (say, "76").

4. $count is equal to 76.

Next, you'll start your own per-user counter script using a session.

Starting a Session

Starting a session is a snap. You just call the `session_start()` function, and PHP takes care of the rest—sending the cookie and creating the temporary file.

1. Open a new file in your text editor.

2. Start a PHP block:

```
<?
```

3. Call the `session_start()` function:

```
session_start();
```

NOTE

The `session_start()` function actually performs several important tasks. First, it checks to see if a session has been started for the current user, and it starts one if necessary. It also alerts the PHP engine that session variables and other session-related functions will be used within the specific script.

Because of the dual purpose of `session_start()`, use it at the beginning of all session-related scripts.

---

4. Create a string to hold a message:

```
$msg = "started a session....";
```

5. Close the PHP block:

```
?>
```

6. Type the following HTML:

```
<HTML>
<HEAD>
<TITLE>Start a Session</TITLE>
```

```
</HEAD>
<BODY>
```

7. Display the message string:

```
<? echo "$msg"; ?>
```

8. Add some more HTML so that the document is valid:

```
</BODY>
</HTML>
```

9. Save the file with the name session.php.

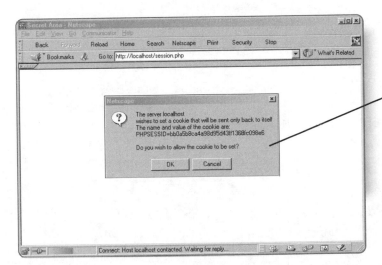

10. Place this file in the document root of your Web server.

11. Open your Web browser and type **http://localhost/ session.php**

If you still have your preferences set to warn before accepting cookies, you'll see a dialog box like this.

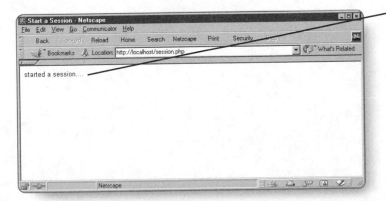

After you click on OK, the message will display.

Was that inspiring, or what? In the next section, you'll register an actual value and watch it change during the course of your session.

Registering and Modifying Session Variables

The goal of this script is to register a variable and change its value during the course of a user session.

1. Open a new file in your text editor.

2. Start a PHP block:

```
<?
```

3. Call the `session_start()` function:

```
session_start();
```

4. Register a variable called count:

```
session_register('count');
```

5. Increment the value of $count to account for the current access:

```
$count++;
```

> **NOTE**
>
> Now, for as long as this session exists, a variable called $count will be available. Currently, the variable has no value.

6. Create a string to hold a message, including the value of $count:

```
$msg = "<P>You've been here $count times. Thanks!</p>";
```

7. Close the PHP block:

```
?>
```

8. Type the following HTML:

```
<HTML>
<HEAD>
<TITLE>Count Me!</TITLE>
</HEAD>
<BODY>
```

9. Display the message string.

```
<? echo "$msg"; ?>
```

10. Add some more HTML so that the document is valid:

```
</BODY>
</HTML>
```

11. Save the file with the name countme.php

12. Place this file in the document root of your Web server.

13. Open your Web browser and type **http://localhost/countme.php**

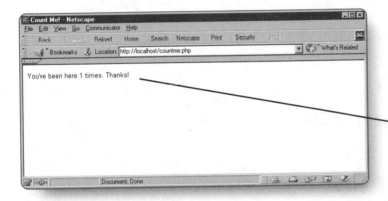

Unless you closed your Web browser between the last script and now, your old session will still be active and you won't see the cookie approval dialog box.

You should just see this.

Reload the page several times, and watch how the counter increments by 1 after each reload.

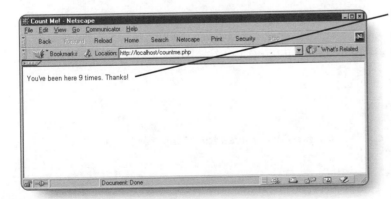

For example, I reloaded the page eight times and finally saw this.

In the next section, you'll handle more than just an access count: you'll set and display user preferences during a user session.

Managing User Preferences with Sessions

Moving beyond the simple access counter, you can use sessions to manage your users' preferences when they visit your site. In this three-step example, you'll start a session, ask a user for his font family and base font size preferences, display those preferences on subsequent pages, and allow the user to change his mind and reset the values.

Starting a Session and Registering Defaults

In this script, you'll start a session and register the font_family and font_size variables. The displayed HTML will be a form that allows you to change your preferences.

1. Open a new file in your text editor.

2. Start a PHP block:

```
<?
```

3. Call the `session_start()` function:

```
session_start();
```

4. Start an `if...else` block to handle the registration of the two session variables, font_family and font_size. First, check for the presence of a value of `$PHPSESSID`:

```
if (!$PHPSESSID) {
```

5. If `$PHPSESSID` does not contain a value, register the two variables:

```
session_register('font_family');
session_register('font_size');
```

6. Continue the block to check for previous values for `$font_family` and `$font_size`:

```
} else if ((!$font_family) || (!$font_size)) {
```

7. If previous values do not exist, register the two variables and close the block:

```
session_register('font_family');
session_register('font_size');
}
```

NOTE

Since the user will come back to this script to reset his display preferences, you have to take into account the fact that the values of the variables must always be extracted from the session itself.

If you simply registered the variables without checking for previous values, each time the page were loaded, the value of these variables would be overwritten as an empty string.

---

8. Set default values for the registered session variables if no previous values exist:

```
if (!$font_family) {
    $font_family = "sans-serif";
}
if (!$font_size) {
    $font_size = "10";
}
```

9. Close the PHP block:

```
?>
```

10. Type the following HTML:

```
<HTML>
<HEAD>
<TITLE>My Display Preferences</TITLE>
```

11. Create a stylesheet block, starting with the opening <STYLE> tag:

```
<STYLE type="text/css">
```

278 CHAPTER 17: SESSION BASICS

12. Add a stylesheet entry for the BODY, P, and A tags. Mingle HTML and PHP to display the current values of $font_family and $font_size:

```
BODY, P, A {font-family:<? echo "$font_family"; ?>;font-size:<? echo
"$font_size"; ?>pt;font-weight:normal;}
```

13. Add a stylesheet entry for the H1 tag. Mingle HTML and PHP to display the value of $font_family and a modified value of $font_size (base value plus 4):

```
H1 {font-family:<? echo "$font_family"; ?>;font-size:<? echo $font_size + 4;
?>pt;font-weight:bold;}
```

14. Close the </STYLE> tag:

```
</STYLE>
```

15. Continue with the HTML, adding a heading and beginning a form. Assume that the form method is post and the action is session02.php:

```
</HEAD>
<BODY>
<H1>Set Your Display Preferences</H1>
<FORM METHOD="POST" ACTION="session02.php">
```

16. Create a set of radio buttons from which the user can choose a new font family:

```
<P>Pick a Font Family:<br>
<input type="radio" name="sel_font_family" value="serif"> serif
<input type="radio" name="sel_font_family" value="sans-serif" checked> sans-
serif
<input type="radio" name="sel_font_family" value="Courier"> Courier
<input type="radio" name="sel_font_family" value="Wingdings"> Wingdings
</p>
```

17. Create a set of radio buttons from which the user can choose a new base font size:

```
<P>Pick a Base Font Size:<br>
<input type="radio" name="sel_font_size" value="8"> 8pt
<input type="radio" name="sel_font_size" value="10" checked> 10pt
<input type="radio" name="sel_font_size" value="12"> 12pt
<input type="radio" name="sel_font_size" value="14"> 14pt
</p>
```

18. Add a submit button and close the form:

```
<P><input type="submit" name="submit" value="Set Display Preferences"></p>
</FORM>
```

19. Add some more HTML so that the document is valid:

```
</BODY>
</HTML>
```

20. Save the file with the name session01.php.

21. Place this file in the document root of your Web server.

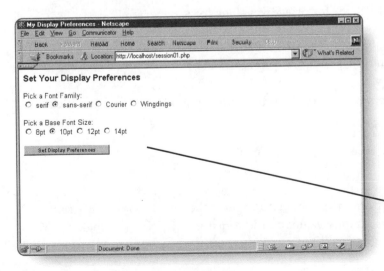

Now open your Web browser and type **http://localhost/session01.php**

Unless you closed your Web browser between the last script and now, your old session will still be active and you won't see the cookie approval dialog box.

You should just see this.

In the next section, you'll create the script that handles the preference changes.

Making Preference Changes

In this script, you'll assign the new values to `$font_family` and `$font_size` and display a confirmation that the changes have been made.

1. Open a new file in your text editor.

2. Start a PHP block:

```
<?
```

3. Call the `session_start()` function:

```
session_start();
```

4. Start an `if...else` block to handle the registration of the two session variables, font_family and font_size. First, check for the presence of a value of `$PHPSESSID`:

```
if (!$PHPSESSID) {
```

5. If `$PHPSESSID` does not contain a value, register the two variables:

```
session_register('font_family');
session_register('font_size');
```

6. Continue the block to check for previous values for `$font_family` and `$font_size`:

```
} else if ((!$font_family) || (!$font_size)) {
```

7. If previous values do not exist, register the two variables and close the block:

```
session_register('font_family');
session_register('font_size');
}
```

8. The selected values from the previous form have the names `$sel_font_family` and `$sel_font_size`. Assign their values to the registered session variables:

```
$font_family = $sel_font_family;
$font_size = $sel_font_size;
```

9. Set default values for the registered session variables if no previous values exist:

```
if (!$font_family) {
        $font_family = "sans-serif";
}
if (!$font_size) {
        $font_size = "10";
}
```

10. Close the PHP block:

```
?>
```

> **NOTE**
>
> For very important security reasons, you can't directly change the value of a registered session variable using POST or GET. You must, in your script, explicitly reassign the values as we have done here.

11. Type the following HTML:

```
<HTML>
<HEAD>
<TITLE>My Display Preferences</TITLE>
```

12. Create a stylesheet block, starting with the opening <STYLE> tag:

```
<STYLE type="text/css">
```

13. Add a stylesheet entry for the BODY, P, and A tags. Mingle HTML and PHP to display the current value of $font_family and $font_size:

```
BODY, P, A {font-family:<? echo "$font_family"; ?>;font-size:<? echo
"$font_size"; ?>pt;font-weight:normal;}
```

14. Add a stylesheet entry for the H1 tag. Mingle HTML and PHP to display the value of $font_family and a modified value of $font_size (base value plus 4):

```
H1 {font-family:<? echo "$font_family"; ?>;font-size:<? echo $font_size + 4;
?>pt;font-weight:bold;}
```

15. Close the </STYLE> tag:

```
</STYLE>
```

16 Continue with the HTML, displaying the values of the two registered session variables:

```
</HEAD>
<BODY>
<H1>Your Preferences Have Been Set</H1>
<P>As you can see, your selected font family is now <? echo "$font_family";
?>, with a base size of <? echo "$font_size" ?> pt.</p>
```

17. Provide a link back to session01.php in case the user wants to change preferences again:

```
<P>Please feel free to <a href="session01.php">change your preferences</a>
again.</p>
```

18 Add some more HTML so that the document is valid:

```
</BODY>
</HTML>
```

19. Save the file with the name session02.php.

20. Place this file in the document root of your Web server.

Unless you closed your Web browser between the last script and now, you should still be staring at the font family and font size selection form.

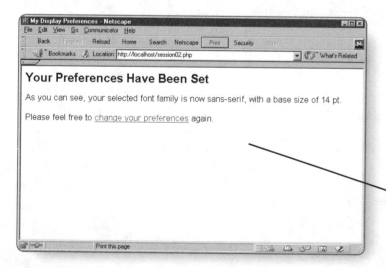

21. Select sans-serif for the font family.

22. Select 14pt for the base font size.

23. Click on the Set Display Preferences button.

The page is displayed using your selected font family and base font size, and the changes are confirmed.

Displaying Changes

This is getting fun! With your Web browser still open to the confirmation screen for the initial preference changes, click on the "change your preferences" link.

The selection form is also displayed using your new font family and base font size.

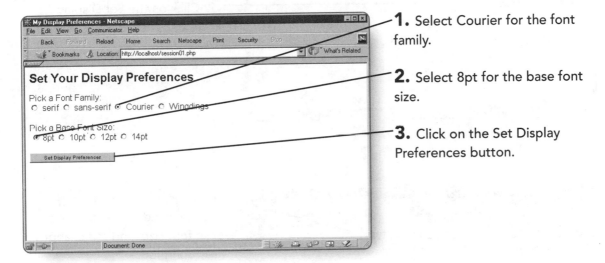

1. Select Courier for the font family.

2. Select 8pt for the base font size.

3. Click on the Set Display Preferences button.

The page is displayed using your selected font family and base font size, and the changes are confirmed.

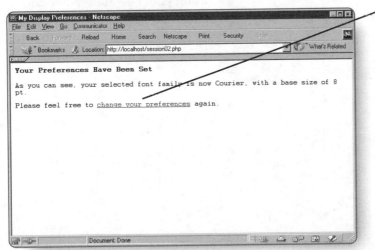

Click on the "change your preferences" link, and the selection form will be displayed using your new font family and base font size.

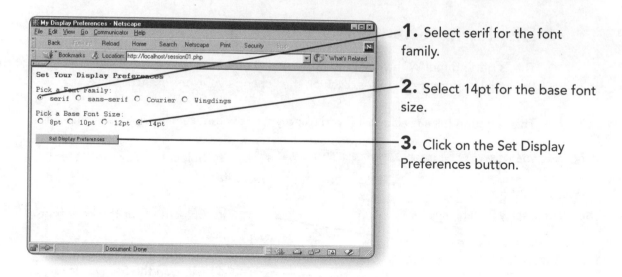

1. Select serif for the font family.

2. Select 14pt for the base font size.

3. Click on the Set Display Preferences button.

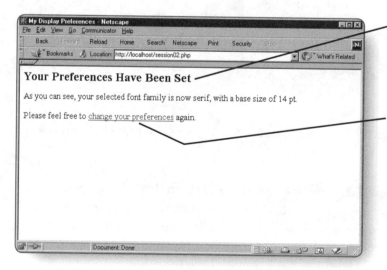

The page is displayed using your selected font family and base font size, and the changes are confirmed.

Click on the "change your preferences" link, and the selection form will be displayed using your new font family and base font size.

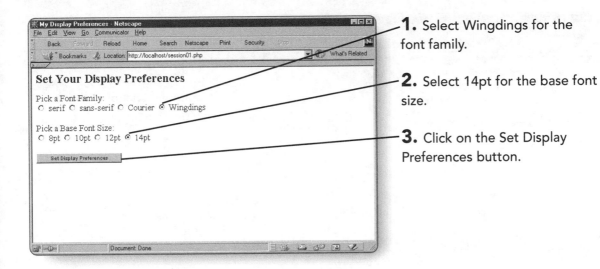

1. Select Wingdings for the font family.

2. Select 14pt for the base font size.

3. Click on the Set Display Preferences button.

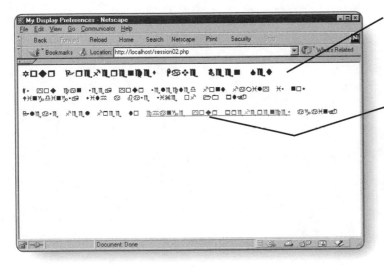

The page is displayed using your selected font family and base font size, and the changes are confirmed.

4. Click on the "change your preferences" link.

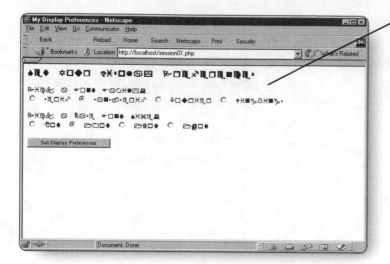

The selection form is displayed using your new font family and base font size.

I recommend changing this again, posthaste!

PART VI

Creating Your Own Contact Management System

18

Planning Your System

The first step in good application design is having a plan. Although improvisation along the way is sometimes a good thing, it's best to start with a solid foundation and a series of goals. The next several chapters will help you create a contact management system—an online address book. In this chapter, you'll learn how to do the following:

- Define administrative tasks and create a menu
- Modify the table-creation script sequence to account for primary keys and auto-incrementing fields
- Define and create the my_contacts table

Planning and Creating the Administration Menu

Not only will you be able to view data within your system, but you'll also be able to add, modify, and delete contacts. A menu would be good—one that provides links to all your action scripts and that adds some authentication to the mix so that only you can see the data. Now create all that in one script!

1. Open a new file in your text editor.

2. Start a PHP block:

```
<?
```

3. Start a session, or continue a session if one currently exists:

```
session_start();
```

4. Start an `if...else` block that checks for the value of the $op variable, which is a hidden variable in the login form you'll soon create:

```
if ($op == "ds") {
```

5. If the value of $op is "ds", the user has completed the form. Start another `if...else` block that checks the validity of the username and password entered by the user:

```
if (($username != "admin") || ($password != "abc123")) {
```

> **NOTE**
>
> You can use any username and password you'd like. This script will check that the username is "admin" and that the password is "abc123".

6. If either the username or password is incorrect, create a variable called $msg to hold an error message:

```
$msg = "<P><font color=\"#FF0000\"><strong>Bad Login - Try
Again</strong></font></P>";
```

7. Create a variable called $show_form, and give it a value of "yes". This value will be checked later in the script, to determine what to display:

```
$show_form = "yes";
```

8. Continue the `if...else` statement:

```
} else {
```

9. If the user makes it this far, the username and password are correct. Register a session variable called valid:

```
session_register('valid');
```

10. Give a value to `$valid`:

```
$valid = "yes";
```

11. Create a variable called `$show_menu`, and give it a value of "yes". This value will be checked later in the script, to determine what to display:

```
$show_menu = "yes";
```

12. Close the inner `if...else` block:

```
}
```

13. Continue the outer `if...else` block:

```
} else {
```

14. If the user is within this section of the outer `if...else` block, he has reached this script without going through the form. Check for the value of `$valid`, and determine what to show—menu or form:

```
if ($valid == "yes") {
    $show_menu = "yes";
} else {
    $show_form = "yes";
}
```

15. Close the outer `if...else` block:

```
}
```

16. Create the form block, which will be shown if the user has not logged in, or if the login is incorrect. Start by creating the variable and printing a header:

```
$form_block = "
<h1>Login</h1>
```

17. Start the form. In this case, the method is post and the action is a variable called $PHP_SELF:

```
<form method=post action=\"$PHP_SELF\">
```

18. Print the value of $msg:

```
$msg
```

19. Create an input field for the username with a text label:

```
<P><strong>username:</strong><br>
<input type=\"text\" name=\"username\"
size=15 maxlength=25></P>
```

20. Create an input field for the password with a text label:

```
<P><strong>password:</strong><br>
<input type=\"password\" name=\"password\" size=15 maxlength=25></P>
```

21. Add the hidden field for $op:

```
<input type=\"hidden\" name=\"op\" value=\"ds\">
```

22. Add some spacing, add the submit button, and close the form and string:

```
<br>
<P><input type=\"submit\" name=\"submit\" value=\"login\"></P>
</FORM>
";
```

> **NOTE**
>
> $PHP_SELF is a global variable whose value is equal to the name of the current script. By using $PHP_SELF as a form action, you're essentially saying, "When the submit button is clicked, reload me."

> **NOTE**
>
> If the login is incorrect, $msg will contain a value, and that value will be printed in this space. If $msg was not created or a value was not given, nothing will print, so it doesn't hurt anything by being present.

23. Create the menu block that will be shown if a user has logged in and is valid. Start by creating the variable and printing a header:

```
$menu_block = "
<h1>My Contact Administration System</h1>
```

24. Add several menu items, and then close the string:

```
<P><strong>Administration</strong>
<ul>
<li><a href=\"show_addcontact.php\">Add a Contact</a>
<li><a href=\"pick_modcontact.php\">Modify a Contact</a>
<li><a href=\"pick_delcontact.php\">Delete a Contact</a>
</ul>

<P><strong>View Records</strong>
<ul>
<li><a href=\"show_contactsbyname.php\">Show Contacts, Ordered by Name</a>
</ul>
";
```

25. Use an `if...else` block to perform a final check, to see which should be displayed—`$form_block` or `$menu_block`. Whichever should be displayed should be the value of a new variable called `$display_block`:

```
if ($show_form == "yes") {
    $display_block = $form_block;
} else if ($show_menu == "yes") {
    $display_block = $menu_block;
}
```

26. Close your PHP block:

```
?>
```

27. Add this HTML:

```
<HTML>
<HEAD>
<TITLE>My Contact Management System</TITLE>
</HEAD>
<BODY>
```

28. Display the results:

```
<? echo "$display_block"; ?>
```

29. Add some more HTML to make a valid document:

```
</BODY>
</HTML>
```

30. Save the file with the name contact_menu.php.

31. Place this file in the document root of your Web server.

Logging in to the Administration Menu

Log in to the administration menu.

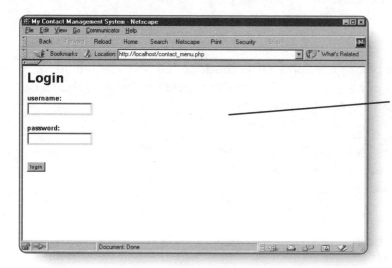

1. Open your Web browser and type **http://localhost/ contact_menu.php**

You will see the login form, with text fields for the username and password, as well as a submit button.

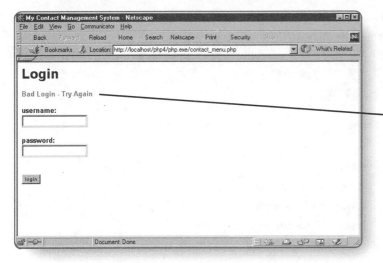

2. Type a bad username and/or a bad password in the appropriate fields, and then click on the login button.

You will see the login form again, with a red error message displayed.

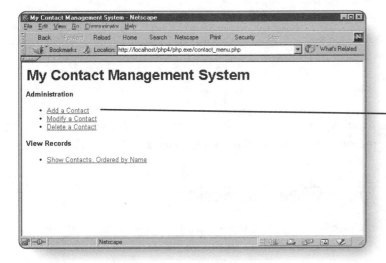

3. Type the correct username (admin) and the correct password (abc123), and then click on the login button.

You will see the Administrative Menu for your contact management system.

In the next section, you'll take a step back and create the my_contacts table so that you can perform all the tasks listed in this fancy administration menu!

Defining the my_contacts Table

Take a moment to think about the kinds of things you'd want in a contact management system: names, addresses, telephone numbers of all sorts, e-mail addresses, and maybe even the person's birthday.

I thought about what I wanted for my own table, which I've decided to call my_contacts. This information appears in the table below.

Field Name	Description
id	Creates a unique ID number for the entry
fname	The person's first name
lname	The person's last name
address1	First line of the address
address2	Second line of the address
address3	Third line of the address
postcode	Zip or postal code
country	Country in which the person resides
prim_tel	Primary telephone number
sec_tel	Secondary telephone number
email	E-mail address
birthday	The person's birthday

In the next section, you'll modify the table-creation scripts from Chapter 12. You'll add the ability to name primary keys and auto-incrementing fields.

Modifying the Table-Creation Scripts

With a few minor modifications to two of the three scripts in the table-creation sequence from Chapter 12, you can add check boxes to the form to handle primary keys and auto-incrementing fields. These types of fields are incredibly useful for ID fields.

1. Open do_showfielddef.php in your text editor.

2. Find the section of $form_block that prints table headings, and add the following before the end of the row:

```
<TH>PRIMARY KEY?</TH><TH>AUTO-INCREMENT?</TH>
```

3. In the `$form_block` within the for loop, the next-to-last line prints a text field with a name of `field_length[]`. After that line, and before the end of the table row, put these two lines:

```
<TD ALIGN=CENTER><INPUT TYPE=\"checkbox\" NAME=\"primary[]\" VALUE=\"Y\"></TD>
<TD ALIGN=CENTER><INPUT TYPE=\"checkbox\" NAME=\"auto_increment[]\"
VALUE=\"Y\"></TD>
```

4. Save this file.

Next, you will modify the final part of the table-creation script.

5. Open do_createtable.php in your text editor.

6. Within the `for` loop, the first line appends text to the `$sql` variable, which holds the SQL statement for table creation. Since you've added two check boxes, for additional elements of the SQL statement, you need to check for them. Start by creating an `if[...]else` block that checks whether the auto_increment check box has been checked:

```
if ($auto_increment[$i] == "Y") {
```

7. If the auto_increment check box has been checked, create a variable to hold additional SQL options:

```
$additional = "NOT NULL auto_increment";
```

> **NOTE**
> When you define a field as auto_increment, it must also be defined as NOT NULL.

8. If the auto_increment check hasn't been checked, create the variable but do not place any text in it, and then close the block. This will assist in resetting the value of the string to an empty value as the looping continues:

```
} else {
        $additional = "";
}
```

9. Create an `if...else` block that checks whether the primary key check box has been checked:

```
if ($primary[$i] == "Y") {
```

10. If the primary key check box has been checked, append the primary key syntax to the `$additional` variable:

```
$additional .= ", primary key
($field_name[$i])";
```

11. If the primary key check box hasn't been checked, append an empty value to the `$additional` value, and then close the block:

```
} else {
      $additional = "";
}
```

> **NOTE**
> The syntax for naming a field as a primary key is separated by a comma from the initial field definition. It looks something like this: primary key (field_name)

12. The last change is to the preexisting loop that checks for field length and creates part of the SQL statement. Find the line that looks like this:

```
$sql .= " ($field_length[$i]),";
```

13. Change the line so that it looks like the following. This ensures that the `$additional` string is placed in the proper section of the SQL statement:

```
$sql .= " ($field_length[$i]) $additional ,";
```

14. Similarly, find a line that looks like the followingp:

```
$sql .= ",";
```

15. Change the line so that it looks like the following:

```
$sql .= " $additional ,";
```

16. Save the file.

In the next section, you'll use these new scripts to create the my_contacts table.

Creating the my_contacts Table

It's time to create the my_contacts table, complete with one primary key and auto-incrementing field!

1. Open your Web browser and type **http://localhost/show_createtable.html**

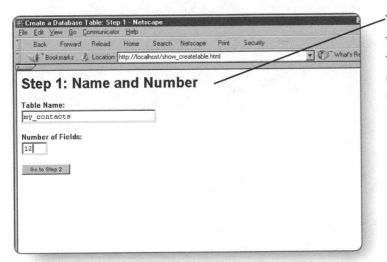

You will see the first form in the table-creation sequence, with text fields for table name and number of fields, as well as a submit button.

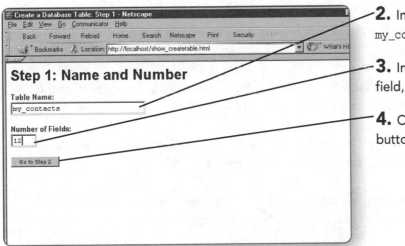

2. In the Table Name field, type my_contacts

3. In the Number of Fields field, type 12

4. Click on the Go to Step 2 button.

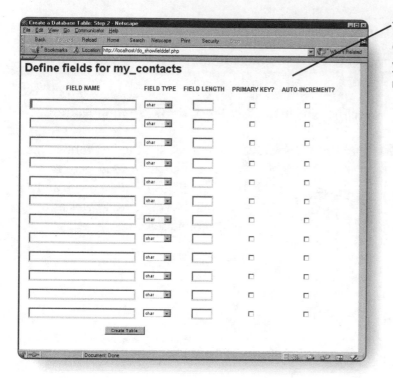

You will see a form with 12 rows, corresponding to the 12 fields you want to create in the my_contacts table.

Populate the fields in these next steps:

5. In the first row, type **id** for the Field Name, select int from the Field Type drop-down menu, check the check box for Primary Key, and check the check box for Auto-Increment.

6. In the second row, type **fname** for the Field Name, select varchar from the Field Type drop-down menu, and specify a Field Length of 75.

7. In the third row, type **lname** for the Field Name, select varchar from the Field Type drop-down menu, and specify a Field Length of 75.

8. In the fourth row, type **address1** for the Field Name, select varchar from the Field Type drop-down menu, and specify a Field Length of 100.

9. In the fifth row, type **address2** for the Field Name, select varchar from the Field Type drop-down menu, and specify a Field Length of 100.

10. In the sixth row, type **address3** for the Field Name, select varchar from the Field Type drop-down menu, and specify a Field Length of 100.

11. In the seventh row, type **postcode** for the Field Name, select varchar from the Field Type drop-down menu, and specify a Field Length of 25.

12. In the eighth row, type **country** for the Field Name, select varchar from the Field Type drop-down menu, and specify a Field Length of 100.

13. In the ninth row, type **prim_tel** for the Field Name, select varchar from the Field Type drop-down menu, and specify a Field Length of 35.

14. In the tenth row, type **sec_tel** for the Field Name, select varchar from the Field Type drop-down menu, and specify a Field Length of 35.

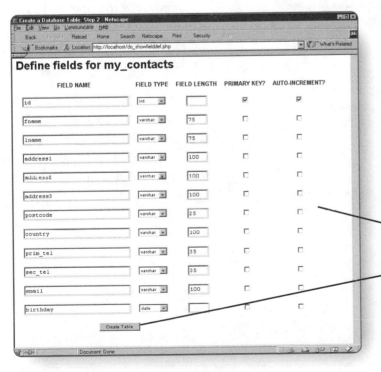

15. In the eleventh row, type **email** for the Field Name, select varchar from the Field Type drop-down menu, and specify a Field Length of 100.

16. In the twelfth row, type **birthday** for the Field Name and select date from the Field Type drop-down menu.

The completed form should look like this.

17. Click on the Create Table button to create the my_contacts table.

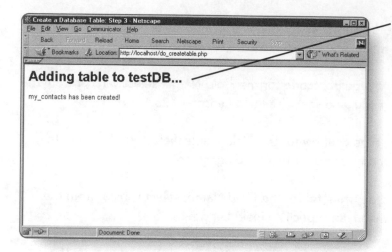

Congratulations! The table has been created.

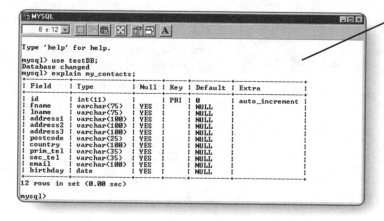

You can verify the primary key and auto-incrementing field using the explain command in the MySQL Monitor.

In the next chapter, you'll create the record addition interface for this table. You'll be well on your way to creating a contact management system!

19

Adding Contacts

You're one step down the development path: You have the my_contacts database all created, waiting for contacts to be added. In this chapter, you'll learn how to do the following:

- Create an administrative interface for adding a record
- Create a script to insert the record into your table
- Require session-based authentication before the script can be viewed or the record can be added

Creating the Record-Addition Form

The HTML form will contain an input field for each column in the my_contacts database table. In the previous chapter, you created 12 fields, which correspond to 12 columns. Your record-addition interface should have a space for each of these fields, except the id field, which can be left blank.

1. Open a new file in your text editor.

2. Start a PHP block:

```
<?
```

3. Start a session, or continue a session if a session currently exists:

```
session_start();
```

> **NOTE**
> Because the id field is an auto-incrementing field, if you add a record and leave the field blank, MySQL will place the next-highest number in that field.

4. Start an if...else block that checks the value of $valid and performs a particular action based on the result. If the value is not "yes", the user didn't go through the proper authentication channels:

```
if ($valid != "yes") {
```

5. Send the user back to the login form, and exit this script:

```
header("Location: http://localhost/contact_menu.php");
exit;
```

6. Continue the if...else block to register the session variable $valid, and then close the block:

```
} else {
    session_register('valid');
}
```

7. Close your PHP block:

```
?>
```

8. Type this HTML to start building the record-addition form:

```
<HTML>
<HEAD>
```

```
<TITLE>My Contact Management System: Add a Contact</TITLE>
</HEAD>
<BODY>

<h1>My Contact Management System</h1>
<h2><em>Add a Contact</em></h2>
```

9. Begin your form. Assume that the method is post and the action is a script called do_addcontact.php:

```
<FORM METHOD="post" ACTION="do_addcontact.php">
```

10. Begin an HTML table to assist in layout. Start a new table row, add two column headings, and then close that row:

```
<table cellspacing=3 cellpadding=5>
<tr>
<th>NAME & ADDRESS INFORMATION</th>
<th>OTHER CONTACT/PERSONAL INFORMATION</th>
</tr>
```

11. Start a new table row and table data cell, and then create an input field for the person's first name with a text label:

```
<tr>
<td valign=top>
<P><STRONG>First Name:</STRONG><BR>
<INPUT TYPE="text" NAME="fname" SIZE=35 MAXLENGTH=75></P>
```

12. In the same table data cell, create an input field for the person's last name with a text label:

```
<P><STRONG>Last Name:</STRONG><BR>
<INPUT TYPE="text" NAME="lname" SIZE=35 MAXLENGTH=75></P>
```

13. In the same table data cell, create an input field for the person's address (first line) with a text label:

```
<P><STRONG>Address Line 1:</STRONG><BR>
<INPUT TYPE="text" NAME="address1" SIZE=35 MAXLENGTH=100></P>
```

14. In the same table data cell, create an input field for the person's address (second line) with a text label:

```
<P><STRONG>Address Line 2:</STRONG><BR>
<INPUT TYPE="text" NAME="address2" SIZE=35 MAXLENGTH=100></P>
```

15. In the same table data cell, create an input field for the person's address (third line) with a text label:

```
<P><STRONG>Address Line 3:</STRONG><BR>
<INPUT TYPE="text" NAME="address3" SIZE=35 MAXLENGTH=100></P>
```

16. In the same table data cell, create an input field for the person's zip/postal code with a text label:

```
<P><STRONG>Zip/Postal Code:</STRONG><BR>
<INPUT TYPE="text" NAME="postcode" SIZE=35 MAXLENGTH=25></P>
```

17. In the same table data cell, create an input field for the person's country with a text label. Close the table data cell after this input field:

```
<P><STRONG>Country:</STRONG><BR>
<INPUT TYPE="text" NAME="country" SIZE=35 MAXLENGTH=100></P>
</td>
```

18. In a new table data cell, create an input field for the person's primary telephone number with a text label:

```
<td valign=top>
<P><STRONG>Primary Telephone Number:</STRONG><BR>
<INPUT TYPE="text" NAME="prim_tel" SIZE=35 MAXLENGTH=35></P>
```

19. In the same table data cell, create an input field for the person's secondary telephone number with a text label:

```
<P><STRONG>Secondary Telephone Number:</STRONG><BR>
<INPUT TYPE="text" NAME="sec_tel" SIZE=35 MAXLENGTH=35></P>
```

20. In the same table data cell, create an input field for the person's e-mail address with a text label:

```
<P><STRONG>E-mail Address:</STRONG><BR>
<INPUT TYPE="text" NAME="email" SIZE=35 MAXLENGTH=100></P>
```

21. In the same table data cell, create an input field for the person's birthday with a text label. Close the table data cell and the table row after this input field:

```
<P><STRONG>Birthday (YYYY-MM-DD):</STRONG><BR>
<INPUT TYPE="text" NAME="birthday" SIZE=10
MAXLENGTH=10></P>
</td>
</tr>
```

22. Start a new table row and table data cell that spans two columns. Inside, add a submit button as well as a link back to the main menu. Close the table data cell, the table row, and the table itself:

```
<tr>
<td align=center colspan=2><br>
<P><INPUT TYPE="SUBMIT" NAME="submit" VALUE="Add Contact to System"></P>
<br>
<p><a href="contact_menu.php">Return to Main Menu</a></p>

</TD>
</TR>
</TABLE>
```

23. Close your form and add some more HTML so that the document is valid:

```
</FORM>
</BODY>
</HTML>
```

24. Save the file with the name show_addcontact.php.

25. Place this file in the document root of your Web server.

In the next section, you'll create the script that takes the form input, creates a SQL statement, and adds the record to the database table.

Creating the Record-Addition Script

This script will add your record to the my_contacts table, taking into consideration the auto-incrementing id field.

1. Open a new file in your text editor.

2. Start a PHP block:

```
<?
```

3. Start an if...else block that checks for values in $fname and $lname. If they don't have values, direct the user back to the form and exit the script:

```
if ((!$fname) || (!$lname)) {
    header( "Location: http://localhost/show_addcontact.php");
    exit;
}
```

4. If the required fields have values, start a session, or continue a session if one currently exists. Then close the block:

```
} else {
    session_start();
}
```

5. Start an if...else block that checks the value of $valid and performs a particular action based on the result. If the value is not "yes", the user didn't go through the proper authentication channels:

```
if ($valid != "yes") {
```

6. Send the user back to the login form, and exit this script:

```
header("Location: http://localhost/contact_menu.php");
exit;
```

7. Continue the if...else block to register the session variable $valid, and then close the block:

```
} else {
    session_register('valid');
}
```

8. Create a variable to hold the name of the database on which the table resides:

```
$db_name = "testDB";
```

9. Create a variable to hold the name of the table you're populating with this script:

```
$table_name = "my_contacts";
```

10. Create a variable to hold the result of the mysql_connect() function. Include the @ to suppress warnings, as well as the die() function to cause the script to end and a message to display if the connection fails:

```
$connection = @mysql_connect("localhost", "sandman", "tQ9472b") or
die("Couldn't connect.");
```

11. Create a variable to hold the result of the mysql_select_db() function. Include the @ to suppress warnings, as well as the die() function to cause the script to end and a message to display if the selection of the database fails:

```
$db = @mysql_select_db($db_name, $connection) or die("Couldn't select
database.");
```

12. Create the SQL statement. The first parenthetical statement gives the names of the fields to populate (in order), and the second parenthetical statement sends the actual strings:

> **NOTE**
>
> Leaving a blank slot for the id field will ensure that the field auto-increments on its own.

```
$sql = "INSERT INTO $table_name
(id, fname, lname, address1, address2,
address3, postcode, country, prim_tel, sec_tel, email, birthday)
VALUES
(\"\",
\"$fname\",\"$lname\",\"$address1\",\"$address2\",\"$address3\",\"$postcode\",
\"$country\", \"$prim_tel\", \"$sec_tel\", \"$email\", \"$birthday\")
";
```

13. Create a variable to hold the result of the mysql_query() function. Include the @ to suppress warnings, as well as the die() function to cause the script to end and a message to display if the query fails:

```
$result = @mysql_query($sql,$connection) or die("Couldn't execute query.");
```

14. Close your PHP block:

```
?>
```

15. Add this HTML:

```
<HTML>
<HEAD>
<TITLE>My Contact Management System: Contact Added</TITLE>
</HEAD>
<BODY>
<h1>My Contact Management System</h1>
<h2><em>Add a Contact - Contact Added</em></h2>
```

16. Add a confirmation statement. Mingle HTML and PHP to include the value of the $table_name variable:

```
<P>The following information was successfully added to <? echo "$table_name"; ?></P>
```

17. Next, you'll re-create the layout used in show_addcontact.php, only it won't contain form fields. Instead, you'll mingle HTML and PHP to show the values that were entered. Start a new table row, add two column headings, and then close that row:

```
<table cellspacing=3 cellpadding=5>
<tr>
<th>NAME & ADDRESS INFORMATION</th>
<th>OTHER CONTACT/PERSONAL INFORMATION</th>
</tr>
```

18. Start a new table row and table data cell, and then display a text label and value for the person's first name:

```
<tr>
<td valign=top>
<P><STRONG>First Name:</STRONG><BR>
<? echo "$fname"; ?></P>
```

19. In the same table data cell, display a text label and value for the person's last name:

```
<P><STRONG>Last Name:</STRONG><BR>
<? echo "$lname"; ?></P>
```

20. In the same table data cell, display a text label and value for the person's address (first line):

```
<P><STRONG>Address Line 1:</STRONG><BR>
<? echo "$address1"; ?></P>
```

21. In the same table data cell, display a text label and value for the person's address (second line):

```
<P><STRONG>Address Line 2:</STRONG><BR>
<? echo "$address2"; ?></P>
```

22. In the same table data cell, display a text label and value for the person's address (third line):

```
<P><STRONG>Address Line 3:</STRONG><BR>
<? echo "$address3"; ?></P>
```

23. In the same table data cell, display a text label and value for the person's zip/postal code:

```
<P><STRONG>Zip/Postal Code:</STRONG><BR>
<? echo "$postcode"; ?></P>
```

24. In the same table data cell, display a text label and value for the person's country. Close the table data cell displaying the value:

```
<P><STRONG>Country:</STRONG><BR>
<? echo "$country"; ?></P>
</td>
```

25. Start a new table data cell, and then display a text label and value for the person's primary telephone number:

```
<td valign=top>
<P><STRONG>Primary Telephone Number:</STRONG><BR>
<? echo "$prim_tel"; ?></P>
```

26. In the same table data cell, display a text label and value for the person's secondary telephone number:

```
<P><STRONG>Secondary Telephone Number:</STRONG><BR>
<? echo "$sec_tel"; ?></P>
```

27. In the same table data cell, display a text label and value for the person's e-mail address:

```
<P><STRONG>E-mail Address:</STRONG><BR>
<? echo "$email"; ?></P>
```

28. In the same table data cell, display a text label and value for the person's birthday. Close the table data cell and table row after displaying the value:

```
<P><STRONG>Birthday (YYYY-MM-DD):</STRONG><BR>
<? echo "$birthday"; ?></P>
</td>
</tr>
```

29. Start a new table row and table data cell that spans two columns. Inside, add a link back to the main menu. Close the table data cell, the table row, and the table itself:

```
<tr>
<td align=center colspan=2><br>
<p><a href="contact_menu.php">Return to Main Menu</a></p>
</TD>
</TR>
</TABLE>
```

30. Add some more HTML so that the document is valid:

```
</BODY>
</HTML>
```

31. Save the file with the name do_addcontact.php.

32. Place this file in the document root of your Web server.

Go on to the next step and start adding contacts!

Populating Your Table

To start populating the my_contacts table, type **http://localhost/contact_menu.php** in the Location box. If you've already logged in, you'll see your administrative menu. Otherwise, log in using the username (admin) and password (abc123).

1. Select the Add a Contact menu item.

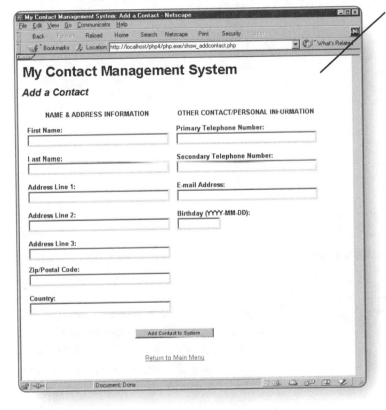

You will see a blank form containing numerous fields for adding contact information, as well as a submit button and a link back to the Main Menu.

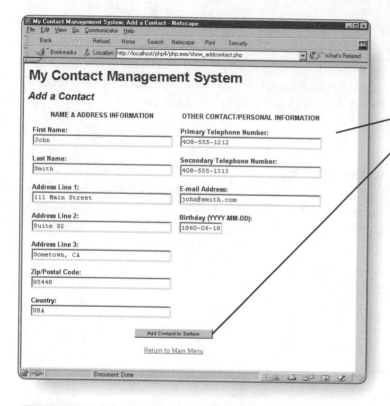

2. Complete the form. Only two fields are required (unless you changed that on your own): first name and last name.

Here's a sample contact.

3. Click on the Add Contact to System button.

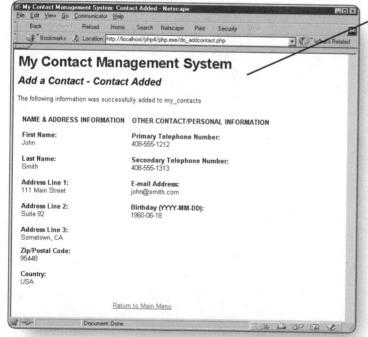

You should see a confirmation screen.

Add several of your own contacts to the system. Make some mistakes, because in the next chapter, you'll create a set of record-modification scripts.

20

Modifying Contacts

Now that you have contacts in your database table, you need a simple way to modify information. People move, change e-mail accounts—you'll need to update your records now and then. In this chapter, you'll learn how to do the following:

- Create an administrative interface for modifying a record

- Create a script to update the record in your table

- Require session-based authentication before the script can be viewed or the record can be modified

Creating the Record-Selection Form

You have a number of entries in the my_contacts table, so you'll need a quick way to select a single record for modification. The next script will create a drop-down menu of all the people in your database, from which you select one record to modify.

1. Open a new file in your text editor.

2. Start a PHP block:

```
<?
```

3. Start a session, or continue a session if one currently exists:

```
session_start();
```

4. Start an if...else block that checks the value of $valid and performs a particular action based on the result. If the value is not "yes", the user didn't go through the proper authentication channels:

```
if ($valid != "yes") {
```

5. Send the user back to the login form, and exit the following script:

```
header("Location: http://localhost/contact_menu.php");
exit;
```

6. Continue the if...else block to register the session variable $valid, and then close the block:

```
} else {
    session_register('valid');
}
```

7. Create a variable to hold the name of the database on which the table resides:

```
$db_name = "testDB";
```

8. Create a variable to hold the name of the table you're populating with this script:

```
$table_name = "my_contacts";
```

9. Create a variable to hold the result of the mysql_connect() function. Include the @ to suppress warnings, as well as the die() function to cause the script to end and a message to display if the connection fails:

```
$connection = @mysql_connect("localhost", "sandman", "tQ9472b") or
die("Couldn't connect.");
```

10. Create a variable to hold the result of the mysql_select_db() function. Include the @ to suppress warnings, as well as the die() function to cause the script to end and a message to display if the selection of the database fails:

```
$db = @mysql_select_db($db_name, $connection) or die("Couldn't select
database.");
```

11. Create the SQL statement. You want to select just the ID number, first name, and last name of each record in the table:

```
$sql = "SELECT id, fname, lname FROM $table_name ORDER BY lname";
```

12. Create a variable to hold the result of the mysql_query() function. Include the @ to suppress warnings, as well as the die() function to cause the script to end and a message to display if the query fails:

```
$result = @mysql_query($sql,$connection) or die("Couldn't execute query.");
```

13. Start the while loop. The while loop will create an array called $row for each record in the result set ($result):

```
while ($row = mysql_fetch_array($result)) {
```

14. Get the individual elements of the record, and give them good names:

```
$id = $row['id'];
$fname = $row['fname'];
$lname = $row['lname'];
```

15. Create a variable called `$option_block`, which will contain the individual elements in the drop-down menu:

```
$option_block .= "<option value=\"$id\">$lname, $fname</option>";
```

16. Close the `while` loop:

```
}
```

17. Create a variable called `$display_block`, which will hold the form. Begin your form. Assume that the method is post and the action is a script called show_modcontact.php:

```
$display_block = "
<FORM METHOD=\"post\" ACTION=\"show_modcontact.php\">
```

18. Create a text label for the drop-down menu:

```
<P><strong>Contact:</strong>
```

19. Start the drop-down menu:

```
<select name=\"id\">
```

20. Place the `$option_block` string inside the `<select> </select>` tag pair. It should contain at least one `<option>` element:

```
$option_block
```

21. Finish the drop-down menu:

```
</select>
```

22. Add a submit button:

```
<INPUT TYPE=\"SUBMIT\" NAME=\"submit\" VALUE=\"Select this Contact\"></P>
```

23. Close your form, the string, and the PHP block:

```
</form>
";
?>
```

24. Add the following HTML:

```
<HTML>
<HEAD>
<TITLE>My Contact Management System: Modify a Contact</TITLE>
</HEAD>
<BODY>
<h1>My Contact Management System</h1>
<h2><em>Modify a Contact - Select from List</em></h2>
<P>Select a contact from the list below, to modify the contact's record.</P>
```

25. Display the contents of `$display_block`:

```
<? echo "$display_block"; ?>
```

26. Add a link back to the main menu:

```
<p><a href="contact_menu.php">Return to Main Menu</a></p>
```

27. Add some more HTML so that the document is valid:

```
</BODY>
</HTML>
```

28. Save the file with the name pick_modcontact.php.

29. Place this file in the document root of your Web server.

In the next section, you'll create the record-modification form, which looks strikingly similar to the record-addition form.

Creating the Record-Modification Form

The record-modification form is based on the record-addition form created in the previous chapter. The difference lies in the prepopulation of values in the form fields. In other words, if there's already data in a record, you can see what you have before you change it.

1. Open a new file in your text editor.

2. Start a PHP block:

```
<?
```

3. Start an `if...else` block that checks for a value for `$id`, the one variable sent from the record-selection form. If a value doesn't exist, direct the user back to the selection form, and exit the script:

```
if (!$id) {
    header( "Location: http://localhost/pick_modcontact.php");
    exit;
}
```

4. If the required field has a value, start a session, or continue a session if one currently exists. Then close the block:

```
} else {
    session_start();
}
```

5. Start an `if...else` block that checks the value of `$valid` and performs a particular action based on the result. If the value is not "yes", the user didn't go through the proper authentication channels:

```
if ($valid != "yes") {
```

6. Send the user back to the login form, and exit this script:

```
header("Location: http://localhost/contact_menu.php");
exit;
```

7. Continue the if...else block to register the session variable $valid, and then close the block:

```
} else {
    session_register('valid');
}
```

8. Create a variable to hold the name of the database on which the table resides:

```
$db_name = "testDB";
```

9. Create a variable to hold the name of the table you're populating with this script:

```
$table_name = "my_contacts";
```

10. Create a variable to hold the result of the mysql_connect() function. Include the @ to suppress warnings, as well as the die() function to cause the script to end and a message to display if the connection fails:

```
$connection = @mysql_connect("localhost", "sandman", "tQ9472b") or
die("Couldn't connect.");
```

11. Create a variable to hold the result of the mysql_select_db() function. Include the @ to suppress warnings, as well as the die() function to cause the script to end and a message to display if the selection of the database fails:

```
$db = @mysql_select_db($db_name, $connection) or die("Couldn't select
database.");
```

12. Create the SQL statement. You want to select all of the fields in the database except id for the record with an ID equal to the value of $id:

```
$sql = "SELECT
fname, lname, address1, address2, address3, postcode, country, prim_tel,
sec_tel, email, birthday
FROM $table_name
WHERE id = \"$id\"
";
```

13. Create a variable to hold the result of the `mysql_query()` function. Include the @ to suppress warnings, as well as the `die()` function to cause the script to end and a message to display if the query fails:

```
$result = @mysql_query($sql,$connection) or die("Couldn't execute query.");
```

14. Start the `while` loop. The `while` loop will create an array called $row for each record in the result set ($result):

```
while ($row = mysql_fetch_array($result)) {
```

15. Get the individual elements of the record, and give them good names:

```
$fname = $row['fname'];
$lname = $row['lname'];
$address1 = $row['address1'];
$address2 = $row['address2'];
$address3 = $row['address3'];
$postcode = $row['postcode'];
$country = $row['country'];
$prim_tel = $row['prim_tel'];
$sec_tel = $row['sec_tel'];
$email = $row['email'];
$birthday = $row['birthday'];
```

> **NOTE**
> Now that you have the current values for the selected record, you will use them later in the script to populate the form fields.

16. Close the `while` loop:

```
}
```

17. Close your PHP block:

```
?>
```

18. Type this HTML to start building the record-modification form:

```
<HTML>
<HEAD>
<TITLE>My Contact Management System: Modify a Contact</TITLE>
</HEAD>
<BODY>
```

```
<h1>My Contact Management System</h1>
<h2><em>Modify a Contact</em></h2>
```

19. Begin your form. Assume that the method is post and the action is a script called do_modcontact.php:

```
<FORM METHOD="post" ACTION="do_modcontact.php">
```

20. Add a hidden field to hold the value of $id:

```
<INPUT TYPE="hidden" name="id" value="<? echo "$id"; ?>">
```

21. Begin an HTML table to assist in layout. Start a new table row, add two column headings, and then close that row:

```
<table cellspacing=3 cellpadding=5>
<tr>
<th>NAME & ADDRESS INFORMATION</th>
<th>OTHER CONTACT/PERSONAL INFORMATION</th>
</tr>
```

22. Start a new table row and table data cell, and then create an input field for the person's first name with a text label. Add the value attribute, and mingle HTML and PHP to echo the actual value:

```
<tr>
<td valign=top>
<P><STRONG>First Name:</STRONG><BR>
<INPUT TYPE="text" NAME="fname" VALUE="<? echo "$fname"; ?>" SIZE=35
MAXLENGTH=75></P>
```

23. In the same table data cell, create an input field for the person's last name with a text label. Add the value attribute, and mingle HTML and PHP to echo the actual value:

```
<P><STRONG>Last Name:</STRONG><BR>
<INPUT TYPE="text" NAME="lname" VALUE="<? echo "$lname"; ?>" SIZE=35
MAXLENGTH=75></P>
```

24. In the same table data cell, create an input field for the person's address (first line) with a text label. Add the value attribute, and mingle HTML and PHP to echo the actual value:

```
<P><STRONG>Address Line 1:</STRONG><BR>
<INPUT TYPE="text" NAME="address1" VALUE="<? echo "$address1"; ?>" SIZE=35
MAXLENGTH=100></P>
```

25. In the same table data cell, create an input field for the person's address (second line) with a text label. Add the value attribute, and mingle HTML and PHP to echo the actual value:

```
<P><STRONG>Address Line 2:</STRONG><BR>
<INPUT TYPE="text" NAME="address2" VALUE="<? echo "$address2"; ?>" SIZE=35
MAXLENGTH=100></P>
```

26. In the same table data cell, create an input field for the person's address (third line) with a text label. Add the value attribute, and mingle HTML and PHP to echo the actual value:

```
<P><STRONG>Address Line 3:</STRONG><BR>
<INPUT TYPE="text" NAME="address3" VALUE="<? echo "$address3"; ?>" SIZE=35
MAXLENGTH=100></P>
```

27. In the same table data cell, create an input field for the person's zip/postal code with a text label. Add the value attribute, and mingle HTML and PHP to echo the actual value:

```
<P><STRONG>Zip/Postal Code:</STRONG><BR>
<INPUT TYPE="text" NAME="postcode" VALUE="<? echo "$postcode"; ?>" SIZE=35
MAXLENGTH=25></P>
```

28. In the same table data cell, create an input field for the person's country with a text label. Add the value attribute, and mingle HTML and PHP to echo the actual value. Close the table data cell after this input field:

```
<P><STRONG>Country:</STRONG><BR>
<INPUT TYPE="text" NAME="country" VALUE="<? echo "$country"; ?>" SIZE=35
MAXLENGTH=100></P>
</td>
```

29. In a new table data cell, create an input field for the person's primary telephone number with a text label. Add the value attribute, and mingle HTML and PHP to echo the actual value:

```
<td valign=top>
<P><STRONG>Primary Telephone Number:</STRONG><BR>
<INPUT TYPE="text" NAME="prim_tel" VALUE="<? echo "$prim_tel"; ?>" SIZE=35
MAXLENGTH=35></P>
```

30. In the same table data cell, create an input field for the person's secondary telephone number with a text label. Add the value attribute, and mingle HTML and PHP to echo the actual value:

```
<P><STRONG>Secondary Telephone Number:</STRONG><BR>
<INPUT TYPE="text" NAME="sec_tel" VALUE="<? echo "$sec_tel"; ?>" SIZE=35
MAXLENGTH=35></P>
```

31. In the same table data cell, create an input field for the person's e-mail address with a text label. Add the value attribute, and mingle HTML and PHP to echo the actual value:

```
<P><STRONG>E-mail Address:</STRONG><BR>
<INPUT TYPE="text" NAME="email" VALUE="<? echo "$email"; ?>" SIZE=35
MAXLENGTH=100></P>
```

32. In the same table data cell, create an input field for the person's birthday with a text label. Add the value attribute, and mingle HTML and PHP to echo the actual value. Close the table data cell and the table row after this input field:

```
<P><STRONG>Birthday (YYYY-MM-DD):</STRONG><BR>
<INPUT TYPE="text" NAME="birthday" VALUE="<? echo "$birthday"; ?>" SIZE=10
MAXLENGTH=10></P>
</td>
</tr>
```

33. Start a new table row and table data cell that spans two columns. Inside, add a submit button as well as a link back to the main menu. Close the table data cell, the table row, and the table itself:

```
<tr>
<td align=center colspan=2><br>
<P><INPUT TYPE="SUBMIT" NAME="submit" VALUE="Update Contact Record"></P>
<br>
<p><a href="contact_menu.php">Return to Main Menu</a></p>

</TD>
</TR>
</TABLE>
```

34. Close your form and add some more HTML so that the document is valid:

```
</FORM>
</BODY>
</HTML>
```

35. Save the file with the name show_modcontact.php.

36. Place this file in the document root of your Web server.

In the next section, you'll create the script that takes the form input, creates a SQL statement, and updates the record in the database table.

Creating the Record-Modification Script

This script will update the record in the my_contacts table, using the value of $id as the primary key (which it is!).

1. Open a new file in your text editor.

2. Start a PHP block:

> **NOTE**
>
> You can have as many (or as few) required fields as you'd like.

```
<?
```

3. Start an `if...else` block that checks for values in `$fname` and `$lname`. If they don't have values, direct the user back to the selection form, and exit the script:

```
if ((!$fname) || (!$lname)) {
    header("Location: http://localhost/pick_modcontact.php");
    exit;
}
```

4. If the required fields have values, start a session, or continue a session if one currently exists. Then close the block:

```
} else {
    session_start();
}
```

5. Start an `if...else` block that checks the value of `$valid` and performs a particular action based on the result. If the value is not "yes", the user didn't go through the proper authentication channels:

```
if ($valid != "yes") {
```

6. Send the user back to the login form, and exit this script:

```
header("Location: http://localhost/contact_menu.php");
exit;
```

7. Continue the `if...else` block to register the session variable `$valid`, and then close the block:

```
} else {
    session_register('valid');
}
```

8. Create a variable to hold the name of the database on which the table resides:

```
$db_name = "testDB";
```

9. Create a variable to hold the name of the table you're populating with this script:

```
$table_name = "my_contacts";
```

10. Create a variable to hold the result of the `mysql_connect()` function. Include the @ to suppress warnings, as well as the `die()` function to cause the script to end and a message to display if the connection fails:

```
$connection = @mysql_connect("localhost", "sandman", "tQ9472b") or
die("Couldn't connect.");
```

11. Create a variable to hold the result of the `mysql_select_db()` function. Include the @ to suppress warnings, as well as the `die()` function to cause the script to end and a message to display if the selection of the database fails:

```
$db = @mysql_select_db($db_name, $connection) or die("Couldn't select
database.");
```

12. Create the SQL statement. This statement uses UPDATE to SET fields to specific values:

```
$sql = "UPDATE $table_name
    SET
    fname = \"$fname\",
    lname = \"$lname\",
    address1 = \"$address1\",
    address2 = \"$address2\",
    address3 = \"$address3\",
    postcode = \"$postcode\",
    country = \"$country\",
    prim_tel = \"$prim_tel\",
    sec_tel = \"$sec_tel\",
    email = \"$email\",
    birthday = \"$birthday\"
    WHERE id = \"$id\"
";
```

13. Create a variable to hold the result of the `mysql_query()` function. Include the @ to suppress warnings, as well as the `die()` function to cause the script to end and a message to display if the query fails:

```
$result = @mysql_query($sql,$connection) or die("Couldn't execute query.");
```

14. Close your PHP block:

```
?>
```

15. Add this HTML:

```
<HTML>
<HEAD>
<TITLE>My Contact Management System: Contact Updated</TITLE>
</HEAD>
<BODY>
<h1>My Contact Management System</h1>
<h2><em>Modify a Contact - Contact Updated</em></h2>
```

16. Add a confirmation statement. Mingle HTML and PHP to include the value of the $table_name variable:

```
<P>The following information was successfully updated in <? echo
"$table_name"; ?></P>
```

17. Next, you'll re-create the layout used in show_modcontact.php, only it won't contain form fields. Instead, you'll mingle HTML and PHP to show the values that were entered. Start a new table row, add two column headings, and then close that row:

```
<table cellspacing=3 cellpadding=5>
<tr>
<th>NAME & ADDRESS INFORMATION</th>
<th>OTHER CONTACT/PERSONAL INFORMATION</th>
</tr>
```

18. Start a new table row and table data cell, and then display a text label and value for the person's first name:

```
<tr>
<td valign=top>
<P><STRONG>First Name:</STRONG><BR>
<? echo "$fname"; ?></P>
```

19. In the same table data cell, display a text label and value for the person's last name:

```
<P><STRONG>Last Name:</STRONG><BR>
<? echo "$lname"; ?></P>
```

20. In the same table data cell, display a text label and value for the person's address (first line):

```
<P><STRONG>Address Line 1:</STRONG><BR>
<? echo "$address1"; ?></P>
```

21. In the same table data cell, display a text label and value for the person's address (second line):

```
<P><STRONG>Address Line 2:</STRONG><BR>
<? echo "$address2"; ?></P>
```

22. In the same table data cell, display a text label and value for the person's address (third line):

```
<P><STRONG>Address Line 3:</STRONG><BR>
<? echo "$address3"; ?></P>
```

23. In the same table data cell, display a text label and value for the person's zip/postal code:

```
<P><STRONG>Zip/Postal Code:</STRONG><BR>
<? echo "$postcode"; ?></P>
```

24. In the same table data cell, display a text label and value for the person's country. Close the table data cell displaying the value.

```
<P><STRONG>Country:</STRONG><BR>
<? echo "$country"; ?></P>
</td>
```

25. Start a new table data cell, and then display a text label and value for the person's primary telephone number:

```
<td valign=top>
<P><STRONG>Primary Telephone Number:</STRONG><BR>
<? echo "$prim_tel"; ?></P>
```

26. In the same table data cell, display a text label and value for the person's secondary telephone number:

```
<P><STRONG>Secondary Telephone Number:</STRONG><BR>
<? echo "$sec_tel"; ?></P>
```

27. In the same table data cell, display a text label and value for the person's e-mail address:

```
<P><STRONG>E-mail Address:</STRONG><BR>
<? echo "$email"; ?></P>
```

28. In the same table data cell, display a text label and value for the person's birthday. Close the table data cell and table row after displaying the value:

```
<P><STRONG>Birthday (YYYY-MM-DD):</STRONG><BR>
<? echo "$birthday"; ?></P>
</td>
</tr>
```

29. Start a new table row and table data cell that spans two columns. Inside, add a link back to the main menu. Close the table data cell, the table row, and the table itself:

```
<tr>
<td align=center colspan=2><br>
<p><a href="contact_menu.php">Return to Main Menu</a></p>
</TD>
</TR>
```

```
</TABLE>
```

30. Add some more HTML so that the document is valid:

```
</BODY>
</HTML>
```

31. Save the file with the name do_modcontact.php.

32. Place this file in the document root of your Web server.

Go on to the next step—modifying some of the contacts in your database table.

Modifying Contacts

To start modifying contacts in the my_contacts table, open http://localhost/contact_menu.php. If you've already logged in, you'll see your administrative menu. Otherwise, log in using the username (admin) and password (abc123).

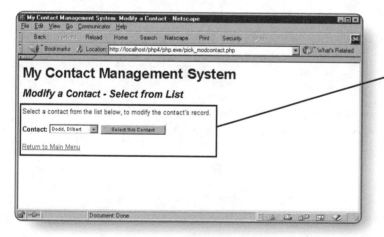

1. Select the Modify a Contact menu item.

You will see a drop-down menu of the contacts in the system, as well as a submit button and a link back to the Main Menu.

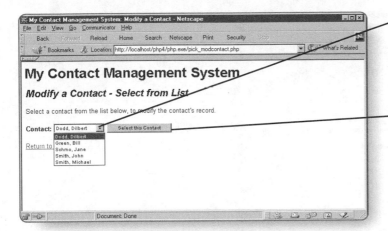

2. Click on Contact menu down arrow. The drop-down menu displays all of the contacts in the system, ordered by last name.

3. Select a contact from the list and click on the Select this Contact button. I selected a sample from my own list. It's a complete example, with a value in every field.

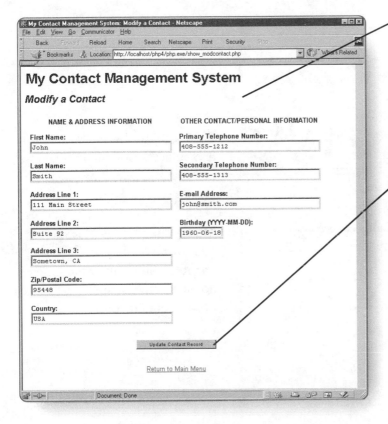

You will see the record modification form, with fields pre-populated with existing values.

4. Change something in the record. In my sample, I changed Address 2 to "Suite 92-A."

5. Click on the Update Contact Record button.

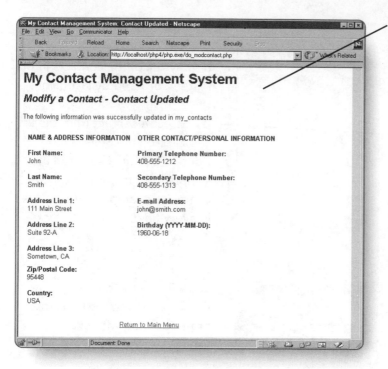

You should see a confirmation screen.

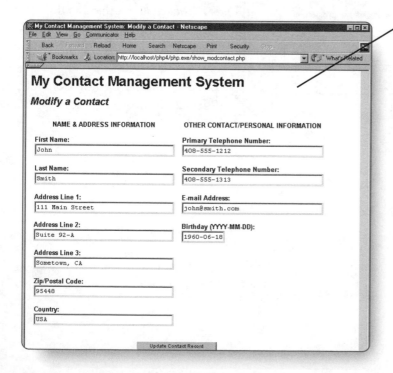

6. Return to the selection form and select your contact again to see that the value has really changed:

Modify the records of some of your own contacts. In the next chapter, you'll create the administrative scripts used to delete some records.

21

Deleting Contacts

There have been plenty of times when I've wanted to delete people from my address book for one reason or another. You should be able to delete people from your online contact management system, too. In this chapter, you'll learn how to do the following:

- Create an administrative interface for deleting a record
- Create a script to delete the record from your table
- Require session-based authentication before the script can be viewed or the record can be deleted

Using the Record-Selection Form

The script that creates a selection form for record deletion is virtually identical to the script used to select a record for modification. This section will be very easy for you to skim through.

1. Open a new file in your text editor.

2. Start a PHP block:

```
<?
```

3. Start a session, or continue a session if one currently exists:

```
session_start();
```

4. Start an `if...else` block that checks the value of $valid and performs a particular action based on the result. If the value is not "yes", the user didn't go through the proper authentication channels:

```
if ($valid != "yes") {
```

5. Send the user back to the login form, and exit this script:

```
header("Location: http://localhost/contact_menu.php");
exit;
```

6. Continue the `if...else` block to register the session variable $valid, and then close the block:

```
} else {
    session_register('valid');
}
```

7. Create a variable to hold the name of the database on which the table resides:

```
$db_name = "testDB";
```

8. Create a variable to hold the name of the table you're populating with this script:

```
$table_name = "my_contacts";
```

9. Create a variable to hold the result of the `mysql_connect()` function. Include the @ to suppress warnings, as well as the `die()` function to cause the script to end and a message to display if the connection fails:

```
$connection = @mysql_connect("localhost", "sandman", "tQ9472b") or
die("Couldn't connect.");
```

10. Create a variable to hold the result of the `mysql_select_db()` function. Include the @ to suppress warnings, as well as the `die()` function to cause the script to end and a message to display if the selection of the database fails:

```
$db = @mysql_select_db($db_name, $connection) or die("Couldn't select
database.");
```

11. Create the SQL statement. You want to select just the ID number, first name, and last name of each record in the table:

```
$sql = "SELECT id, fname, lname FROM $table_name ORDER BY lname";
```

12. Create a variable to hold the result of the `mysql_query()` function. Include the @ to suppress warnings, as well as the `die()` function to cause the script to end and a message to display if the query fails:

```
$result = @mysql_query($sql,$connection) or die("Couldn't execute query.");
```

13. Start the `while` loop. The `while` loop will create an array called `$row` for each record in the result set (`$result`):

```
while ($row = mysql_fetch_array($result)) {
```

14. Get the individual elements of the record, and give them good names:

```
$id = $row['id'];
$fname = $row['fname'];
$lname = $row['lname'];
```

15. Create a variable called $option_block, which will contain the individual elements in the drop-down menu:

```
$option_block .= "<option value=\"$id\">$lname, $fname</option>";
```

16. Close the while loop:

```
}
```

17. Create a variable called $display_block, which will hold the form. Begin your form. Assume that the method is post and the action is a script called show_delcontact.php:

```
$display_block = "
<FORM METHOD=\"post\" ACTION=\"show_delcontact.php\">
```

18. Create a text label for the drop-down menu:

```
<P><strong>Contact:</strong>
```

19. Start the drop-down menu:

```
<select name=\"id\">
```

20. Place the $option_block string inside the <select> </select> tag pair. It should contain at least one <option> element:

```
$option_block
```

21. Finish the drop-down menu:

```
</select>
```

22. Add a submit button:

```
<INPUT TYPE=\"SUBMIT\" NAME=\"submit\" VALUE=\"Select this Contact\"></P>
```

23. Close your form, the string, and the PHP block:

```
</form>
";
?>
```

24. Add this HTML:

```
<HTML>
<HEAD>
<TITLE>My Contact Management System: Delete a Contact</TITLE>
</HEAD>
<BODY>
<h1>My Contact Management System</h1>
<h2><em>Delete a Contact - Select from List</em></h2>
<P>Select a contact from the list below, to delete the contact's record.</p>
```

25. Display the contents of `$display_block`:

```
<? echo "$display_block"; ?>
```

26. Add a link back to the main menu:

```
<p><a href="contact_menu.php">Return to Main Menu</a></p>
```

27. Add some more HTML so that the document is valid:

```
</BODY>
</IITML>
```

28. Save the file with the name pick_delcontact.php.

29. Place this file in the document root of your Web server:

In the next section, you'll create a pre-deletion confirmation screen that shows all the current values of the selected record.

Creating the Record-Deletion Form

The record deletion form isn't a form in the usual sense of the word—you aren't typing anything into a form field. Instead, this screen will display the existing record in read-only format, and include hidden form fields and submit button. By viewing the record before deleting it, you're certain to delete the correct record.

1. Open a new file in your text editor.

2. Start a PHP block:

```
<?
```

3. Start an `if...else` block that checks for a value for `$id`, the one variable sent from the record-selection form. If a value doesn't exist, direct the user back to the selection form, and exit the script:

```
if (!$id) {
    header( "Location: http://localhost/pick_delcontact.php");
    exit;
}
```

4. If the required field has a value, start a session, or continue a session if one currently exists. Then close the block.

```
} else {
    session_start();
}
```

5. Start an `if...else` block that checks the value of `$valid` and performs a particular action based on the result. If the value is not "yes", the user didn't go through the proper authentication channels:

```
if ($valid != "yes") {
```

6. Send the user back to the login form, and exit this script:

```
header("Location: http://localhost/contact_menu.php");
exit;
```

7. Continue the if...else block to register the session variable $valid, and then close the block:

```
} else {
        session_register('valid');
}
```

8. Create a variable to hold the name of the database on which the table resides:

```
$db_name = "testDB";
```

9. Create a variable to hold the name of the table you're populating with this script:

```
$table_name = "my_contacts";
```

10. Create a variable to hold the result of the mysql_connect() function. Include the @ to suppress warnings, as well as the die() function to cause the script to end and a message to display if the connection fails:

```
$connection = @mysql_connect("localhost", "sandman", "tQ9472b") or
die("Couldn't connect.");
```

11. Create a variable to hold the result of the mysql_select_db() function. Include the @ to suppress warnings, as well as the die() function to cause the script to end and a message to display if the selection of the database fails:

```
$db = @mysql_select_db($db_name, $connection) or die("Couldn't select
database.");
```

12. Create the SQL statement. You want to select all the fields in the database except id, for the record with an ID equal to the value of $id:

```
$sql = "SELECT
fname, lname, address1, address2, address3, postcode, country, prim_tel,
sec_tel, email, birthday
FROM $table_name
WHERE id = \"$id\"
";
```

13. Create a variable to hold the result of the `mysql_query()` function. Include the @ to suppress warnings, as well as the `die()` function to cause the script to end and a message to display if the query fails:

```
$result = @mysql_query($sql,$connection) or die("Couldn't execute query.");
```

14. Start the `while` loop. The while loop will create an array called `$row` for each record in the result set (`$result`):

```
while ($row = mysql_fetch_array($result)) {
```

15 Get the individual elements of the record, and give them good names:

```
$fname = $row['fname'];
$lname = $row['lname'];
$address1 = $row['address1'];
$address2 = $row['address2'];
$address3 = $row['address3'];
$postcode = $row['postcode'];
$country = $row['country'];
$prim_tel = $row['prim_tel'];
$sec_tel = $row['sec_tel'];
$email = $row['email'];
$birthday = $row['birthday'];
```

16. Close the `while` loop:

```
}
```

17. Close your PHP block:

```
?>
```

18. Type this HTML to start building the record-confirmation screen:

```
<HTML>
<HEAD>
<TITLE>My Contact Management System: Delete a Contact</TITLE>
</HEAD>
<BODY>
```

```
<h1>My Contact Management System</h1>
<h2><em>Delete a Contact</em></h2>

<FORM METHOD="post" ACTION="do_delcontact.php">
<INPUT TYPE="hidden" name="id" value="<? echo
"$id"; ?>">
<INPUT TYPE="hidden" name="fname" value="<?
echo "$fname"; ?>">
<INPUT TYPE="hidden" name="lname" value="<? echo "$lname"; ?>">
```

> **NOTE**
>
> The hidden form fields carry useful information from step to step.

19. Begin your form. Assume that the method is post and the action is a script called do_delcontact.php:

```
<FORM METHOD="post" ACTION="do_delcontact.php">
```

20. Add a hidden field to hold the value of $id:

```
<INPUT TYPE="hidden" name="id" value="<? echo "$id"; ?>">
```

21. Add two more hidden fields to hold the value of $fname and $lname. You'll use these fields for display purposes in the final confirmation screen, after the deletion has occurred:

```
<INPUT TYPE="hidden" name="fname" value="<? echo "$fname"; ?>">
<INPUT TYPE="hidden" name="lname" value="<? echo "$lname"; ?>">
```

22. Next, you'll re-create the layout used in the record-addition and modification forms, mingling HTML and PHP to show the values for the selected record. Start a new table row, add two column headings, and then close that row:

```
<table cellspacing=3 cellpadding=5>
<tr>
<th>NAME & ADDRESS INFORMATION</th>
<th>OTHER CONTACT/PERSONAL INFORMATION</th>
</tr>
```

23. Start a new table row and table data cell, and then display a text label and value for the person's first name:

```
<tr>
<td valign=top>
<P><STRONG>First Name:</STRONG><BR>
<? echo "$fname"; ?></P>
```

24. In the same table data cell, display a text label and value for the person's last name:

```
<P><STRONG>Last Name:</STRONG><BR>
<? echo "$lname"; ?></P>
```

25. In the same table data cell, display a text label and value for the person's address (first line):

```
<P><STRONG>Address Line 1:</STRONG><BR>
<? echo "$address1"; ?></P>
```

26. In the same table data cell, display a text label and value for the person's address (second line):

```
<P><STRONG>Address Line 2:</STRONG><BR>
<? echo "$address2"; ?></P>
```

27. In the same table data cell, display a text label and value for the person's address (third line):

```
<P><STRONG>Address Line 3:</STRONG><BR>
<? echo "$address3"; ?></P>
```

28. In the same table data cell, display a text label and value for the person's zip/postal code:

```
<P><STRONG>Zip/Postal Code:</STRONG><BR>
<? echo "$postcode"; ?></P>
```

29. In the same table data cell, display a text label and value for the person's country. Close the table data cell displaying the value:

```
<P><STRONG>Country:</STRONG><BR>
<? echo "$country"; ?></P>
</td>
```

30. Start a new table data cell, and then display a text label and value for the person's primary telephone number:

```
<td valign=top>
<P><STRONG>Primary Telephone Number:</STRONG><BR>
<? echo "$prim_tel"; ?></P>
```

31. In the same table data cell, display a text label and value for the person's secondary telephone number:

```
<P><STRONG>Secondary Telephone Number:</STRONG><BR>
<? echo "$sec_tel"; ?></P>
```

32. In the same table data cell, display a text label and value for the person's e-mail address:

```
<P><STRONG>E-mail Address:</STRONG><BR>
<? echo "$email"; ?></P>
```

33. In the same table data cell, display a text label and value for the person's birthday. Close the table data cell and table row after displaying the value:

```
<P><STRONG>Birthday (YYYY-MM-DD):</STRONG><BR>
<? echo "$birthday"; ?></P>
</td>
</tr>
```

34. Start a new table row and table data cell that spans two columns. Inside, add a submit button and a link back to the main menu. Close the table data cell, the table row, and the table itself:

```
<tr>
<td align=center colspan=2><br>
<P><INPUT TYPE="SUBMIT" NAME="submit" VALUE="Delete this Contact"></P>
<p><a href="contact_menu.php">Return to Main Menu</a></p>
</TD>
</TR>
</TABLE>
```

35. Close the form and add some more HTML so that the document is valid:

```
</FORM>
</BODY>
</HTML>
```

36. Save the file with the name show_delcontact.php.

37. Place this file in the document root of your Web server.

In the next section, you'll create the script that takes value of $id (currently held in a hidden form field) and deletes the corresponding record from the database table.

Creating the Record-Deletion Script

This script will delete the record in the my_contacts table, using the value of $id as the primary key.

1. Open a new file in your text editor.

2. Start a PHP block:

```
<?
```

3. Start an if...else block that checks for a value for $id. If no value is present, direct the user back to the selection form, and exit the script:

```
if (!$id) {
    header("Location: http://localhost/pick_delcontact.php");
    exit;
}
```

4. If the required field has a value, start a session, or continue a session if one currently exists. Then close the block.

```
} else {
    session_start();
}
```

5. Start an `if...else` block that checks the value of `$valid` and performs a particular action based on the result. If the value is not "yes", the user didn't go through the proper authentication channels:

```
if ($valid != "yes") {
```

6. Send the user back to the login form, and exit this script:

```
header("Location: http://localhost/contact_menu.php");
exit;
```

7. Continue the `if...else` block to register the session variable `$valid`, and then close the block:

```
} else {
    session_register('valid');
}
```

8. Create a variable to hold the name of the database on which the table resides:

```
$db_name = "testDB";
```

9. Create a variable to hold the name of the table you're populating with this script:

```
$table_name = "my_contacts";
```

10. Create a variable to hold the result of the `mysql_connect()` function. Include the @ to suppress warnings, as well as the `die()` function to cause the script to end and a message to display if the connection fails:

```
$connection = @mysql_connect("localhost", "sandman", "tQ9472b") or
die("Couldn't connect.");
```

11. Create a variable to hold the result of the `mysql_select_db()` function. Include the @ to suppress warnings, as well as the `die()` function to cause the script to end and a message to display if the selection of the database fails:

```
$db = @mysql_select_db($db_name, $connection) or die("Couldn't select
database.");
```

12. Create the SQL statement to delete the record:

```
$sql = "DELETE FROM $table_name WHERE id = \"$id\"";
```

13. Create a variable to hold the result of the `mysql_query()` function. Include the @ to suppress warnings, as well as the `die()` function to cause the script to end and a message to display if the query fails:

```
$result = @mysql_query($sql,$connection) or die("Couldn't execute query.");
```

14 Close your PHP block:

```
?>
```

15. Add this HTML:

```
<HTML>
<HEAD>
<TITLE>My Contact Management System: Contact Deleted</TITLE>
</HEAD>
<BODY>

<h1>My Contact Management System</h1>
<h2><em>Delete a Contact - Contact Deleted</em></h2>
```

16. Add a confirmation statement. Mingle HTML and PHP to include the values of the `$fname`, `$lname`, and `$table_name` variables:

```
<P><? echo "$fname $lname"; ?> has been deleted from <? echo "$table_name";
?></p>
```

17. Add a link back to the main menu, and then add some more HTML so that the document is valid:

```
<p><a href="contact_menu.php">Return to Main Menu</a></p>
</BODY>
</HTML>
```

18. Save the file with the name do_delcontact.php.

19. Place this file in the document root of your Web server.

Go on to the next step and delete some of the contacts in your database table.

Deleting Contacts

To start deleting contacts in the my_contacts table, open http://localhost/
contact_menu.php. If you've already logged in, you'll see your administrative menu.
Otherwise, log in using the username (admin) and password (abc123).

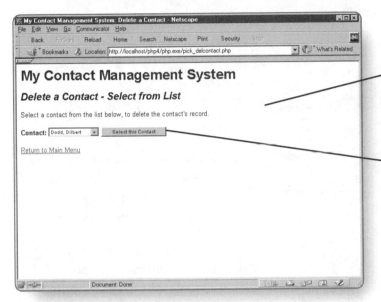

1. Select the Delete a Contact
menu item.

You will see a drop-down menu
of the contacts in the system, as
well as a submit button and a
link back to the Main Menu.

2. Select a contact from the list
and click on the Select this
Contact button. I selected a
sample from my own list.

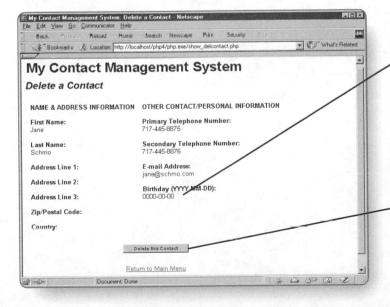

NOTE

The birthday in the
displayed record shows
0000-00-00 because no
date was entered in the
original record. MySQL
uses a default date for
date fields.

3. Click on the Delete this
Contact button.

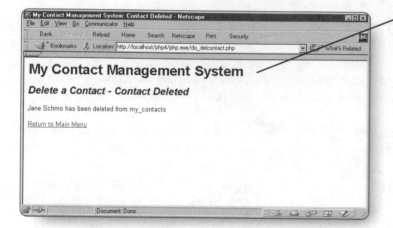

You should see a confirmation screen.

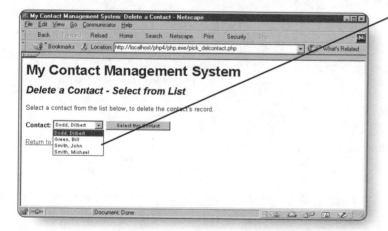

4. Return to the selection form and select your contact again to see that the record no longer exists in the drop-down menu.

Delete a record or two, and then move on to the next chapter, where you'll create the read-only contact information screens.

22

Working with Contacts

You have all of this information in a table, and I haven't shown you how to create any scripts for selecting and displaying read-only data. It's time to remedy that. In this chapter, you'll learn how to do the following:

- Count and display the number of contacts in your system
- DIsplay the current date
- Check for birthdays in the current month, and display special text
- Display read-only contact details
- Require session-based authentication before the script can be viewed or the record is deleted

Modifying Your Administration Menu

The next few sections show some modifications you can make to the original contact_menu.php to display elements such as the current date, the number of contacts in the database, and other pieces of information that make your system more customized.

Showing the Number of Contacts

The following modifications will modify the contact_menu.php script so that it displays the current number of contacts in the my_contacts table.

1. Open contact_menu.php in your text editor.

2. Find this block of code, highlight it, and cut it out of the file (prepare to paste):

```
$form_block = "
<h1>Login</h1>
<form method=post action=\"$PHP_SELF\">
$msg
<P><strong>username:</strong><br>
<input type=\"text\" name=\"username\" size=15 maxlength=25></P>

<P><strong>password:</strong><br>
<input type=\"password\" name=\"password\" size=15 maxlength=25></P>

<input type=\"hidden\" name=\"op\" value=\"ds\">
<br>
<P><input type=\"submit\" name=\"submit\" value=\"login\"></P>
</FORM>
";
```

3. Find the `if...else` block that looks like the following:

```
if ($show_form == "yes") {
    $display_block = $form_block;
} else if ($show_menu == "yes") {
    $display_block = $menu_block;
}
```

4. Replace the following line with the section you cut in step 2:

```
$display_block = $form_block;
```

5. Rename the variable `$form_block` to `$display_block`.

6. The `if...else` block should look like this:

```
if ($show_form == "yes") {
    $display_block = "
    <h1>Login</h1>
    <form method=post action=\"$PHP_SELF\">
    $msg
    <P><strong>username:</strong><br>
    <input type=\"text\" name=\"username\" size=15 maxlength=25></P>

    <P><strong>password:</strong><br>
    <input type=\"password\" name=\"password\" size=15 maxlength=25></P>

    <input type=\"hidden\" name=\"op\" value=\"ds\">
    <br>
    <P><input type=\"submit\" name=\"submit\" value=\"login\"></P>
    </FORM>
    ";
} else if ($show_menu == "yes") {
    $display_block = $menu_block;
}
```

7. Find this block of code, highlight it, and cut it out of the file (prepare to paste):

```
$menu_block = "
<h1>My Contact Management System</h1>
<P><strong>Administration</strong>
<ul>
<li><a href=\"show_addcontact.php\">Add a Contact</a>
<li><a href=\"pick_modcontact.php\">Modify a Contact</a>
<li><a href=\"pick_delcontact.php\">Delete a Contact</a>
</ul>

<P><strong>View Records</strong>
<ul>
```

```
<li><a href=\"show_contactsbyname.php\">Show Contacts, Ordered by Name</a>
</ul>
";
```

8. Find the `if...else` block that contains the following:

```
} else if ($show_menu == "yes") {
    $display_block = $menu_block;
}
```

9. Replace the next line with the section you cut in step 7:

```
$display_block = $menu_block;
```

10. Rename the variable $menu_block to $display_block.

11. The complete `if...else` block should look like this:

```
if ($show_form == "yes") {
    $display_block = "
    <h1>Login</h1>
    <form method=post action=\"$PHP_SELF\">
    $msg
    <P><strong>username:</strong><br>
    <input type=\"text\" name=\"username\" size=15 maxlength=25></P>

    <P><strong>password:</strong><br>
    <input type=\"password\" name=\"password\" size=15 maxlength=25></P>

    <input type=\"hidden\" name=\"op\" value=\"ds\">
    <br>
    <P><input type=\"submit\" name=\"submit\" value=\"login\"></P>
    </FORM>
    ";
} else if ($show_menu == "yes") {
    $display_block = "
<h1>My Contact Management System</h1>
<P><strong>Administration</strong>
<ul>
<li><a href=\"show_addcontact.php\">Add a Contact</a>
```

```
<li><a href=\"pick_modcontact.php\">Modify a Contact</a>
<li><a href=\"pick_delcontact.php\">Delete a Contact</a>
</ul>

<P><strong>View Records</strong>
<ul>
<li><a href=\"show_contactsbyname.php\">Show Contacts, Ordered by Name</a>
</ul>
";
}
```

12. Save your changes before going any further.

None of those changes modified the display in any way. They simply organized your code a little bit better in preparation for the next changes.

These next changes will all take place within the second part of the if...else block you just modified.

13. Find this line, because the rest of the changes go right after it:

```
} else if ($show_menu == "yes") {
```

14. Create a variable to hold the name of the database on which the table resides:

```
$db_name = "testDB";
```

15. Create a variable to hold the name of the table you're populating with this script:

```
$table_name = "my_contacts";
```

16. Create a variable to hold the result of the mysql_connect() function. Include the @ to suppress warnings, as well as the die() function to cause the script to end and a message to display if the connection fails:

```
$connection = @mysql_connect("localhost", "sandman", "tQ9472b") or
die("Couldn't connect.");
```

17. Create a variable to hold the result of the `mysql_select_db()` function. Include the @ to suppress warnings, as well as the u function to cause the script to end and a message to display if the selection of the database fails:

```
$db = @mysql_select_db($db_name, $connection) or die("Couldn't select
database.");
```

18. Create a SQL statement counts the number of entries in the id field:

```
$sql = "SELECT count(id) FROM $table_name";
```

19. Create a variable to hold the result of the `mysql_query()` function. Include the @ to suppress warnings, as well as the `die()` function to cause the script to end and a message to display if the query fails:

```
$result = @mysql_query($sql,$connection) or die("Couldn't execute query.");
```

20. Create a variable to hold the specific value within the result:

```
$count = mysql_result($result,0,"count(id)");
```

21. The next modification is primarily aesthetic. Take the string within `$display_block` and replace it with the following HTML, creating a two-column table for menu options:

> **NOTE**
>
> If you're working with a one-cell result, the `mysql_result()` function is simpler than fetching an entire row. This function requires the result of a valid query, a row (starting at 0), and the field name.

```
$display_block = "
<h1>My Contact Management System</h1>

<table cellspacing=3 cellpadding=3>
<tr>
<td valign=top>
<P><strong>Administration</strong>
<ul>
<li><a href=\"show_addcontact.php\">Add a Contact</a>
<li><a href=\"pick_modcontact.php\">Modify a Contact</a>
<li><a href=\"pick_delcontact.php\">Delete a Contact</a>
</ul>
```

```
<P><strong>View Records</strong>
<ul>
<li><a href=\"show_contactsbyname.php\">Show Contacts, Ordered by Name</a>
</ul>
</td>

<td valign=top>
<P><strong>Miscellaneous</strong></P>

</td>
</tr>
</table>
";
```

22. In the new `$display_block` string, find the section for Miscellaneous. Start a bullet list, and then print a list item with a text label and a bold representation of the value of `$count`. After that list item, close the list itself:

```
<ul>
<li>Contacts in system: <strong>$count</strong>
</ul>
```

23. Save your changes.

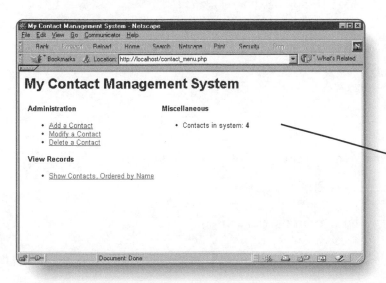

Open http://localhost/contact_menu.php. If you've already logged in, you'll see your administrative menu. Otherwise, log in using the username (admin) and password (abc123).

You should now see a new layout for the menu, as well as the number of contacts in the table, in the appropriate places.

In the next section, you'll display the current date on your menu.

Displaying Today's Date

Compared to the previous section, the changes needed to display the current date are a snap! The `date()` function is highly customizable once you know all the options.

1. Open contact_menu.php in your text editor.

2. Find this line, because the rest of the changes go in this block:

```
} else if ($show_menu == "yes") {
```

> **NOTE**
>
> You can find a list of `date()` function options in Appendix B.

3. After the line that assigns a value to the $count variable, add this line to create a variable called $today, containing a formatted date string:

```
$today = date("l, F jS Y");
```

The date format options are interpreted as follows:

Format Option	Description
l,	Long name of day (literal comma)
F	Long name of month
j	Day of month (2-digit)
S	Ordinal suffix
Y	Year (4-digit)

4. Find the following line in the $display_block string:

```
<h1>My Contact Management System</h1>
```

5. After it, add the following to print the date string:

```
<p><em>Today is $today</em></p>
```

6. Save your file.

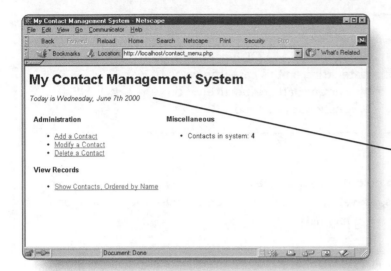

Open http://localhost/contact_menu.php. If you've already logged in, you'll see your administrative menu. Otherwise, log in using the username (admin) and password (abc123).

You should now see a line of text that says "Today is [your date here]".

In the next section, you'll do some neat SQL to find the number of contacts whose birthdays occur during the current month, and you'll print their names in a list. This is helpful for people like me, who can't remember their own mother's birthday, let alone anyone else's!

Showing the Birthdays in the Current Month

One of the fields in your database is a field for the person's birthday. It's not required, but if you take the time to enter someone's birthday, chances are good that you actually want to remember it. This next section will print the number of contacts who have birthdays in the current month, as well as the person's name and birthday and a link to his or her contact details. Nifty!

1. Open contact_menu.php in your text editor.

2. Find this line, because the rest of the changes go in this block:

```
} else if ($show_menu == "yes") {
```

3. Now find the line that assigns a value to the $today variable, because you'll start typing things after this line:

```
$today = date("l, F jS Y");
```

4. Create a SQL statement that gets the number of people who have birthdays in the current month:

```
$get_birthday_count = "SELECT count(id) FROM $table_name WHERE MONTH(birthday)
= MONTH(NOW())";
```

> **NOTE**
>
> The MONTH() and NOW() functions are MySQL functions used to get the month out of a date string (in this case, the value of the birthday field) and the current date, respectively. You can learn more about MySQL functions in Appendix C.

5. Create a variable to hold the result of the mysql_query() function. Include the @ to suppress warnings, as well as the die() function to cause the script to end and a message to display if the query fails:

```
$birthday_count_res = @mysql_query($get_birthday_count,$connection) or
die("Couldn't execute query.");
```

6. Create a variable to hold the specific value within the result:

```
$birthday_count = mysql_result($birthday_count_res, 0, "count(id)");
```

7. Inside $display_block, within the bullet list under the Miscellaneous heading, add this list item:

```
<li>Birthdays this month: <strong>$birthday_count</strong>
```

8. Save your file.

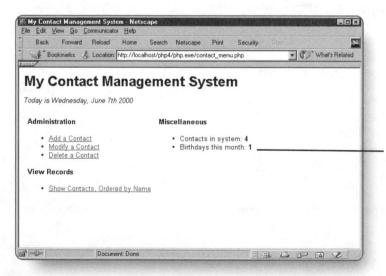

Open http://localhost/contact_menu.php. If you've already logged in, you'll see your administrative menu. Otherwise, log in using the username (admin) and password (abc123).

You should now see a list item for the number of birthdays in the current month, and a value after it.

Enhancing the Menu Display

Next, you'll have more fun with SQL. If the number of contacts who have birthdays in the current month is one or more, you'll create a string that includes the person's name and birthday and a link to his or her contact details.

1. Open contact_menu.php in your text editor.

2. Find this line, because the rest of the changes go in this block:

```
} else if ($show_menu == "yes") {
```

3. Find the line that assigns a value to the $birthday_count variable, because you'll start typing things after this line:

```
$birthday_count = mysql_result($birthday_count_res, 0, "count(id)");
```

4. Create an if statement that will be executed if the value is true. In this case, it's looking for a positive value for $birthday_count:

```
if ($birthday_count != "0") {
```

5. You'll create a bullet list within a while block in a moment. Start the bullet list outside the while block:

```
$bd_string = "<ul>";
```

6. Create a SQL statement that selects the id, first name, last name, month of the birthday, and day of the birthday and that orders the result set by birthday:

```
$get_contacts_bd = "
SELECT id, fname, lname, MONTH(birthday) as month, DAYOFMONTH(birthday) as date
FROM $table_name
WHERE MONTH(birthday) = MONTH(NOW())
ORDER BY birthday
";
```

> **NOTE**
>
> You can select fields or parts of fields and assign a new name to them using "as [new name]" within your SQL statement. In the previous statement, you're extracting the month of a birthday and giving it a name of "month," and you're extracting the day of a birthday and giving it a name of "date."

7. Create a variable to hold the result of the `mysql_query()` function. Include the @ to suppress warnings, as well as the `die()` function to cause the script to end and a message to display if the query fails:

```
$contacts_bd_res = @mysql_query($get_contacts_bd,$connection) or die("Couldn't
execute query.");
```

8. Start the `while` loop. The `while` loop will create an array called `$contacts_bd` for each record in the result set (`$contacts_bd_res`):

```
while ($contacts_bd = mysql_fetch_array($contacts_bd_res)) {
```

9. Get the individual elements of the record, and give them good names:

```
$contact_id = $contacts_bd['id'];
$contact_fname = $contacts_bd['fname'];
$contact_lname = $contacts_bd['lname'];
$contact_bd_month = $contacts_bd['month'];
$contact_bd_date = $contacts_bd['date'];
```

10. Append a list item to `$bd_string` that contains the person's name and birthday. Create a link to a script called show_contact.php, which you'll create in the next section:

```
$bd_string .= "<li><a href=\"show_contact.php?id=$contact_id\">$contact_fname
$contact_lname</a> ($contact_bd_month"."-"."$contact_bd_date)";
```

11. Close the `while` loop:

```
}
```

12. Close the bullet list you created in `$bd_string`:

```
$bd_string .= "</ul>";
```

13. Close the if statement:

```
}
```

14. Inside `$display_block`, within the bullet list under the Miscellaneous heading, and under the "Birthdays this month" list item, add the following:

```
$bd_string
```

15. Save your file.

Open http://localhost/contact_menu.php. If you've already logged in, you'll see your administrative menu. Otherwise, log in using the username (admin) and password (abc123).

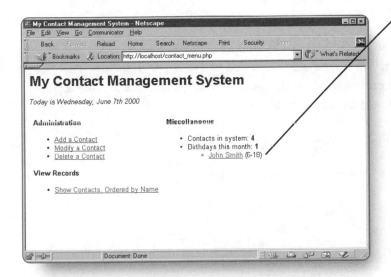

If you have any contacts in your database table whose birthdays are in the current month, you should see their names and birthdays listed.

In the next section, you'll create the contact details script to display all the contact information you've been putting in the my_contacts table.

Selecting Data from the my_contacts Table

Now that all the difficult scripting is out of the way, it's time to do some simple SQL selects to display the data in the my_contacts table. You'll start by listing the contacts, and then you'll show the contact details.

Displaying the Record List

The goal of this script is to display a bulleted list of the contacts in your database table, complete with a link to the show_contact.php script.

1. Open a new file in your text editor.

2. Start a PHP block:

```
<?
```

3. Start a session, or continue a session if one currently exists:

```
session_start();
```

4. Start an `if...else` block that checks the value of `$valid` and performs a particular action based on the result. If the value is not "yes", the user didn't go through the proper authentication channels:

```
if ($valid != "yes") {
```

5. Send the user back to the login form, and exit this script:

```
header("Location: http://localhost/contact_menu.php");

exit;
```

6. Continue the `if...else` block to register the session variable `$valid`, and then close the block:

```
} else {
    session_register('valid');
}
```

7. Create a variable to hold the name of the database on which the table resides:

```
$db_name = "testDB";
```

8. Create a variable to hold the name of the table you're populating with this script:

```
$table_name = "my_contacts";
```

9. Create a variable to hold the result of the `mysql_connect()` function. Include the @ to suppress warnings, as well as the `die()` function to cause the script to end and a message to display if the connection fails:

```
$connection = @mysql_connect("localhost", "sandman", "tQ9472b") or
die("Couldn't connect.");
```

10. Create a variable to hold the result of the `mysql_select_db()` function. Include the @ to suppress warnings, as well as the `die()` function to cause the script to end and a message to display if the selection of the database fails:

```
$db = @mysql_select_db($db_name, $connection) or die("Couldn't select
database.");
```

11. Create the SQL statement. You want to select just the ID number, first name, and last name of each record in the table:

```
$sql = "SELECT id, fname, lname FROM $table_name ORDER BY lname";
```

12. Create a variable to hold the result of the `mysql_query()` function. Include the @ to suppress warnings, as well as the `die()` function to cause the script to end and a message to display if the query fails:

```
$result = @mysql_query($sql,$connection) or die("Couldn't execute query.");
```

13. You'll create a bulleted list within a `while` block in a moment. Start the bulleted list outside the `while` block:

```
$contact_list = "<ul>";
```

14. Start the while loop. The while loop will create an array called $row for each record in the result set ($result):

```
while ($row = mysql_fetch_array($result)) {
```

15. Get the individual elements of the record, and give them good names:

```
$id = $row['id'];
$fname = $row['fname'];
$lname = $row['lname'];
```

16. Append a list item to $contact_list that contains the person's name within a link to a script called show_contact.php:

```
$contact_list .= "<li><a href=\"show_contact.php?id=$id\">$lname, $fname</a>";
```

17. Close the while loop:

```
}
```

18. Close the bullet list you created in $contact_list:

```
$contact_list .= "</ul>";
```

19. Close the PHP block:

```
?>
```

20. Add the following HTML:

```
<HTML>
<HEAD>
<TITLE>My Contact Management System: Contacts Listed by Name</TITLE>
</HEAD>
<BODY>
<h1>My Contact Management System</h1>
<P>Select a contact from the list below, to view the contact's record.</P>
```

21. Display the contents of $contact_list:

```
<? echo "$contact_list"; ?>
```

22. Add a link back to the main menu:

```
<p><a href="contact_menu.php">Return to Main Menu</a></p>
```

23. Add some more HTML so that the document is valid:

```
</BODY>
</HTML>
```

24. Save the file with the name show_contactsbyname.php.

25. Place this file in the document root of your Web server.

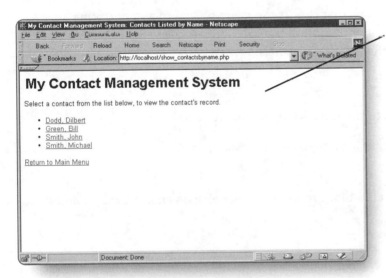

Open http://localhost/contact_menu.php. If you've already logged in, you'll see your administrative menu. Otherwise, log in using the username (admin) and password (abc123). Select the Show Contacts, Ordered by Name link.

In the next section, you'll create the contact display page, show_contact.php.

Displaying Read-Only Records

It's the moment of truth: displaying your contacts!

1. Open a new file in your text editor.

2. Start a PHP block:

```
<?
```

3. Start an `if...else` block that checks for a value for `$id`, the one variable sent in the link's query string. If a value doesn't exist, direct the user back to the menu, and exit the script:

```
if (!$id) {
    header("Location: http://localhost/contact_menu.php");
    exit;
}
```

4. If the required field has a value, start a session or continue a session if one currently exists, and then close the block:

```
} else {
    session_start();
}
```

5. Start an `if...else` block that checks the value of `$valid` and performs a particular action based on the result. If the value is not "yes", the user didn't go through the proper authentication channels:

```
if ($valid != "yes") {
```

6. Send the user back to the login form, and exit this script:

```
header("Location: http://localhost/contact_menu.php");
exit;
```

7. Continue the `if...else` block to register the session variable `$valid`, and then close the block:

```
} else {
    session_register('valid');
}
```

8. Create a variable to hold the name of the database on which the table resides:

```
$db_name = "testDB";
```

9. Create a variable to hold the name of the table you're populating with this script:

```
$table_name = "my_contacts";
```

10. Create a variable to hold the result of the `mysql_connect()` function. Include the @ to suppress warnings, as well as the `die()` function to cause the script to end and a message to display if the connection fails:

```
$connection = @mysql_connect("localhost", "sandman", "tQ9472b") or
die("Couldn't connect.");
```

11. Create a variable to hold the result of the `mysql_select_db()` function. Include the @ to suppress warnings, as well as the `die()` function to cause the script to end and a message to display if the selection of the database fails:

```
$db = @mysql_select_db($db_name, $connection) or die("Couldn't select
database.");
```

12. Perform some validation on the value of `$id`. You want to make sure that the number really exists in the system before you run SQL queries using a bad key!

```
$chk_id = "SELECT id FROM $table_name WHERE id = \"$id\"";
```

13. Create a variable to hold the result of the `mysql_query()` function. Include the @ to suppress warnings, as well as the `die()` function to cause the script to end and a message to display if the query fails:

```
$chk_id_res = @mysql_query($chk_id,$connection) or die("Couldn't execute
query.");
```

14. Create a variable to count the number of rows within the result. There should be one row:

```
$chk_id_num = mysql_num_rows($chk_id_res);
```

15. Start an `if...else` block to deal with the results of the validation. The first section checks the row count. The correct answer is 1:

```
if ($chk_id_num == "0") {
```

16. If the row count is 0, the id was invalid. Redirect the user to the menu, and exit the script:

```
header("Location: http://localhost/contact_menu.php");
exit;
```

17. Continue the `if...else` statement, now preparing to act on a valid result:

```
} else {
```

18. Create the SQL statement. You want to select all the fields in the database except id for the record that has an ID equal to the value of `$id`:

```
$sql = "
SELECT fname, lname, address1, address2, address3, postcode, country,
prim_tel, sec_tel, email, birthday
FROM $table_name
WHERE id = \"$id\"
";
```

19. Create a variable to hold the result of the `mysql_query()` function. Include the `@` to suppress warnings, as well as the `die()` function to cause the script to end and a message to display if the query fails:

```
$result = @mysql_query($sql,$connection) or die("Couldn't execute query.");
```

20. Start the `while` loop. The `while` loop will create an array called `$row` for each record in the result set (`$result`):

```
while ($row = mysql_fetch_array($result)) {
```

21. Get the individual elements of the record, and give them good names:

```
$fname = $row['fname'];
$lname = $row['lname'];
$address1 = $row['address1'];
$address2 = $row['address2'];
$address3 = $row['address3'];
$postcode = $row['postcode'];
$country = $row['country'];
$prim_tel = $row['prim_tel'];
$sec_tel = $row['sec_tel'];
$email = $row['email'];
$birthday = $row['birthday'];
```

22. Close the `while` loop:

```
}
```

23. Close your PHP block:

```
?>
```

24. Type the following HTML to start building the record details screen:

```
<HTML>
<HEAD>
<TITLE>My Contact Management System: Read-Only Contact Details</TITLE>
</HEAD>
<BODY>
<h1>My Contact Management System</h1>
```

25. Mingle HTML and PHP to show a nice title, with the contact's full name:

```
<h2>Contact Details for <? echo "$fname $lname"; ?></h2>
```

26. Start a paragraph with a text label:

```
<P><strong>Name & Address:</strong><br>
```

27. Display all the individual elements for name and address:

```
<? echo "$fname $lname"; ?><br>
<? echo "$address1"; ?><br>
<? echo "$address2"; ?><br>
<? echo "$address3"; ?><br>
<? echo "$postcode"; ?><br>
<? echo "$country"; ?></P>
```

28. Start a paragraph, and print text labels and results for the telephone and e-mail fields:

```
<P><strong>Tel 1:</strong> <? echo "$prim_tel"; ?><br>
<strong>Tel 2:</strong> <? echo "$sec_tel"; ?><br>
<strong>E-Mail:</strong> <? echo "<a href=\"mailto:$email\">$email</a>"; ?></P>
```

29. Start a paragraph, and print a text label and result for the birthday:

```
<P><strong>Birthday:</strong> <? echo "$birthday"; ?></P>
```

30. Add a link back to the main menu, then add some more HTML so that the document is valid:

```
<br>
<p><a href="contact_menu.php">Return to Main Menu</a></p>

</BODY>
</HTML>
```

31. Save the file with the name show_contact.php.

32. Place this file in the document root of your Web server.

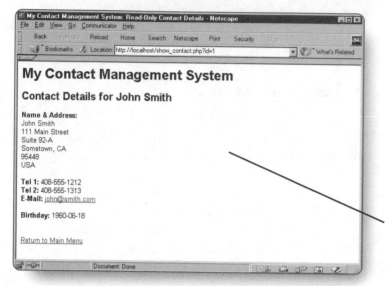

Open http://localhost/contact_menu.php. If you've already logged in, you'll see your administrative menu. Otherwise, log in using the username (admin) and password (abc123). Select the Show Contacts, Ordered by Name link, and then select one of your contacts from the list.

Looks good! This is a contact in my database table that's complete.

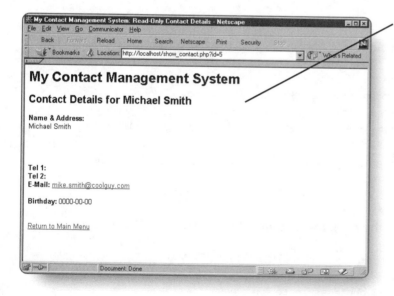

But here's what happens when the contact isn't complete and no birthday has been entered. Pretty ugly! Make some modifications to show_contact.php to take into account the fact that only two fields (first name and last name) are required.

Enhancing the Record Display

1. Open show_contact.php.

2. Scroll down to the Name & Address section:

3. Delete the following section:

```
<? echo "$address1"; ?><br>
<? echo "$address2"; ?><br>
<? echo "$address3"; ?><br>
<? echo "$postcode"; ?><br>
<? echo "$country"; ?></P>

<P><strong>Tel 1:</strong> <? echo "$prim_tel"; ?><br>
<strong>Tel 2:</strong> <? echo "$sec_tel"; ?><br>
<strong>E-Mail:</strong> <? echo "<a href=\"mailto:$email\">$email</a>";
?></P>

<P><strong>Birthday:</strong> <? echo "$birthday"; ?></P>
```

4. Type the following series of `if` statements, which look for a value of the specific variable and print the line only if a value is present:

```
<?
    if ($address1 != "") {
        echo "$address1 <br>";
    }
    if ($address2 != "") {
        echo "$address2 <br>";
    }
    if ($address3 != "") {
        echo "$address3 <br>";
    }
    if ($postcode != "") {
        echo "$postcode <br>";
    }
    if ($country != "") {
        echo "$country <br>";
    }
?>
```

```
</P>
<P>
<?

   if ($prim_tel != "") {
       echo "<strong>Tel 1:</strong> $prim_tel <br>";
   }
   if ($sec_tel != "") {
       echo "<strong>Tel 2:</strong> $sec_tel <br>";
   }
   if ($email != "") {
       echo "<strong>E-Mail:</strong> <a href=\"mailto:$email\">$email</a>
<br>";
   }
?>
</P>
<?

   if ($birthday != "0000-00-00") {
       echo "<P><strong>Birthday:</strong> $birthday </P>";
   }
?>
```

5. Save this file.

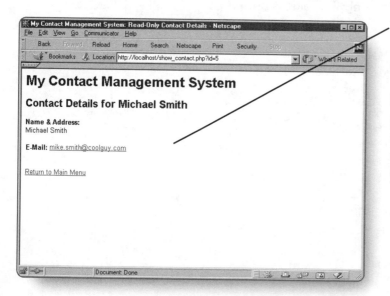

Now when I view an incomplete record, I don't see all that white space.

So there you have it—a complete online contact management system using sessions and user authentication. Put that on your resume!

Appendices

A

Additional Configuration Options

The installation instructions at the beginning of this book detailed a simple configuration of PHP. If you feel like venturing out on your own by adding additional extensions (on Windows) or recompiling PHP (on Linux), this appendix gives you a brief rundown of some of your options.

Windows Extensions

The following support is compiled into the Windows binary release of PHP4.0.0:

- Regular expression support
- Dynamic library support
- Internal Sendmail support
- Perl-compatible regular expression support
- ODBC support
- Session support
- XML support
- MySQL support

To get additional functionality, additional extensions (.dll files) are required. Some possibilities are listed in the following table.

Filename	Description
php_calendar.dll	Calendar conversion functions
php_crypt.dll	Crypt support
php_dbase.dll	DBase support
php_filepro.dll	Read-only access to Filepro databases
php_ftp.dll	FTP-related functions
php_gd.dll	GD Library functions for graphic manipulation
php_imap.dll	IMAP support
php_java.dll	Java support
php_ldap.dll	LDAP functions
php_mcrypt.dll	Mcrypt support
php_mssql65.dll	Microsoft SQL Server 6.5 support
php_mssql70.dll	Microsoft SQL Server 7.0 support
php_nsmail.dll	Netscape mail functions
php_oci8.dll	Oracle 8 support
php_oracle.dll	Oracle support
php_zlib.dll	ZLib functions

The only files included in the PHP4.0.x distribution package are php_calendar.dll, php_imap.dll, and php_ldap.dll. Short of building from Windows source, you're currently limited to the kindness of others within the Open Source movement. One developer keeps reasonably up-to-date extensions at http://download.swwwing. com/php4/modules/.

To use Windows extensions, simply place them in your PHP directory and then modify the php.ini file.

1. Find a section that starts like this:

```
;Windows Extensions
```

2. For each extension you want to use, take away the semicolon before the name if the file is in the list.

3. If the file is not in the list, add it:

```
extension=[your_extension_name].dll
```

4. After changing anything in the php.ini file, check the output of phpinfo() to verify your changes.

Linux Configuration Options

Here is the configuration line used in Chapter 3 to build PHP:

```
./configure --with-mysql=/usr/local/mysql-3.22.32-pc-linux-gnu-i686/ --with-apxs=/usr/local/apache_1.3.12/bin/apxs
```

This line tells PHP to include support for MySQL and to build as a dynamic module. Many other configuration options are available to you, many of which you'll never use (I know I don't). The table below lists them in case you want to fiddle with your installation. Remember, since PHP is an Apache dynamic module, you don't have to recompile Apache when making changes to PHP.

Configuration Options

Option	Description
--enable-bcmath	Includes BCMATH support
--enable-ftp	Enables FTP support
--enable-magic-quotes	Enables magic quotes by default
--enable-safe mode	Enables safe mode by default
--enable-track-vars	Enables GET/POST/Cookie track variables by default
--enable-trans-sid	Enables transparent session id propagation
--with-aspell[=DIR]	Includes ASPELL support
--with-cybercash[=DIR]	Includes CyberCash support. DIR is the CyberCash MCK installation directory
--with-dom[=DIR]	Includes DOM support (requires libxml >= 1.0). DIR is the libxml installation directory
--with-gd[=DIR]	Includes GD support (DIR is GD's installation directory)
--with-imap[=DIR]	Includes IMAP support. DIR is the IMAP include and c-client.a directory
--with-java[=DIR]	Includes Java support. DIR is the base installation directory for the JDK
--with-ldap[=DIR]	Includes LDAP support. DIR is the LDAP base installation directory
--with-mcal[=DIR]	Includes MCAL support
--with-mcrypt[=DIR]	Includes mcrypt support. DIR is the mcrypt installation directory
--with-mhash[=DIR]	Includes mhash support. DIR is the mhash installation directory
--with-servlet[=DIR]	Includes servlet support. DIR is the base installation directory for the JSDK

B

Essential PHP Language Reference

This appendix is by no means a copy of the PHP Manual (found at http://www.php.net/manual/), which contains user-submitted comments and code samples. Instead, this appendix serves as an "essential" reference—it contains the elements of PHP that (in my opinion) you can't live without. The PHP Development Team and all of the documentation contributors have done a wonderful job with the entire PHP Manual, and there's no need to reinvent the wheel. However, since this appendix touches on only a small percentage of all there is to know about PHP, check the PHP Manual before asking a question on one of the PHP mailing lists.

PHP Start and End Tags

To combine PHP code with HTML, the PHP code must be *escaped*, or set apart, from the HTML. The PHP engine will consider anything within the tag pairs shown in the table below as PHP code.

Basic PHP Start and End Tags

Opening Tag	Closing Tag
<?php	?>
<?	?>
<script language="php">	</script>

Variables

You create variables to represent data. For instance, the following variable holds a value for sales tax:

```
$sales_tax = 0.0875;
```

This variable holds a SQL statement:

```
$sql = "SELECT * FROM MY_TABLE";
```

You can refer to the value of other variables when determining the value of a new variable:

```
$tax_total = $sales_tax * $sub_total;
```

The following are true of variable names:

- They begin with a dollar sign ($).
- They cannot begin with a numeric character.
- They are case-sensitive.

Here are some common variable types:

- arrays
- floats
- integers
- strings

These types are determined by PHP, based on the context in which they appear.

Arrays

In the following example, $fave_colors is an array that contains strings representing array elements. In this case, the array elements (0 to 3) are names of colors.

```
$fave_colors[0] = "red";
$fave_colors[1] = "blue";
$fave_colors[2] = "black";
$fave_colors[3] = "white";
```

Array elements are counted with 0 as the first position.

Floats

Each of the following variables is a float, or floating-point number. Floats are also known as "numbers with decimal points."

```
$a = 1.552;
$b = 0.964;
$sales_tax = 0.875;
```

Integers

Integers are positive or negative whole numbers, or "numbers without decimal points." Each of the following variables is an integer:

```
$a = 15;
$b = -521;
```

Strings

A series of characters grouped within double quotation marks is considered a string:

```
$a = "I am a string.";
$b = "<P>This book is <strong>cool</strong>!";
```

You can also reference other variables within your string, which will be replaced when your script is executed. For example:

```
$num = 57; // an integer
$my_string = "I read this book $num times!"; // a string
```

When you run the script, `$my_string` will become "I read this book 57 times!".

Variables from HTML Forms

Depending on the method of your HTML form (GET or POST), the variables will be part of the `$HTTP_POST_VARS` or `$HTTP_GET_VARS` global associative array. The name of the input field will become the name of the variable. For example, the following input field produces the variable `$first_name`:

```
<input type="text" name="first_name" size="20">
```

If the method of this form were POST, this variable could also be referenced as `$HTTP_POST_VARS["first_name"]`. If the method were GET, you could also use `$HTTP_GET_VARS["first_name"]`.

Variables from Cookies

Like variables from forms, variables from cookies are kept in a global associative array called `$HTTP_COOKIE_VARS`. If you set a cookie called "user" with a value of "Joe Smith", like so:

```
SetCookie ("user", "Joe Smith", time()+3600);
```

a variable called $user is placed in `$HTTP_COOKIE_VARS`, with a value of "Joe Smith". You can refer to `$user` or `$HTTP_COOKIE_VARS['user']` to get that value.

Environment Variables

When a Web browser makes a request of a Web server, it sends along with the request a list of extra variables called *environment variables*. They can be very useful for displaying dynamic content or authorizing users.

By default, environment variables are available to PHP scripts as `$VAR_NAME`. However, to be absolutely sure that you're reading the correct value, you can use the `getenv()` function to assign a value to a variable of your choice. The following are some common environment variables.

`REMOTE_ADDR` gets the IP address of the machine making the request. For example:

```
<?
    $remote_address = getenv("REMOTE_ADDR");
    echo "Your IP address is $remote_address.";
?>
```

`HTTP_USER_AGENT` gets the browser type, browser version, language encoding, and platform. For example:

```
<?
    $browser_type = getenv("HTTP_USER_AGENT");
    echo "You are using $browser_type.";
?>
```

For a list of HTTP environment variables and their descriptions, visit http://hoohoo.ncsa.uiuc.edu/cgi/env.html.

Operators

An operator is a symbol that represents a specific action. For example, the + arithmetic operator adds two values, and the = assignment operator assigns a value to a variable.

Arithmetic Operators

Arithmetic operators bear a striking resemblance to simple math, as shown in the table below.

Operator	Example	Action
+	$b = $a + 3;	Adds values together
-	$b = $a - 3;	Subtracts values
*	$b = $a * 3;	Multiplies values
/	$b = $a / 3;	Divides values
%	$b – $a % 3;	Returns the modulus, or remainder

Assignment Operators

The = is the basic assignment operator:

```
$a = 124; // the value of $a is 124
```

Other assignment operators are shown in the table below.

Assignment Operators

Operator	Example	Action
+=	$a += 3;	Changes the value of a variable to the current value plus the value on the right side
-=	$a -= 3;	Changes the value of the variable to the current value minus the value on the right side
.=	$a .= "string";	Concatenates (adds on to) the value on the right side with the current value

Comparison Operators

It should come as no surprise that comparison operators compare two values. A value of true or false is returned by the comparison. The comparison operators are shown in the table below.

Comparison Operators

Operator	Definition
==	Equal to
!=	Not equal to
>	Greater than
<	Less than
>=	Greater than or equal to
<=	Less than or equal to

Increment/Decrement Operators

The increment/decrement operators do just what their name implies: add or subtract from a variable.

Increment/Decrement Operators

Operator	Usage	Definition
Pre-increment	++$a	Increments by 1 and returns $a
Post-increment	$a++	Returns $a and then increments $a by 1
Pre-decrement	--$a	Decrements by 1 and returns $a
Post-decrement	$a--	Returns $a and then decrements $a by 1

Logical Operators

Logical operators allow your script to determine the status of conditions and, in the context of your if...else or while statements, execute certain code based on which conditions are true and which are false.

Logical Operators

Operator	Example	Result
!	!$a	TRUE if $a is not true
&&	$a && $b	TRUE if both $a and $b are true
||	$a || $b	TRUE if either $a or $b is true

Control Structures

Programs are essentially a series of statements. Control structures, as their name implies, control how those statements are executed. Control structures are usually built around a series of conditions, such as "If the sky is blue, go outside and play." In this example, the condition is "If the sky is blue" and the statement is "go outside and play."

Control structures use curly braces ({ and }) to separate the groups of statements from the remainder of the program. Examples of common control structures follow; memorizing these will make your life much easier.

if...elseif...else

The `if...elseif...else` construct executes a statement based on the value of the expression being tested. In the following sample if statement, the expression being tested is "$a is equal to 10."

```
if ($a == "10") {
        // execute some code
}
```

After $a is evaluated, if it is found to have a value of 10 (that is, if the condition is TRUE), the code inside the curly braces will execute. If $a is found to be something other than 10 (if the condition is FALSE), the code will be ignored, and the program will continue.

To offer an alternative series of statements, should $a not have a value of 10, add an else statement to the structure, to execute a section of code when the condition is FALSE:

```
if ($a == "10") {
        echo "a equals 10";
} else {
        echo "a does not equal 10";
}
```

The `elseif` (or two words: "else if") statement can be added to the structure to evaluate an alternative expression before heading to the final else statement. For example, the following structure first evaluates whether $a is equal to 10. If that condition is FALSE, the `elseif` statement is evaluated. If it is found to be TRUE, the code within its curly braces executes. Otherwise, the program continues to the final else statement:

```
if ($a == "10") {
        echo "a equals 10";
} elseif ($b == "8") {
        echo "b equals 8";
} else {
        echo "a does not equal 10 and b does not equal 8.";
}
```

You can use if statements alone or as part of an if...else or if...elseif...else statement. Whichever you choose, you will find this structure to be an invaluable element in your programs!

while

Unlike the if...elseif...else structure, in which each expression is evaluated once and an action is performed based on its value of true or false, the while statement continues to loop until an expression is false. In other words, the while loop continues while the expression is true.

For example, in the following while loop, the value of $a is printed on the screen and is incremented by 1 as long as the value of $a is less than or equal to 3:

```
$a = 0 // set a starting point
while ($a <= "3") {
        echo "a equals $a<br>";
        $a++;
}
```

for

Like while loops, for loops evaluate the set of conditional expressions at the beginning of each loop. Here is the syntax of the for loop:

```
for (expr1; expr2; expr3) {
        // code to execute
}
```

At the beginning of each loop, the first expression is evaluated, followed by the second expression. If the second expression is true, the loop continues by executing the code and then evaluating the third expression. If the second expression is false, the loop does not continue, and the third expression is never evaluated.

Take the counting example used in the while loop, and rewrite it using a for loop:

```
for ($a = 0; $a <= "3"; $a++) {
        echo "a equals $a<br>";
}
```

Built-In Functions

All of the following functions are part of the numerous functions that make up the PHP language. These really are just a small number of the PHP functions; they are the ones I use on a regular basis. Depending on the types of things you'll be doing with PHP, you may or may not need more functions, but please visit the PHP Manual at http://www.php.net/manual/ and familiarize yourself with what is available.

Array Functions

Numerous PHP functions are available for use with arrays. Only a few are noted here—those that I find absolutely essential, and those that form a foundation of knowledge for working with arrays.

array()

The `array()` function allows you to manually assign values to an array. Here is the syntax of the `array()` function:

```
$array_name = array("val1", "val2", "val3", ...);
```

array_push()

The `array_push()` function allows you to add one or more elements to the end of an existing array. Its syntax is

```
array_push($array_name, "element 1", "element 2", ...);
```

array_pop()

The `array_pop()` function allows you to take (pop) off the last element of an existing array. Its syntax is

```
array_pop($array_name);
```

array_unshift()

The `array_unshift()` function allows you to add elements to the beginning of an existing array. Its syntax is

```
array_unshift($array_name, "element 1", "element 2", ...);
```

array_shift()

The `array_shift()` function allows you to take (pop) off the first element of an existing array. Its syntax is

```
array_shift($array_name);
```

array_merge()

The `array_merge()` function allows you to combine two or more existing arrays. Its syntax is

```
array_merge($array1, $array2, ...);
```

array_keys()

The `array_keys()` function returns an array of all the key names in an existing array. Its syntax is

```
array_keys($array_name);
```

array_values()

The `array_values()` function returns an array of all the values in an existing array. Its syntax is

```
array_values($array_name);
```

count()

The `count()` function counts the number of elements in a variable. It's usually used to count the number of elements in an array, because any variable that is not an array has only one element—itself.

In the following example, `$a` is assigned a value equal to the number of elements in the `$colors` array:

```
$a = count($colors);
```

If `$colors` contains the values "blue", "black", "red", and "green", `$a` will be assigned a value of 4.

each() and list()

The each() and list() functions usually appear together, in the context of stepping through an array and returning its keys and values. Here is the syntax for these functions:

```
each(arrayname);
list(val1, val2, val3, ...);
```

For example, when you submit an HTML form via the GET method, each key/value pair is placed in the global variable $HTTP_GET_VARS. If your form input fields are named first_name and last_name and the user enters values of Joe and Smith, the key/value pairs are first_name/Joe and last_name/Smith. In the $HTTP_GET_VARS array, these variables are represented as the following:

```
$HTTP_GET_VARS["first_name"] // value is "Joe"
$HTTP_GET_VARS["last_name"] // value is "Smith"
```

You can use the each() and list() functions to step through the array in this fashion, printing the key and value for each element in the array:

```
while (list($key, $val) = each($HTTP_GET_VARS)) {
    echo "$key has a value of $val<br>";
}
```

reset()

The reset() function rewinds the pointer to the beginning of the array. Its syntax is

```
reset($array_name);
```

shuffle()

The shuffle() function randomizes the elements of a given array. Its syntax is

```
shuffle($array_name);
```

sizeof()

The sizeof() function counts the number of elements in an array. In the following example, $a is assigned a value equal to the number of elements in the $colors array:

```
$a = sizeof($colors);
```

If $colors contains the values "blue", "black", "red", and "green", $a is assigned a value of 4.

Database Connectivity Functions for MySQL

Numerous PHP functions exist for connecting to and querying a MySQL server. Following are some basic functions and their syntax. See the PHP Manual at http://www.php.net/manual/ for a complete listing of MySQL functions—there are plenty!

mysql_connect()

This function opens a connection to MySQL. It requires a server name, username, and password.

```
$connection = mysql_connect("servername","username","password");
```

mysql_create_db()

This function creates a database on the MySQL server. It requires a valid established connection.

```
mysql_create_db("myDB");
```

mysql_drop_db()

This function drops a database on the MySQL server. It requires a valid established connection.

```
mysql_drop_db("myDB");
```

mysql_select_db()

This function selects a database on the MySQL server for use by subsequent queries. It requires a valid established connection.

```
$db = mysql_select_db("myDB", $connection);
```

mysql_query()

This function issues the SQL statement. It requires an open connection to the database.

```
$sql_result = mysql_query("SELECT * FROM SOMETABLE",$connection);
```

mysql_error()

This function returns a meaningful error message when something goes wrong with your connection or query. It's usually used in the context of the die() function, like this:

```
$sql_result = mysql_query("SELECT * FROM SOMETABLE",$connection)
    or die(mysql_error());
```

mysql_fetch_array()

This function automatically places the SQL statement result row into an array.

```
$row = mysql_fetch_array($sql_result);
```

mysql_num_rows()

This function returns the number of rows in a result set.

```
$num = mysql_num_rows($sql_result);
```

mysql_free_result()

This function frees the memory resources used by a database query.

```
mysql_free_result($sql_result);
```

mysql_close()

This function explicitly closes a database connection.

```
mysql_close($connection);
```

Date and Time Functions

The basic PHP date and time functions let you easily format timestamps for use in database queries and calendar functions, as well as for simply printing the date on an order form receipt.

date()

The date() function returns the current server timestamp, formatted according to a given set of parameters. Its syntax is

```
date(format, [timestamp]);
```

If the timestamp parameter is not provided, the current timestamp is assumed. The following table shows the available formats.

date( ) Function Formats

Character	Meaning
a	Prints "am" or "pm"
A	Prints "AM" or "PM"
h	Hour in 12-hour format (01 to 12)
H	Hour in 24-hour format (00 to 23)
g	Hour in 12-hour format without a leading zero (1 to 12)
G	Hour in 24-hour format without a leading zero (0 to 23)
i	Minutes (00 to 59)
s	Seconds (00 to 59)
Z	Time zone offset in seconds (-43200 to 43200)
U	Seconds since the Epoch (January 1, 1970 00:00:00 GMT)
d	Day of the month in two digits (01 to 31)
j	Day of the month in two digits without a leading zero (1 to 31)
d	Day of the week in text (Mon to Sun)
l	Day of the week in long text (Monday to Sunday)
w	Day of the week in numeric, Sunday to Saturday (0 to 6)
F	Month in long text (January to December)
m	Month in two digits (01 to 12)
n	Month in two digits without a leading zero (1 to 12)
M	Month in three-letter text (Jan to Dec)
Y	Year in four digits (2000)
y	Year in two digits (00)
z	Day of the year (0 to 365)
t	Number of days in the given month (28 to 31)
S	English ordinal suffix (th, nd, st)

checkdate()

The `checkdate()` function validates a given date. Successful validation means that the year is between 0 and 32767, the month is between 1 and 12, and the proper number of days are in each month (leap years are accounted for). Its syntax is

```
checkdate(month, day, year);
```

mktime()

The `mktime()` function returns the UNIX timestamp as a long integer (in the format of seconds since the Epoch) for a given date. Thus, the primary use of `mktime()` is to format dates in preparation for mathematical functions and date validation. Its syntax is

```
mktime(hour, minute, second, month, day, year);
```

time() and microtime()

The `time()` function returns the current system time, measured in seconds since the Epoch. The syntax of `time()` is simply

```
time();
```

You could get a result such as 958950466.

Using `microtime()` adds a count of microseconds, so instead of just receiving a result like 958950466, you would get a result like 0.93121600 958950466, at the exact moment you asked for the time since the Epoch (this includes both seconds and microseconds).

Filesystem Functions

The built-in filesystem functions can be very powerful tools—or weapons, if used incorrectly. Be very careful when using filesystem functions, especially if you have PHP configured to run as root or some other system-wide user. For example, using a PHP script to issue an `rm -R` command while at the root level of your directory structure would be a very bad thing.

chmod(), chgrp(), and chown()

Like the shell commands of the same name, the chmod(), chgrp(), and chown() functions modify the permissions, group, and owner of a directory or file. Here is the syntax of these functions:

```
chmod("filename", mode);
chmgrp("filename", newgroup);
chown("filename", newowner);
```

In order to change permissions, groups, and owners, the PHP user must be the owner of the file, or the permissions must already be set to allow such changes by that user.

copy()

The copy() function works much like the cp shell command: It needs a file name and a destination in order to copy a file. The syntax of copy() is

```
copy("source filename", "destination");
```

The PHP user must have permission to write into the destination directory, or the copy() function will fail.

fopen()

The fopen() function opens a specified file or URL for reading and/or writing. The syntax of fopen() is

```
fopen("filename", "mode")
```

To open a URL, use http:// or ftp:// at the beginning of the file name string. You can open URLs only for reading, not writing.

If the file name begins with anything else, the file is opened from the filesystem, and a file pointer to the opened file is returned. Otherwise, the file is assumed to reside on the local filesystem.

The specified mode determines whether the file is opened for reading, writing, or both. The following table lists the valid modes.

fopen( ) Function Modes	
Mode	**Description**
r	Read-only. The file pointer is at the beginning of the file.
r+	Reading and writing. The file pointer is at the beginning of the file.
w	Write-only. The file pointer is at the beginning of the file, and the file is truncated to zero length. If the file does not exist, attempt to create it.
w+	Reading and writing. The file pointer is at the beginning of the file, and the file is truncated to zero length. If the file does not exist, attempt to create it.
a	Write-only. The file pointer is at the end of the file (it appends content to the file). If the file does not exist, attempt to create it.
a+	Reading and writing. The file pointer is at the end of the file (it appends content to the file). If the file does not exist, attempt to create it.

fread( )

Use the fread() function to read a specified number of bytes from an open file pointer. Its syntax is

```
fread(filepointer, length);
```

fputs( )

The fputs() function writes to an open file pointer. Its syntax is

```
fputs(filepointer, content, [length]);
```

The file pointer must be open in order to write to the file. The length parameter is optional. If it isn't specified, all specified content is written to the file.

fclose()

Use the `fclose()` function to close an open file pointer. Its syntax is

```
fclose(filepointer);
```

mkdir()

Like the `mkdir` shell command, the `mkdir()` function creates a new directory on the filesystem. Its syntax is

```
mkdir("pathname", mode);
```

The PHP user must have write permission in the specified directory.

rename()

As its name suggests, the `rename()` function attempts to give a new name to an existing file. Its syntax is

```
rename("oldname", "newname");
```

The PHP user must have permission to modify the file.

rmdir()

Like the `rmdir` shell command, the `rmdir()` function removes a directory from the filesystem. Its syntax is

```
rmdir("pathname");
```

The PHP user must have write permission in the specified directory.

symlink()

The `symlink()` function creates a symbolic link from an existing file or directory on the filesystem to a specified link name. Its syntax is

```
symlink("targetname", "linkname");
```

The PHP user must have write permission in the specified directory.

unlink()

The `unlink()` function deletes a file from the filesystem. Its syntax is

```
unlink("filename");
```

The PHP user must have write permission for this file.

HTTP Functions

The built-in functions for sending specific HTTP headers and cookie data are crucial aspects of developing large Web-based applications in PHP. Luckily, the syntax for these functions is quite easy to understand and implement.

header()

The `header()` function outputs an HTTP header string, such as a location redirection. This output must occur before any other data is sent to the browser, including HTML tags.

NOTE

This information bears repeating: do not attempt to send information of any sort to the browser before sending a `header()`. You can perform any sort of database manipulations or other calculations before the `header()`, but you cannot print anything to the screen—not even a newline character.

For example, to use the `header()` function to redirect a user to a new location, use this code:

```
header("Location: http://www.newlocation.com");
exit;
```

TIP

Follow a `header()` statement with the `exit` command. This ensures that the code does not continue to execute.

---

setcookie()

The `setcookie()` function sends a cookie to the user. Cookies must be sent before any other header information is sent to the Web browser. The syntax for `setcookie()` is

```
setcookie("name", "value", "expire", "path", "domain", "secure");
```

For example, you would use the following code to send a cookie called username with a value of joe that is valid for one hour within all directories on the testcompany.com domain:

```
setcookie("username","joe", time()+3600, "/", ".testcompany.com");
```

Mail Function

The PHP mail function makes the interface between your HTML forms and your server's outgoing mail program a snap!

If your server has access to sendmail or an SNMP gateway, the `mail()` function sends mail to a specified recipient. Its syntax is

```
mail("recipient", "subject", "message", "mail headers");
```

For example, the following code sends mail to julie@thickbook.com, with a subject of "I'm sending mail!" and a message body saying "PHP is cool!". The "From:" line is part of the additional mail headers.

```
mail("julie@thickbook.com", "I'm sending mail!", "PHP is cool!", "From:
youremail@yourdomain.com\n");
```

Mathematical Functions

Since I have very little aptitude for mathematics, I find PHP's built-in mathematical functions to be of the utmost importance! In addition to all the functions, the value of pi (3.14159265358979323846) is already defined as a constant in PHP (`M_PI`).

ceil()

The `ceil()` function rounds a fraction up to the next higher integer. Its syntax is

```
ceil(number);
```

decbin() and bindec()

The `decbin()` and `bindec()` functions convert decimal numbers to binary numbers, and binary numbers to decimal numbers, respectively. The syntax of these functions is

```
decbin(number);
bindec(number);
```

dechex() and hexdec()

The `dechex()` and `hexdec()` functions convert decimal numbers to hexadecimal numbers, and hexadecimal numbers to decimal numbers, respectively. The syntax of these functions is

```
dechex(number);
hexdec(number);
```

decoct() and octdec()

The `decoct()` and `octdec()` functions convert decimal numbers to octal numbers, and octal numbers to decimal numbers, respectively. The syntax of these functions is

```
decoct(number);
octdec(number);
```

floor()

The `floor()` function rounds a fraction down to the next lower integer. Its syntax is

```
floor(number);
```

number_format()

The `number_format()` function returns the formatted version of a specified number. Its syntax is

```
number_format("number", "decimals", "dec_point", "thousands_sep");
```

For example, to return a formatted version of the number 12156688, with two decimal places and a comma separating each group of thousands, use

```
echo number_format("12156688","2",".",",");
```

The result is 12,156,688.00.

If only a number is provided, the default formatting does not use a decimal point and puts a comma between every group of thousands.

pow()

The `pow()` function returns the value of a given number, raised to the power of a given exponent. Its syntax is

```
pow(number, exponent);
```

rand()

The `rand()` function generates a random value from a specific range of numbers. Its syntax is

```
rand(min, max);
```

round()

The `round()` function rounds a fraction to the next higher or next lower integer. Its syntax is

```
round(number);
```

sqrt()

The `sqrt()` function returns the square root of a given number. Its syntax is

```
sqrt(number);
```

srand()

The `srand()` function provides the random number generator with a set of possible values. Its syntax is

```
srand(seed);
```

A common practice is to seed the random number generator by using a number of microseconds:

```
srand((double)microtime()*1000000);
```

Miscellaneous Functions

The die() and exit functions provide useful control over the execution of your script, offering an "escape route" for programming errors. Other functions have found their way into this "miscellaneous" category.

die()

The die() function outputs a given message and terminates the script when a returned value is false. Its syntax is

```
die("message");
```

For example, you would use the following code to print a message and stop the execution of your script upon failure to connect to your database:

```
$connection = mysql_connect("servername", "username", "password")
    or die ("Can't connect to database.");
```

exit

The exit statement terminates the execution of the current script at the point where the exit statement is made.

sleep() and usleep()

The sleep() and usleep() functions put a pause, or a delay, at a given point in the execution of your PHP code. The syntax of these functions is

```
sleep(seconds);
usleep(microseconds);
```

The only difference between sleep() and usleep() is that the given wait period for sleep() is in seconds, and the wait period for usleep() is in microseconds.

uniqid()

The uniqid() function generates a unique identifier, with a prefix if you want one. Its syntax is

```
uniqid("prefix");
```

That's boring, though. Suppose you want a unique ID with a prefix of "phpuser." You would use

```
$id = uniqid("phpuser");
echo "$id";
```

and you would get something like phpuser38b320a6b5482.

But if you use something really cool like

```
$id = md5(uniqid(rand()));
echo "$id";
```

you would get an ID like 999d8971461bedfc7caadcab33e65866.

Program Execution Functions

You can use PHP's built-in program execution functions to use programs residing on your system, such as encryption programs, third-party image manipulation programs, and so forth. For all program execution functions, the PHP user must have permission to execute the given program.

exec()

The exec() function executes an external program. Its syntax is

```
exec(command, [array], [return_var]);
```

If an array is specified, the output of the exec() function will append to the array. If return_var is specified, it will be assigned a value of the program's return status.

For example, you would use the following code to perform a "ping" of a server five times and print the output:

```
$command = "ping -c5 www.thickbook.com";
exec($command, $result, $rval);
for ($i = 0; $i < sizeof($result); $i++) {
    echo "$result[$i]<br>";
}
```

passthru()

Like the exec() function, the passthru() function executes an external program. The difference between the two is that passthru() returns the raw output of the action. The syntax of passthru() is

```
passthru(command, return_var);
```

If return_var is specified, it will be assigned a value of the program's return status.

system()

The system() function executes an external program and displays output as the command is being executed. Its syntax is

```
system(command, [return_var]);
```

If return_var is specified, it will be assigned a value of the program's return status.

For example, you would use the following code to perform a "ping" of a server five times and print the raw output:

```
$command = "ping -c5 www.thickbook.com";
system($command);
```

Regular Expression Functions

ereg_replace() and eregi_replace()

The ereg_replace() and eregi_replace() functions replace instances of a pattern within a string and return the new string. The ereg_replace() function performs a case-sensitive match, and eregi_replace() performs a case-insensitive match. Here is the syntax for both functions:

```
ereg_replace(pattern, replacement, string);
eregi_replace(pattern, replacement, string);
```

For example, you would use the following code to replace "ASP" with "PHP" in the string "I really love programming in ASP!":

```
$old_string = "I really love programming in ASP!";
$new_string = ereg_replace("ASP", "PHP", $old_string);
echo "$new_string";
```

If "ASP" is mixed case, such as "aSp", use the `eregi_replace()` function:

```
$old_string = "I really love programming in aSp!";
$new_string = eregi_replace("ASP", "PHP", $old_string);
echo "$new_string";
```

split()

The `split()` function splits a string into an array using a certain separator (comma, colon, semicolon, and so on). Its syntax is

```
split(pattern, string, [limit]);
```

If a limit is specified, the `split()` function stops at the named position—for example, at the tenth value in a comma-delimited list.

Session-Handling Functions

Session handling is a way of holding on to data as a user navigates your Web site. Data can be variables or entire objects. These simple functions are just a few of the session-related functions in PHP; see the PHP Manual at http://www.php.net/manual/ for more.

session_start()

The `session_start()` function starts a session if one has not already been started, or it resumes a session if the session ID is present for the user. This function takes no arguments and is called simply by placing the following at the beginning of your code:

```
session_start();
```

session_register()

The `session_register()` function registers a variable within the current session. In other words, if you want to keep track of the value of a variable called `$username` within a user's session, you must first register `$username` as a session variable. Its syntax is

```
session_register("variable_name");
```

For example, to register $username as a global session variable, use this:

```
session_register("username");
```

session_unregister()

The `session_unregister()` function unregisters, or "forgets," a variable within the current session. Its syntax is

```
session_unregister("variable_name");
```

For example, to forget about the global session variable called $username, use this:

```
session_unregister("username");
```

session_destroy()

The `session_destroy()` function effectively destroys all the variables and values registered for the current session. This function takes no arguments and is called simply by placing the following in your code:

```
session_destroy();
```

String Functions

This section only scratches the surface of PHP's built-in string manipulation functions, but if you understand these common functions, your programming life will be quite a bit easier!

addslashes() and stripslashes()

The `addslashes()` and `stripslashes()` functions are very important when inserting and retrieving data from a database. Often, text inserted into a database will contain special characters (single quotes, double quotes, backslashes, NULL) that must be "escaped" before being inserted. The `addslashes()` function does just that, using this syntax:

```
addslashes(string);
```

Similarly, the `stripslashes()` function returns a string with the slashes taken away, using this syntax:

```
stripslashes(string);
```

chop(), ltrim(), and trim()

All three of these functions remove errant white space from a string. The chop() function removes white space from the end of a string, and ltrim() removes white space from the beginning of a string. The trim() function removes both leading and trailing white space from a string. Here is the syntax of these functions:

```
chop(string);
ltrim(string);
trim(string);
```

echo()

The echo() function returns output. The syntax of echo() is

```
echo (parameter1, parameter 2, ...)
```

For example:

```
echo "I'm using PHP!"; // output is: I'm using PHP!
echo 2+6;              // output is: 8
```

The parentheses are not required when using echo.

explode() and implode()

The explode() function splits a string using a given separator and returns the values in an array. The syntax of explode() is

```
explode("separator", "string");
```

For example, the following code takes a string called $color_list, containing a comma-separated list of colors, and places each color into an array called $my_colors:

```
$color_list = "blue,black,red,green,yellow,orange";
$mycolors = explode(",", $color_list);
```

Conversely, the implode() function takes an array and makes it into a string, using a given separator. The syntax of implode() is

```
implode("separator", "string");
```

For example, the following code takes an array called `$color_list` and then creates a string called `$mycolors`, containing the values of the `$color_list` array, separated by commas:

```
$mycolors = implode(",", $color_list);
```

htmlspecialchars() and htmlentities()

The `htmlspecialchars()` and `htmlentities()` functions convert special characters and HTML entities within strings into their acceptable entity representations. The `htmlspecialchars()` function converts only the less-than sign (< becomes <), greater-than sign (> becomes >), double quotes ("" becomes "), and the ampersand (& becomes &).

The `htmlentities()` function converts the characters in the ISO-8859-1 character set to the proper HTML entity. Here is the syntax of these functions:

```
htmlspecialchars(string);
htmlentities(string);
```

nl2br()

The `nl2br()` function replaces all ASCII newlines with the HTML line break (<BR>). The syntax of the `nl2br()` function is

```
nl2br(string);
```

sprintf()

The `sprintf()` function returns a string that has been formatted according to a set of directives, as listed in the table on the next page. The syntax of `sprintf()` is

```
sprintf(directives, string);
```

strlen()

The `strlen()` function returns the length of a given string. Its syntax is

```
strlen(string);
```

sprintf() Function Formatting Directives

Directive	Result
%	Adds a percent sign.
b	Considers the string an integer and formats it as a binary number.
c	Considers the string an integer and formats it with that ASCII value.
d	Considers the string an integer and formats it as a decimal number.
f	Considers the string a double and formats it as a floating-point number.
o	Considers the string an integer and formats it as an octal number.
s	Considers and formats the string as a string.
x	Considers the string an integer and formats it as a hexadecimal number (lowercase letters).
X	Considers the string an integer and formats it as a hexadecimal number (uppercase letters).

strtolower()

The strtolower() function returns a given string with all alphabetic characters in lowercase. Its syntax is

```
strtolower(str);
```

strtoupper()

The strtoupper() function returns a given string with all alphabetic characters in uppercase. Its syntax is

```
strtoupper (str);
```

substr()

The substr() function returns a portion of a string, given a starting position and optional ultimate length. Its syntax is

```
substr(string, start, [length]);
```

If the start position is a positive number, the starting position is counted from the beginning of the string. If the start position is negative, the starting position is counted from the end of the string.

Similarly, if the optional length parameter is used and is a positive number, the length is counted from the beginning of the string. If the length parameter is used and is a negative number, the length is counted from the end of the string.

For example:

```
$new_string = substr("PHP is great!", 1);    // returns "HP is great!"
$new_string = substr("PHP is great!", 0, 7); // returns "PHP is "
$new_string = substr("PHP is great!", -1);   // returns "!"
$new_string = substr("PHP is great!", -6, 5);        // returns "great"
```

ucfirst()

The `ucfirst()` function changes the first alphabetic character in a string to an uppercase character. Its syntax is

```
ucfirst(string);
```

ucwords()

The `ucwords()` function changes the first letter of each word in a string to uppercase. Its syntax is

```
ucwords(string);
```

Variable Functions

The two basic variable functions, `isset()` and `unset()`, help you manage your variables within the scope of an application.

The `isset()` function determines whether a variable exists. The `unset()` function explicitly destroys the named variable. Here is the syntax of each:

```
isset(var);
unset(var);
```

The `isset()` function returns true if the variable exists and false if it does not.

Basic MySQL
Reference

This appendix is a very brief glance at the Structured Query Language (SQL) and some basic functions you can use with MySQL to make development a lot easier. See the MySQL Manual at http://www.mysql.com/ for a comprehensive list of MySQL functions and language elements.

CREATE or DROP a Database

Starting with something simple, you can use the CREATE command to create a new database. The syntax is

```
CREATE DATABASE IF NOT EXISTS yourDBName;
```

When you create a database with this command, you're really just creating a directory that will hold the files that make up the tables in the database.

To delete an entire database from the system, use the DROP command:

```
DROP DATABASE IF EXISTS yourDBName;
```

Be extremely careful when using the DROP command, because once you DROP the database, all of the tables are dropped as well!

CREATE or DROP a Table

You can also use the CREATE command to create a table within the current database. The syntax is:

```
CREATE TABLE yourTableName (fieldName1
[type], fieldName2 [type], ...) [options]
```

To delete a table from the current database, use the DROP command:

```
DROP TABLE yourTableName;
```

Be extremely careful when using the DROP command, because once you DROP the tables, they're gone!

> **NOTE**
>
> Some common data types are int, float, char, varchar, date, time, datetime, text, and blob. Refer to the MySQL manual for a list of supported data types and any size and data restrictions, or see the tutorial at http://www.thickbook.com/extra/php_datatypes.phtml.

ALTER a Table

The ALTER command gives you the opportunity to modify elements of a particular table, such as renaming columns, changing the type of a column, adding columns, deleting columns, and so on. Following are some common uses:

- To add a column to a table, use this:

  ```
  ALTER TABLE yourTableName ADD newColumn fieldDefinition;
  ```

- To delete a column from a table, use this:

  ```
  ALTER TABLE yourTableName DROP columnName;
  ```

- To change a column from one type to another, use this:

  ```
  ALTER TABLE yourTableName CHANGE columnName newfieldDefinition;
  ```

- To make a unique column in your table, use this:

  ```
  ALTER TABLE yourTableName ADD UNIQUE columnName (columnName);
  ```

- To index a column in your table, use this:

  ```
  ALTER TABLE yourTableName ADD INDEX columnName (columnName);
  ```

Using the ALTER command alleviates the need to delete an entire table and re-create it just because you spelled a field name incorrectly or made other minor mistakes.

INSERT, UPDATE, or REPLACE within a Table

The INSERT and REPLACE commands populate your tables one record at a time. The syntax of INSERT is:

```
INSERT INTO yourTableName (fieldName1, fieldName2, ...)
    VALUES ('[value of fieldName1]', '[value of fieldName2]'...);
```

When inserting records, be sure to separate your strings with single quotes or double quotes. If you use single quotes around your strings, and the data you are adding contains apostrophes, avoid errors by escaping the apostrophe (\') within the INSERT statement. Similarly, if you use double quotes around your strings and you want to include double quotes as part of the data, escape them (\") within your INSERT statement.

The REPLACE command has the same syntax and requirements as the INSERT command. The only difference is that you use REPLACE to overwrite a record in a table, based on a unique value:

```
REPLACE INTO yourTableName (fieldName1, fieldName2, ...)
    VALUES ('[value of fieldName1]', '[value of fieldName2]'...);
```

The UPDATE command modifies parts of a record without replacing the entire record. To update an entire column in a table with the same new value, use this:

```
UPDATE yourTableName SET fieldName = '[new value]';
```

If you want to update only specific rows, use a WHERE clause:

```
UPDATE yourTableName SET fieldName = '[new value]' WHERE [some expression];
```

UPDATE can be a very powerful SQL command. For example, you can perform string functions and mathematical functions on existing records and use the UPDATE command to modify their values.

DELETE from a Table

Like the DROP command, using DELETE without paying attention to what you're doing can have horrible consequences in a production environment. Once you DROP a table or DELETE a record, it's gone forever. Don't be afraid; just be careful. To delete all the contents of a table, use the following:

```
DELETE FROM yourTableName;
```

If you want to delete only specific rows, use a WHERE clause:

```
DELETE FROM yourTableName WHERE [some expression];
```

If you're going to start deleting records, be sure you have a backup, just in case something goes wrong. Everyone screws up once.

SELECT from a Table

When creating database-driven Web sites, the SELECT command will likely be the most often-used command in your arsenal. The SELECT command causes certain records in your table to be chosen, based on criteria that you define. Here is the basic syntax of SELECT:

```
SELECT [field names] FROM [table name]
WHERE [some expression]
ORDER BY [field names];
```

To select all the records in a table, use this:

```
SELECT * FROM yourTableName;
```

To select just the entries in a given column of a table, use this:

```
SELECT columnName FROM yourTableName;
```

To select all the records in a table and have them returned in a particular order, use an expression for ORDER BY. For example, if you have a date field for record entries and you want to see all the record entries ordered by newest to oldest, use this:

```
SELECT * FROM yourTableName ORDER BY dateField DESC;
```

DESC stands for "descending." To view from oldest to newest, use ASC for "ascending." ASC is the default order.

You can also perform mathematical and string functions within SQL statements, thereby using SELECT to do more than just echo existing data. Some examples follow.

A Few String Functions

This list contains only a few of the many string-related functions listed in the MySQL Manual. Visit http://www.mysql.com/ and check out the entire manual for more information.

- You can concatenate values using the CONCAT() function. The syntax is
  ```
  SELECT CONCAT(field1,field2,...) AS newName FROM yourTableName;
  ```

- Convert your results to lowercase using the LOWER() function. The syntax is
  ```
  SELECT LOWER(field1,field2,...) FROM yourTableName;
  ```

- Convert your results to uppercase using the UPPER() function. The syntax is
  ```
  SELECT UPPER(field1,field2,...) FROM yourTableName;
  ```

A Few Date and Time Functions

This list contains only a few of the many date and time-related functions listed in the MySQL Manual. Visit http://www.mysql.com/ and check out the entire manual for more information.

- Get the day of the week (1 = Sunday, 2 = Monday, ...) from a date field using the DAYOFWEEK() function. The syntax is

  ```
  SELECT DAYOFWEEK(date) FROM yourTableName;
  ```

- Get the weekday (0 = Monday, 1 = Tuesday, ...) from a date field using the WEEKDAY() function. The syntax is

  ```
  SELECT WEEKDAY(date) FROM
  yourTableName;
  ```

> **NOTE**
>
> The difference between the DAYOFWEEK() and WEEKDAY() functions is the starting point of the week. When getting the day of the week, the week starts at Day1, which is Sunday. When getting the weekday (or "work week"), the week starts at Day 0, which is Monday.

- Get the day of the month (1 through 31) from a date field using the DAYOFMONTH() function. The syntax is

  ```
  SELECT DAYOFMONTH(date) FROM
  yourTableName;
  ```

- Get the day of the year (1 through 366) from a date field using the DAYOFYEAR() function. The syntax is

  ```
  SELECT DAYOFYEAR(date) FROM
  yourTableName;
  ```

- Get the month (1 through 12) from a date field using the MONTH() function. The syntax is

  ```
  SELECT MONTH(date) FROM yourTableName;
  ```

- Get the month name (January, February, ...) from a date field using the MONTHNAME() function. The syntax is

  ```
  SELECT MONTHNAME(date) FROM yourTableName;
  ```

- Get the day name (Monday, Tuesday, ...) from a date field using the DAYNAME() function. The syntax is

  ```
  SELECT DAYNAME(date) FROM yourTableName;
  ```

- Get the week (0 through 53) from a date field using the WEEK() function. Start the week with Sunday (0) or Monday (1). The syntax is

  ```
  SELECT WEEK(date, [0 or 1]) FROM yourTableName;
  ```

- Get the year (1000 through 9999) from a date field using the YEAR() function. The syntax is

  ```
  SELECT YEAR(date) FROM yourTableName;
  ```

D

Getting Help

One of the greatest aspects of the Open Source community is that people are eager to help you learn as much as you can, so that you can become an Open Source advocate as well. However, you probably should attempt to find answers to your questions before posing them to the community at large. Doing so includes reading available manuals and FAQs, searching through mailing list archives, and visiting Web sites. Chances are good that someone else has had the same question you have.

PHP Resources

PHP-related Web sites, newsgroups, and mailing lists are popping up all over the place. The ones listed here are just a smattering of what's available.

Web Sites

The majority of these sites are maintained by normal people on their own time, so if you use any of their resources, try to give back to the community by helping others with their questions when you can, contributing code snippets to code repositories, and so forth.

www.php.net

The home of PHP is www.php.net. The annotated online manual is here, as well as the PHP FAQ, bug reports, links to ISPs that offer access to PHP, news articles, and much more!

www.zend.com

Zend Technologies, the folks behind the Zend engine of PHP4, have created a portal site for PHP developers. This personalized site not only showcases how you can build a high-traffic, dynamic site using PHP, but it also provides pointers, resources, and lessons on how to maximize the potential of PHP in all your online applications.

www.thickbook.com

I created this Web site as a supplement to my books. You will find additional code samples and tutorials, book errata, downloadable code from the books, a feedback section, and anything else I think up in my spare time.

Webmonkey (hotwired.lycos.com/webmonkey/)

The company that brings us *Wired* magazine also brings us HotWired, which spawned Webmonkey, a developer's resource site with a section devoted to PHP.

Don't limit yourself to the PHP section of Webmonkey, for there's much information to be had in other sections as well. This is one of my favorites, not only because I write for them, but because they're smart folks.

WeberDev (www.weberdev.com)

A longtime favorite of PHP developers, this site contains development tricks and tips for many programming languages (just to be fair) as well as a content management system for everyone to add their own code snippets, tutorials, and more! It has a great weekly newsletter and high traffic. Go contribute!

PHPBuilder (www.phpbuilder.com)

This is a very good tutorial site for intermediate and advanced PHP developers. It contains weekly "How To" columns for real-world applications, such as "Building Dynamic Pages With Search Engines in Mind," "Generating Pronounceable Passwords," and tons more. Recommended!

DevShed (www.devshed.com)

This contains many user-submitted tutorials, news articles, interviews, and competitive analyses of server-side programming languages. Covers PHP as well as many other topics of interest to developers, such as servers and databases.

px.sklar.com

This is a bare-bones code repository, but who needs graphics when all you're looking for are code snippets? Borrowing from the "take a penny, leave a penny" mentality, you grab a code snippet to start with and then add your own when you feel confident in sharing.

PHP KnowledgeBase (php.faqts.com)

The PHP Knowledge Base contains questions and answers posed on PHP mailing lists. Anyone can answer questions at the Web site or ask new ones.

AlbaSoftware PHP Resources (www.albasoftware.com)

This PHP portal is designed for all levels of PHP developers and contains general information, articles, and tutorials for developers. You can also find information on contributing to Open Source projects started by AlbaSoftware.

www.php-center.de and www.dynamic-webpages.de

These are two German-language PHP portals containing FAQs, tutorials, links, and code samples—everything portal sites should be!

www.phpindex.com

Quite like the German PHP portals, PHP Index is a wonderful PHP portal—entirely in French.

Mailing Lists

Several high-traffic mailing lists are available for PHP discussion, in English as well as other languages. Please remember your netiquette when asking a question: Be polite, offer as many examples as you can (if you're describing a problem), provide your system information (if looking for a solution), and did I mention to say please and thank you?

You can find mailing list subscription information in the "Support" section at http://www.php.net/. The English PHP mailing lists are archived and available for searching at http://marc.theaimsgroup.com/. Just look for the PHP-related lists under the "WWW" heading.

User Groups

Sometimes, knowing other developers in real life can prove helpful. You can find a list of PHP user groups at http://www.moewes.com/phpug.php3.

MySQL Resources

Many of the PHP-related Web sites listed earlier also contain information on development with MySQL, but the MySQL Web site at http://www.mysql.com/ is the place to start for comprehensive MySQL information.

The online MySQL Manual is immense, but it's so well-written and useful that its size should not scare you. You can find the manual at http://www.mysql.net/Manual/manual_toc.html.

As with PHP, several high-traffic mailing lists are available for MySQL discussion, in English as well as other languages. You can find mailing list subscription information at http://www.mysql.com/doc.html.. The MySQL mailing lists are archived and available for searching at http://lists.mysql.com/.

Apache Resources

Start at the Apache Foundation Web site, http://www.apache.org/, for server documentation and a list of FAQs. Many of the developer-oriented Web sites offer Apache-specific tutorials—you just have to hunt them down.

E

Using the CD-ROM

The CD that accompanies this book contains versions of Apache, MySQL, and PHP4 for both Windows and Linux, as well as all the code used throughout the chapters. The specially-designed Prima Tech interface will assist you in navigating the CD-ROM and/or installing the contents on your computer.

Running the CD

To make the CD more user-friendly and take up less of your disk space, we've designed the CD-ROM so that you can install or copy only those files that you desire.

Linux

1. Open the CD-ROM tray and insert the CD.

2. As root, type the following at the command line: **mount/dev/cdrom /tmp** (replace */tmp* with wherever you want to mount the CD).

3. Start an X session (**startx** in most cases).

4. Open your Web browser.

5. Navigate through your file system until you find start_here.html, located in the directory where you mounted the CD-ROM.

6. Open start_here.html with your Web browser.

Windows 95/98/2000/NT

1. Open the CD-ROM tray and insert the CD.

2. Open your Web browser.

3. Navigate through your file system until you find start_here.html, on the CD-ROM.

The Prima License

The first window you will see is the Prima License Agreement. Take a moment to read the agreement. If you accept the terms of the agreement, click the I Agree button. If you do not accept the license agreement, click the I Disagree button.

The Prima User Interface

Prima's user interface is designed to make viewing and using the CD-ROM contents quick and easy. The opening screen contains a two-frame window. The left frame contains the structure of the items on the CD-ROM. The right frame displays an informational page for the selected entry in the left frame.

Resizing and Closing the User Interface

As with any window, you can resize the user interface. To do so, position the mouse over any edge or corner, hold down the left mouse button, and drag the edge or corner to a new position.

To close and exit the user interface, close your Web browser using your normal method of closing the application.

Using the User Interface

To extract the source code from the CD-ROM, select a link from the list in the left frame. The right frame will refresh, and will contain links to particular scripts or other files.

Extract the files by right-clicking on the file name and downloading the file to another directory on your hard drive.

Index

License Agreement/Notice of Limited Warranty